Fodor's InFocus

D1559987

ST. MAARTEN, ST. BARTHS & ANGUILLA

1st Edition

Where to Stay and Eat for All Budgets

Must-See Sights and Local Secrets

Ratings You Can Trust

Fodor's Travel Publications   New York, Toronto, London, Sydney, Auckland
www.fodors.com

FODOR'S INFOCUS ST. MAARTEN, ST. BARTHS & ANGUILLA

Series Editor: Douglas Stallings

Editors: Douglas Stallings, Mark Sullivan
Editorial Contributors: Elise Meyer, Roberta Sotonoff

Editorial Production: Carolyn Roth
Maps & Illustrations: David Lindroth, *cartographer*; Bob Blake and Rebecca Baer, *map editors*; William Wu, *information graphics*
Design: Fabrizio LaRocca, *creative director*; Guido Caroti, *art director*; Ann McBride, *designer*; Melanie Marin, *senior picture editor*
Cover Photo: (Anguilla): Chris Caldicott/Axiom Photographic Agency/Getty Images
Production/Manufacturing: Matthew Struble

1st Edition
ISBN 978–1–4000–0758–5
ISSN 1942-7344

SPECIAL SALES

This book is available for special discounts for bulk purchases for sales promotions or premiums. Special editions, including personalized covers, excerpts of existing books, and corporate imprints, can be created in large quantities for special needs. For more information, write to Special Markets/Premium Sales, 1745 Broadway, MD 6-2, New York, NY 10019, or e-mail specialmarkets@randomhouse.com.

AN IMPORTANT TIP & AN INVITATION

Although all prices, opening times, and other details in this book are based on information supplied to us at press time, changes occur all the time in the travel world, and Fodor's cannot accept responsibility for facts that become outdated or for inadvertent errors or omissions. **So always confirm information when it matters,** especially if you're making a detour to visit a specific place. Your experiences—positive and negative—matter to us. If we have missed or misstated something, **please write to us.** We follow up on all suggestions. Contact the St. Maarten, St. Barths & Anguilla editor at editors@fodors.com or c/o Fodor's at 1745 Broadway, New York, NY 10019.

PRINTED IN THE UNITED STATES OF AMERICA
10 9 8 7 6 5 4 3 2 1

Be a Fodor's Correspondent

Your opinion matters. It matters to us. It matters to your fellow Fodor's travelers, too. And we'd like to hear it. In fact, we *need* to hear it. When you share your experiences and opinions, you become an active member of the Fodor's community. Here's how you can help improve Fodor's for all of us.

Tell us when we're right. We rely on local writers to give you an insider's perspective. But our writers and staff editors also depend on you. Your positive feedback is a vote to renew our recommendations for the next edition.

Tell us when we're wrong. We update most of our guides every year. But things change. If any of our descriptions are inaccurate or inadequate, we'll incorporate your changes in the next edition and will correct factual errors at fodors.com *immediately*.

Tell us what to include. You probably have had fantastic travel experiences that aren't yet in Fodor's. Why not share them with a community of like-minded travelers? Share your discoveries and experiences with everyone directly at fodors.com. Your input may lead us to add a new listing or a higher recommendation.

Give us your opinion instantly at our feedback center at www.fodors.com/feedback. You may also e-mail editors@fodors.com with the subject line "St. Maarten, St. Barths & Anguilla Editor." Or send your nominations, comments, and complaints by mail to St. Maarten, St. Barths & Anguilla Editor, Fodor's, 1745 Broadway, New York, NY 10019.

Happy Traveling!

Tim Jarrell, Publisher

CONTENTS

ABOUT
THIS BOOK

Our Ratings

We wouldn't recommend a place that wasn't worth your time, but sometimes a place is so experiential that superlatives don't do it justice: you just have to be there to know. These sights, properties, and experiences get our highest rating, **Fodor's Choice**, indicated by orange stars throughout this book. Black stars highlight sights and properties we deem **Highly Recommended**, places that our writers, editors, and readers praise again and again for consistency and excellence.

Credit Cards

Want to pay with plastic? **AE, D, DC, MC, V** after restaurant and hotel listings indicate whether American Express, Discover, Diners Club, MasterCard, and Visa are accepted.

Restaurants

Unless we state otherwise, restaurants are open for lunch and dinner daily. We mention dress only when there's a specific requirement and reservations only when they're essential or not accepted—it's always best to book ahead.

Hotels

Unless we tell you otherwise, you can assume that the hotels have private bath, phone, TV, and air-conditioning. We always list facilities but not whether you'll be charged an extra fee to use them, so when pricing accommodations, find out what's included.

Many Listings

★	Fodor's Choice
★	Highly recommended
⊠	Physical address
⊹	Directions
⌂	Mailing address
☎	Telephone
🖷	Fax
⊕	On the Web
✉	E-mail
🎫	Admission fee
☉	Open/closed times
Ⓜ	Metro stations
▭	Credit cards

Hotels & Restaurants

🏨	Hotel
🛏	Number of rooms
⚸	Facilities
ⅼⓄⅼ	Meal plans
✕	Restaurant
⌕	Reservations
↘	Smoking
🍷	BYOB
✕🏨	Hotel with restaurant that warrants a visit

Outdoors

⛳	Golf
⛺	Camping

Other

☺	Family-friendly
⇨	See also
⊠	Branch address
☞	Take note

WHEN TO GO

The Caribbean high season is traditionally from December 15 through April 15—when northern weather is at its worst. During this season you're guaranteed that all hotels and restaurants will be open and busy. It's also the most fashionable, the most expensive, and the most popular time to visit. The Christmas holiday season is an especially expensive time to visit Anguilla and St. Barths, and you may very well pay double during this period, not to mention have a one- to two-week minimum rental requirement for villas and even some hotels. If you wait until mid-May or June, prices may be 20% to 50% less, and this is particularly true of St. Barths and Anguilla; however, some hotels close, particularly later in summer and early fall. The period from mid-August through late November is typically the least busy time in all three islands, when many of the major resorts on Anguilla and restaurants on St. Barths close.

Climate
The Caribbean climate is fairly constant. Summer, however, can bring somewhat higher temperatures and more humidity because the trade winds slow. The Atlantic hurricane season begins on June 1 and stretches all the way through November 30. While heavy rains can happen anytime throughout the year, it's during this six-month period when tropical fronts are most likely. Major hurricanes are possible but a relatively rare occurrence, and in recent years building standards have been raised to a much higher level to avoid some of the devastating damage such as that caused in St. Maarten by Hurricane Louis in 1995.

Forecasts **Accuweather** (⊕www.accuweather.com). **Weather Channel** (⊕www.weather.com).

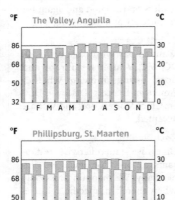

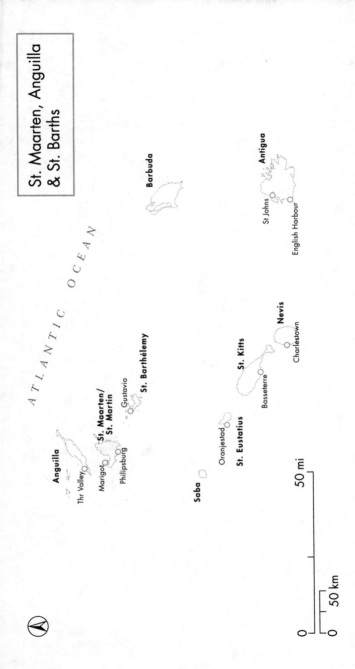

St. Maarten, Anguilla
& St. Barths

ATLANTIC OCEAN

Anguilla

Thr Valley

Marigot
Philipsburg

**St. Maarten/
St. Martin**

Gustavia

St. Barthélemy

Saba

Oranjestad

St. Eustatius

Basseterre

St. Kitts

Nevis

Charlestown

Barbuda

St Johns

Antigua

English Harbour

50 mi

50 km

0

0

St. Maarten/ St. Martin

WORD OF MOUTH

"There are still hidden treasures to be found and special qualities that remain on St. Martin/Maarten."

—Barbara1

"If you want more active night life I would suggest staying on Dutch side, as that where most of it is, including casinos. It is better to drive during the day to French side to explore."

—Snubes

Updated
by Roberta
Sotonoff
THE MAJORITY OF THE YACHT CREW doesn't know the difference between a gaff and a gallow, but that isn't a deterrent for this race. Off they go aboard Dennis Connor's America's Cup winner Stars and Stripes. The wind howls through the sails, and Captain Morgan (not the pirate but a sailor from Jamaica) shouts, "Get ready to tack. We can take the lead." The trimmers, grinders, and winchers man their stations. The boat gets within hearing range of its rival, another America's Cup contender, Canada II, and friendly barbs are exchanged.

The St. Maarten 12-Metre Challenge is a singular experience. Then again, the island of St. Maarten/St. Martin is also quite unique. Where else can you find a 37-square-mi (96-square-km) island that is governed by two nations—the Netherlands and France—with residents from 70 different countries who speak who knows how many languages? Happily for Americans, who make up the majority of visitors, English works in both nations. Dutch St. Maarten will feel particularly comfortable for Americans, and you're as likely to run into an American expat there as anyone else, on the beach or not. But once you pass the meandering, unmarked border into the French side, you can find more pronounced differences. You'll be hard-pressed to find a washcloth unless your lodgings are very upscale, and it's almost necessary to be an engineer to bypass the safety mechanisms in the electrical outlets. And another thing: though U.S. dollars are happily accepted, be ready for wallet shock. Most things are priced in euros.

Almost 4,000 years ago, it was salt and not tourism that drove the little island's economy. Arawak Indians, the island's first known inhabitants, prospered until the warring Caribs invaded, adding the peaceful Arawaks to their list of conquests. Columbus spotted the isle in 1493, but it wasn't populated by Europeans until the 17th century, when it was claimed by the Dutch, French, and Spanish. The Dutch and French finally joined forces to claim the island in 1644, and the Treaty of Concordia partitioned the territory in 1648.

Both sides of the island offer a little European culture along with a lot of laid-back Caribbean ambience. Water sports abound—diving, snorkeling, scuba, sailing, windsurfing, and in late February the Heineken Regatta, with as many as 300 sailboats competing from around the world. (For the experience of a lifetime, some visitors purchase a working berth aboard a regatta vessel.)

With soft trade winds cooling the subtropical climate, it's easy to while away the day relaxing on one of the 37 beaches, strolling Philipsburg's boardwalk, and perusing the shops on Philipsburg's Front Street or the *rues* (streets) of the very French town of Marigot. While luck is an important commodity at St. Maarten's 13 casinos, chance plays no part in finding a good meal at the excellent eateries or after-dark fun in the subtle to sizzling nightlife. Still, the isle's biggest assets are its friendly residents.

Although the island has been heavily developed—especially on the Dutch side—roads could still use work. When cruise ships are in port (and there can be as many as seven at once), shopping areas are crowded and traffic moves at a snail's pace. Still, these are minor inconveniences compared to the feel of the sand between your toes or the breeze through your hair, gourmet food sating your appetite, or having the ability to crisscross between two nations on one island.

EXPLORING ST. MAARTEN/ ST. MARTIN

The best way to explore St. Maarten/St. Martin is by car. Though often congested, especially around Philipsburg and Marigot, the roads are fairly good, though narrow and winding, with some speed bumps, potholes, and an occasional wandering goat herd. Few roads are marked with their names, but destination signs are common. Besides, the island is so small that it's hard to get really lost—at least that is what locals tell you.

A scenic "loop" around the island can take just half a day, including plenty of stops. If you head up the east shoreline from Philipsburg, follow the signs to Dawn Beach and Oyster Pond. The road winds past soaring hills, turquoise waters, quaint West Indian houses, and wonderful views of St. Barths. As you cross over to the French side, the road leads to Grand Case, Marigot, and Sandy Ground. From Marigot, the flat island of Anguilla is visible. Completing the loop brings you past Cupecoy Beach, through Maho and Simpson Bay, where Saba looms in the horizon, and back over the mountain road into Philipsburg.

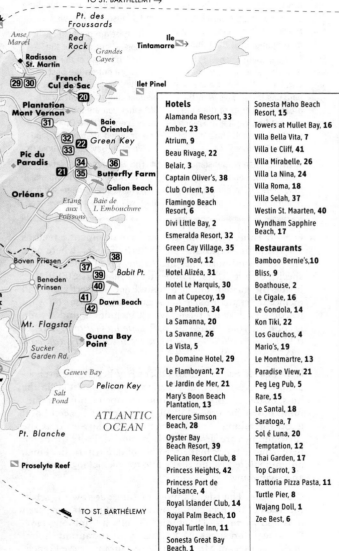

TO ST. BARTHÉLEMY →

Pt. des
Froussards

Anse
Marcel

Red
Rock

Grandes
Cayes

Ile
Tintamarre →

Radisson
St. Martin

29 30

French
Cul de Sac

Ilet Pinel

20

Plantation
Mont Vernon

31

Baie
Orientale

Pic du
Paradis

32
33

22

Green Key

34

36

21

35

Butterfly Farm

Orléans

Galion Beach

Etang
aux
Poissons

Baie de
L. Embouchure

Boven Prinsen

38

37

39

Babit Pt.

Beneden
Prinsen

40

41

Dawn Beach

42

Mt. Flagstaf

Guana Bay
Point

Sucker
Garden Rd.

Geneve Bay

Pelican Key

Salt
Pond

ATLANTIC
OCEAN

Pt. Blanche

Proselyte Reef

TO ST. BARTHÉLEMY
→

Hotels

Alamanda Resort, **33**
Amber, **23**
Atrium, **9**
Beau Rivage, **22**
Belair, **3**
Captain Oliver's, **38**
Club Orient, **36**
Flamingo Beach
Resort, **6**
Divi Little Bay, **2**
Esmeralda Resort, **32**
Green Cay Village, **35**
Horny Toad, **12**
Hotel Alizéa, **31**
Hotel Le Marquis, **30**
Inn at Cupecoy, **19**
La Plantation, **34**
La Samanna, **20**
La Savanne, **26**
La Vista, **5**
Le Domaine Hotel, **29**
Le Flamboyant, **27**
Le Jardin de Mer, **21**
Mary's Boon Beach
Plantation, **13**
Mercure Simson
Beach, **28**
Oyster Bay
Beach Resort, **39**
Pelican Resort Club, **8**
Princess Heights, **42**
Princess Port de
Plaisance, **4**
Royal Islander Club, **14**
Royal Palm Beach, **10**
Royal Turtle Inn, **11**
Sonesta Great Bay
Beach, **1**

Sonesta Maho Beach
Resort, **15**
Towers at Mullet Bay, **16**
Villa Bella Vita, **7**
Villa Le Cliff, **41**
Villa Mirabelle, **26**
Villa La Nina, **24**
Villa Roma, **18**
Villa Selah, **37**
Westin St. Maarten, **40**
Wyndham Sapphire
Beach, **17**

Restaurants

Bamboo Bernie's, **10**
Bliss, **9**
Boathouse, **2**
Le Cigale, **16**
Le Gondola, **14**
Kon Tiki, **22**
Los Gauchos, **4**
Mario's, **19**
Le Montmartre, **13**
Paradise View, **21**
Peg Leg Pub, **5**
Rare, **15**
Le Santal, **18**
Saratoga, **7**
Sol é Luna, **20**
Temptation, **12**
Thai Garden, **17**
Top Carrot, **3**
Trattoria Pizza Pasta, **11**
Turtle Pier, **8**
Wajang Doll, **1**
Zee Best, **6**

St. Maarten/St. Martin Best Bets

A two-nation vacation is what you get with St. Maarten/St. Martin. But the island has much more going for it than that.

■ Phillipsburg is one of the best shopping spots in the Caribbean; though it has fewer bargains these days with the growing strength of the euro, Marigot (the capital of French St. Martin) is still chock-full of interesting stores.

■ Grand Case is the island's gastronomic capital, but good food seeps from almost every island pore. You'll find plenty of

great restaurants in Phillipsburg and Simpson Bay as well.

■ Thirty-seven perfect beaches are spread out all over the island (and most of the island's hotels are not on the best beaches, one reason so many people choose to rent a car). Whether you are looking for the busy scene at Baie Orientale or the deserted stretches of sand at Simpson Bay, each is unique.

■ The wide range of water sports—from sailing to waterskiing, snorkeling to deep-sea fishing—will meet almost any need.

★ **Butterfly Farm.** A serene, tropical environment envelops visitors in the terrarium-like Butterfly Sphere, where dozens of colorful butterflies flit. At any given time, some 40 species of butterflies, numbering as many as 600, flutter inside the garden under a tented net. Butterfly art and memorabilia are for sale in the gift shop. In case you want to come back, your ticket, which includes a guided tour, is good for your entire stay. ⊠*Rte. de Le Galion, Quartier d'Orléans* ☎*590/87–31–21* ⊕*www.thebutterflyfarm.com* ☎*$12* ☉*Daily 9–3.*

French Cul de Sac. North of Orient Bay Beach, the French-colonial mansion of St. Martin's mayor is nestled in the hills. Little red-roof houses look like open umbrellas tumbling down the green hillside. The area is peaceful and good for hiking. There's construction, however, as the surroundings are slowly being developed. From the beach here, shuttle boats make the five-minute trip to **Ilet Pinel,** an uninhabited island that's fine for picnicking, sunning, and swimming.

Grand Case. The island's most picturesque town is set in the heart of the French side on a beach at the foot of green hills and pastures. Though it has only a 1-mi-long (1½-km-long) main street, it's known as the restaurant capital of the Caribbean. More than 27 restaurants serve French,

Italian, Indonesian, and Vietnamese fare here. The budget-minded love the half-dozen lolos—kiosks at the far end of town that sell savory barbecue and seafood. Grand Case Beach Club is at the end of this road and has two beaches where you can take a dip.

Guana Bay Point. On the rugged, windswept east coast about 10 minutes north of Philipsburg, Guana Bay Point offers isolated, untended beaches and a spectacular view of St. Barths. However, because of the undercurrent, this should be more of a turf than a surf destination.

★ **Le Fort Louis.** Though not much remains of the structure itself, the fort, completed by the French in 1789, commands a sweeping view of Marigot, its harbor, and the English island of Anguilla, which alone makes it worth the climb. There are few signs to show the way, so the best way to find the fort is to go to Marigot and look up. ✉ *Marigot*.

Marigot. This town has a southern European flavor, especially its beautiful harborfront, with shopping stalls, open-air cafés, and fresh-food vendors. It's well worth a few hours to explore if you're a shopper, a gourmand, or just a Francophile. Marina Royale is the shopping complex at the port, but rue de la République and rue de la Liberté, which border the bay, are also filled with duty-free shops, boutiques, and bistros. The West Indies Mall offers a deluxe shopping experience. There's less bustle here than in Philipsburg, and the open-air cafés are tempting places to sit and people-watch. Marigot doesn't die at night, so you might wish to stay here into the evening—particularly on Wednesday, when the market opens its art, crafts, and souvenir stalls, and on Thursday, when the shops of Marina Royale remain open until 10 and shoppers enjoy live music. From the harborfront you can catch the ferry for Anguilla or St. Barths. Overlooking the town is Le Fort Louis, from which you get a breathtaking, panoramic view of Marigot and the surrounding area. Every Wednesday and Saturday at the foot of Le Fort Louis, there's an open-air food market where fresh fish, produce, fruits, and spices are sold and crowds sample the goods. Parking can be a real challenge during the business day and even at night during the high season.

Orléans. North of Oyster Pond and the Étang aux Poissons (Fish Lake) is the island's oldest settlement, also known as the French Quarter. You can find classic, vibrantly painted West Indian–style homes with elaborate ginger-bread fretwork.

Philipsburg. The capital of Dutch St. Maarten stretches about a mile (1½ km) along an isthmus between Great Bay and the Salt Pond and has five parallel streets. Most of the village's dozens of shops and restaurants are on Front Street, narrow and cobblestoned, closest to Great Bay. It's generally congested when cruise ships are in port, because of its many duty-free shops and several casinos. Little lanes called *steegjes* connect Front Street with Back Street, which has fewer shops and considerably less congestion. Along the beach is a newly constructed ½-mi-long (1-km-long) boardwalk with restaurants and several Wi-Fi hot spots.

Wathey Square (pronounced watty) is in the heart of the village. Directly across from the square are the town hall and the courthouse, in the striking white building with the cupola. The structure was built in 1793 and has served as the commander's home, a fire station, a jail, and a post office. The streets surrounding the square are lined with hotels, duty-free shops, fine restaurants, and cafés. The **Captain Hodge Pier,** just off the square, is a good spot to view Great Bay and the beach that stretches alongside. The **Sint Maarten Museum** hosts rotating cultural exhibits and a permanent historical display called Forts of St. Maarten–St. Martin. The artifacts range from Arawak pottery shards to objects salvaged from the wreck of the HMS *Proselyte*. ✉7 *Front St., Philipsburg* ☎599/542–4917 ✒*Free* ☉ *Weekdays 10–4, Sat. 10–2.*

Pic du Paradis. From Friar's Bay Beach, a bumpy, tree-canopied road leads inland to this peak. At 1,492 feet, it's the island's highest point. There are two observation areas. From them, the tropical forest unfolds below and the vistas are breathtaking. The road is quite isolated, so it's best to travel in groups. It's also quite steep and not in particularly good shape, becoming a single lane as you near the summit; if you don't have a four-wheel-drive vehicle, don't even try it. Parking at the top is iffy, and it's best if you turn around before you park. It may not be so easy later.

★ Near the bottom of Pic du Paradis is **Loterie Farm,** a peaceful 150-acre private nature preserve opened to the public in 1999 by American expat B. J. Welch. Designed to preserve island habitats, Loterie Farm offers a rare glimpse of Caribbean forest and mountain land. Welch has renovated an old farmhouse and welcomes visitors for hiking, mountain biking, ecotours, or less strenuous activities, such as meditation and yoga. Raves accompany lunch and dinner fare at the Hidden Forest Café since chef Julie Purkis took over the kitchen. The restaurant is open Tuesday through Sunday. The Loterie Farm's newest attraction, the Fly Zone, allows Tarzan wannabes to soar over the forest canopy via a series of ropes, cables, and suspended bridges. The Fly Zone boasts the longest zip lines in the Western Hemisphere. ✉*Rte. de Pic du Paradis* ☎*590/87–86–16 or 590/57–28–55* 🎫*€5* ⏱*Daily sunrise–sunset.*

Plantation Mont Vernon. Wander past indigenous flora, a renovated 1786 cotton plantation, and an old-fashioned rum distillery at a unique outdoor history and ecomuseum. Along the rambling paths of this former wooded estate, bilingual signs give detailed explanations of the island's agricultural history when its economy was dependent on salt, rum, coffee, sugar, and indigo. There's a complimentary coffee bar along the way and a delightful gift shop at the entrance. ✉*Rte. d'Orient-Baie* ☎*590/29–50–62* 🌐*www.plantationmontvernon.com* 🎫*€12* ⏱*Daily 9–5.*

St. Maarten Park. This delightful little enclave houses animals and plants indigenous to the Caribbean and South America, including many birds that were inherited from a former aviary. There's also a bat cave filled with fruit bats. The zoo's lone male collared peccary now has a female to keep him company. A family of cotton-topped tamarins also have taken residence at the zoo. All the animals live among more than 100 different plant species. The Monkey Bar is the zoo's charming souvenir shop and sells Caribbean and zoo mementos. This is a perfect place to take the kids when they need a break from the sand and sea. ✉*Madame Estate, Arch Rd., Philipsburg* ☎*599/543–2030* 🎫*$10* ⏱*Mid-Dec.–mid-Apr., daily 9–5; mid-Apr.–mid-Dec., daily 9:30–6.*

WHERE TO EAT

Although most people come to St. Maarten/St. Martin for sun and fun, they leave craving the cuisine. That's not surprising as the food is so interesting and varied that the island has come to be known as the gourmet capital of the Caribbean. For an island that covers only 37 square mi, there are more than 400 restaurants from which to choose. During your visit you can sample the best dishes

Concordia

The smallest island in the world to be shared between two different countries, St. Maarten/ St. Martin has existed peacefully in its subdivided state for more than 360 years. The Treaty of Concordia, which subdivided the island, was signed in 1648 and was really inspired by the two resident colonies of French and Dutch settlers (not to mention their respective governments) joining forces to repel a common enemy, the Spanish, in 1644. Although the French were promised the side of the island facing Anguilla and the Dutch the south side of the island, the boundary itself wasn't firmly established until 1817 and then after several disputes (16 of them, to be exact).

from France, Thailand, Italy, Vietnam, India, Japan, and, of course, the Caribbean.

Many of the best restaurants are in Grand Case, but you should not limit your culinary adventures to that place. There are great dining options throughout the island, from the bistros of Marigot to the romantic restaurants of Cupecoy to the low-key eateries of Simpson Bay. Whether you enjoy dining on fine china in one of the upscale restaurants or off a paper plate at the island's many *lolos* (roadside eateries), St. Maarten/St. Martin's culinary options are sure to appeal to everyone.

ABOUT THE RESTAURANTS

During high season, it's essential to **make reservations,** and making them a month in advance is advisable for some of the best places. Often restaurants include a 15% service charge, so go over your bill before tipping. Keep in mind that you can't always leave tips on your credit card, so carry enough cash. A taxi is probably the easiest solution to the parking problems in Grand Case, Marigot, and Philipsburg. Grand Case has two lots—each costs $4—at each end of the main boulevard, but they're always packed.

WHAT TO WEAR

Although appropriate dining attire ranges from swimsuits to sport jackets, casual dress is usually appropriate throughout restaurants on the island. For men, a jacket and khakis or jeans will take you anywhere; for women, dressy pants, a skirt, or even fancy shorts are usually acceptable. Jeans are fine in the less formal eateries. In the listings below dress is casual (and chic) unless otherwise noted, but ask when making reservations if you're unsure.

WHAT IT COSTS IN U.S. DOLLARS				
$$$$	$$$	$$	$	¢
RESTAURANTS				
over $30	$20–$30	$12–$20	$8–$12	under $8

Restaurant prices are for a main course, excluding taxes and service charges.

DUTCH SIDE

ASIAN

$$–$$$ ✕**Wajang Doll.** The *wajang*, a puppet used in traditional plays, lends its name to this popular Indonesian restaurant. Standout dishes include the rijsttafel, an Indonesian specialty that includes 15 to 20 small dishes. Other standouts include *nasi goreng* (fried rice) and such seafood dishes as red snapper. ⊠*Royal Village Unit 5, Welfare Rd. 58, Cole Bay* ☎*599/544–2255* ▤*AE, MC, V* ⊙*Closed Sun. No lunch.*

CAFÉS

¢–$ ✕**Au Petit Café Français.** This tiny bistro is found in the quaint shopping area just off Front Street. It only has a small amount of indoor and outdoor seating, but it's worth the visit for a quick, inexpensive snack or for a freshly ground cup of coffee. Watching employees make crepes is half the fun; eating them is the other half. You can also order hearty salads, pizza, and hot or cold sandwiches on fresh bread. It opens at 11 AM. ⊠*120 Old St., Philipsburg* ☎*No phone* ▤*No credit cards* ⊙*Closed Sun. No dinner.*

¢–$ ✕**Kangaroo Court Café.** Grab a table on the lovely back patio of this little café. Almond trees shade it so well that nets are installed to keep nuts and leaves from hitting diners. Although it's best known for coffees, the café also serves great sandwiches, salads, and pizzas. Wash it all down with a fruit frappés, or a selection from one of the island's largest selections of wines by the glass. Incidentally, the odd name comes from the location, next to the courthouse in Philipsburg. ⊠*6 Front St., Philipsburg* ☎*599/542–7557* ▤*AE, D, MC, V* ⊙*Closed Sun. No dinner.*

¢–$ ✕**Zee Best.** This cozy bistro serves one of the best breakfasts on the island. There's a huge selection of sweet and savory

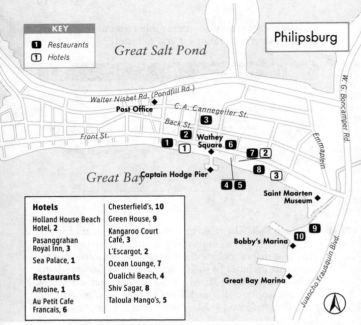

KEY

1 *Restaurants*

1 *Hotels*

Great Salt Pond

Walter Nisbet Rd. (Pondfill Rd.)

Post Office

C.A. Cannegeiter St.

Back St.

Front St.

W. G. Boncamper Rd.

3

2 **Wathey** **6**
Square

7 **2**

1

1

Emmaplein

8

Great Bay **Captain Hodge Pier**

3

4 **5**

Saint Maarten
Museum

9

Bobby's Marina **10**

Juancho Yrausquin Blvd.

Great Bay Marina

Hotels

Holland House Beach
Hotel, **2**

Pasanggrahan
Royal Inn, **3**

Sea Palace, **1**

Restaurants

Antoine, **1**

Au Petit Cafe
Francais, **6**

Chesterfield's, **10**

Green House, **9**

Kangaroo Court
Café, **3**

L'Escargot, **2**

Ocean Lounge, **7**

Oualichi Beach, **4**

Shiv Sagar, **8**

Taloula Mango's, **5**

crepes, omelets, quiches, and freshly baked croissants and other treats from the oven. Specialties include the St. Martin omelet, filled with ham, cheese, mushrooms, onions, green peppers, and tomatoes. Best of all, breakfast is served until 2 PM—perfect for late risers. Lunch includes sandwiches, salads, and the chef's famous spaghetti bolognaise. Grab a table in the dining room or on the terrace; it's a good place to relax with a newspaper and a cup of cappuccino. Zee Best turns into Piccolo restaurant for dinner. ⊠*Plaza del Lago, Simpson Bay* ☎*599/544–2477* ▭*No credit cards.*

CARIBBEAN

\$–\$\$ ✕**Turtle Pier Bar & Restaurant.** The open-air setting, sea breezes, wood-plank floors, and huge lobster tank leave no doubt that you're sitting on a pier in the Caribbean. Unfortunately, the laid-back atmosphere outweighs the average food and slow service. Open seven days a week for breakfast, lunch, and dinner, Turtle Pier has a notable lobster night on Wednesday, buffets on Saturday night, all-you-can-eat rib dinners on Sunday, and live music several nights a week. ⊠*114 Airport Rd., Simpson Bay* ☎*599/545–2562* ▭*AE, D, MC, V.*

CONTINENTAL

$–$$ ✕**Chesterfield's.** On the Great Bay waterfront, Chesterfield's is a St. Maarten institution. A five-minute walk from the cruise-ship pier, nautically themed Chesty's is a great place for relaxed meals on the open-air deck. It serves breakfast, lunch, and dinner at reasonable prices. The main fare is steak and seafood, though the menu includes Duck Chesterfield (roast duckling with fresh pineapple-and-banana sauce), peel-and-eat shrimp, and conch fritters. The Mermaid Bar is popular with yachties, locals, and tourists alike. ⌂*Great Bay Marina, Philipsburg* ☎*599/542–3484* ⊟*MC, V.*

ECLECTIC

$–$$$ ✕**Bamboo Bernies.** This place is many different things: a tiki bar, a concert venue, and a restaurant. The open-air dining area is positioned so that it is almost entirely surrounded by the ocean, so you can be sure to have a good view—especially if you're here to watch the sunset. Favorite dishes include dry-rub barbecue ribs, chicken and shrimp kebabs, and pan-roasted mahimahi. There's also a sushi bar with a few dozen kinds of sushi and sashimi. ⌂*Caranvanerai Resort, 2 Beacon Hill Rd., Maho* ☎*599/545–3622* ⊟*MC, V* ☾*No lunch.*

$$$$ ✕**Bliss.** Part restaurant, part lounge, and nightclub, Bliss is one of the most popular nightspots in St. Maarten. The open-air dining room, decorated in cool Caribbean colors, has great views of the ocean. The contemporary menu features dishes like grilled sirloin, lobster bruschetta, and slow-baked salmon. Stay after dinner and have a drink at the bar, listen to the DJs, or dance under the stars. ⌂*Caranvanerai Resort, 2 Beacon Hill Rd., Maho* ☎*599/545–3996* ⊟*AE, D, MC, V* ☾*No lunch.*

$–$$$ ✕**The Green House.** The famous happy hour is just one of the reasons people flock to the Green House. This waterfront restaurant balances a relaxed atmosphere, reasonable prices, and quality food with a just-right, flavorful bite. All the beef served is Black Angus, and some people say the burgers and steaks are the best on the island. If you're seeking something spicy, try the deep fried calamari. The daily specials, like the Friday-night "lobster mania," are widely popular. ⌂*Bobby's Marina, Philipsburg* ☎*599/542–2941* ⊟*AE, D, MC, V.*

$$–$$$$ ✕**Ocean Lounge.** This restaurant's prime location on the boardwalk in Philipsburg has made it quite a hot spot. The sleek white tablecloths and dark wood columns call to mind

a café on the Mediterranean. Standout dishes include the tilapia fillet and the *Kwekkeboom Kroketten*, (croquettes served with toast and mustard). The dinner dishes include finger foods like chicken sate with spicy peanut sauce and Spanish-style meatballs in tomato sauce. ⊠*Holland House Beach Hotel, 43 Front St., Philipsburg* ☎*599/542–2572* ⊟*AE, D, MC, V.*

$–$$$ ✕**Oualichi Beach Bar & Restaurant.** Conveniently located on the boardwalk, Oualichi has great views of the cruise ships from its nautically themed dining room or outdoor terrace. This is a popular hangout and everyone on the island seems to love the Oualichi pizza. The menu also includes casual fare like sandwiches and wraps. ⊠*Great Bay Beach Boardwalk, Philipsburg* ☎*599/542–4313* ⊟*AE, D, MC, V* ⊙*No lunch Sun.–Wed.*

$$$–$$$$ ✕**Peg Leg Pub.** Overlooking Simpson Bay Lagoon, this place is a cross between your typical beach bar and an English pub. Lunch options include deli-style sandwich platters. For dinner try the mango chicken or the sea-and-land combo featuring a New York strip steak and jumbo garlic shrimp. Good news for beer lovers: Peg Leg Pub serves more than 35 different brews. Best of all, appetizers are half-price during happy hour; try the bacon-wrapped shrimp, jalapeno cheese poppers, or the coconut shrimp. ⊠*3 Palm Plaza, Simpson Bay* ☎*599/544–5859* ⊟*AE, D, MC, V* ⊙*No lunch Sun.*

$$$–$$$$ ✕**Saratoga.** At Simpson Bay Yacht Club, this elegant res-
★ taurant lets you choose between the waterfront terrace and the handsome mahogany-paneled dining room. The menu changes daily, but you can never go wrong with one of chef John Jackson's takes on fresh fish, including wahoo, red snapper, and yellowfin tuna. You might start with a spicy ceviche of snapper with mango and tortilla chips, then segue to grilled grouper fillet. The wine list includes 150 different wines, including many by the glass. ⊠*Simpson Bay Yacht Club, Airport Blvd., Simpson Bay* ☎*599/544–2421* ⌂*Reservations essential* ⊟*AE, D, MC, V* ⊙*Closed Sun. Closed Aug. and Sept. No lunch.*

$$ ✕**Taloula Mango's.** Ribs are the specialty at this casual beachfront restaurant, but the jerk chicken and thin-crust pizza are not to be ignored. There are also vegetarian options, like the tasty falafel. On weekdays lunch is accompanied by live music; every Friday during happy hour a DJ spins tunes. In case you're wondering, the restaurant got its name from the owner's golden retriever. ⊠*Sint Rose Shop-*

ping Mall, off Front St. on beach boardwalk, Philipsburg ☎*599/542–1645* ☐*AE, D, MC, V.*

★ **Fodor's**Choice ✕**Temptation.** If you think you know Caribbean

$$$–$$$$ cuisine, the constantly changing menu at Temptation just might come as a surprise. Chef Dino Jagtiani, who trained at the Culinary Institute of America, is the mastermind behind dishes like tamarind-glazed mahimahi or caramelized onion-crusted Atlantic salmon. The wine list is extensive and features a number of reasonably priced selections. There are also many inventive cocktails, such as the St. Maartini—a refreshing blend of coconut rum, guava puree, passion fruit juice, and peach schnapps. The dining room is cozy and intimate, with low lighting and live piano music. There's outdoor seating as well. ⊠*Atlantis World Casino, Rhine Rd. 106, Cupecoy* ☎*599/545–2254* ☐*AE, D, MC, V* ⊙*Closed Mon. mid-June–Aug. No lunch.*

FRENCH

$$$–$$$$ ✕**Antoine.** You'd be hard-pressed to find a more enjoy-
★ able evening in Philipsburg. Owner Jean Pierre Pomarico's warmth shines through as he greets guests and ushers them into the comfy seaside restaurant. Low-key, blue-accented decor, white bamboo chairs, water-colors lining the walls, and candles—along with the sound of the nearby surf—create a relaxing atmosphere. The lobster thermidor (a succulent tail oozing with cream and Swiss cheese) is a favorite, but other specialties include the seafood linguine and the fillet with shallot butter. At $29, the prix-fixe menu is a great deal. ⊠*119 Front St., Philipsburg* ☎*599/542–2964* ⊕*www.antoinerestaurant.com* ⌂*Reservations essential* ☐*AE, D, MC, V.*

$$$–$$$$ ✕**L'Escargot.** One of the most venerable restaurants in St. Maarten, L'Escargot is in a 150-year-old creole house. The wraparound veranda, the bunches of grapes hanging from the chandeliers, and the Toulouse Lautrec–style murals add to the colorful atmosphere. As the names suggest, snails are the specialty. There are eight different kinds on the menu, but if you can't decide between them just ask owners Jöel and Sonya for the appetizer sampler. You can't go wrong with specialties like rack of lamb and roast duck. There's also a Friday night cabaret show in the tradition of *La Cage aux Folles*. ⊠*96 Front St., Philipsburg* ☎*599/542–2483* ⊕*www.lescargotrestaurant.com* ☐*AE, MC, V.*

$$$–$$$$ ✕**Le Monmartre.** Evoking 19th-century Paris, Le Montmartre is based on an actual bistro. The owners have gone to great lengths to install mirrored walls and crystal chandeliers

for a Parisian bistro feel. The food is creative and inventive, with twists on classic French dishes. Here you'll find grilled Caribbean lobster tail with bacon and pasta in butter sauce and the kangaroo fillet with sweet potato puree and spinach. Save room for desserts like homemade tiramisu or a crisp pastry filled with vanilla crème brûlée and covered with chocolate mousse. ⊠*Atlantis World Casino, Rhine Rd. 106, Cupecoy* ☎*599/544–3939* ⊟*AE, MC, V* ☾*No lunch.*

INDIAN

$$ ✕**Shiv Sagar.** The colors of India—notably yellow and green—enliven this second-floor restaurant in Philipsburg. What it lacks in decor it more than makes up for in flavor. The menu emphasizes northern Indian specialties, including marvelous tandooris and curries, but try one of the less familiar dishes such as *madrasi machi* (red snapper with hot spices) or *saag gosht* (lamb sautéed with spinach). ⊠*20 Front St., opposite First Caribbean International Bank, Philipsburg* ☎*599/542–2299* ⊕*www.shivsagarsxm.com* ⊟*AE, D, DC, MC, V* ☾*Closed Sun. dinner.*

ITALIAN

★ Fodor'sChoice ✕**La Gondola.** Owner Davide Foini started out by
$$$–$$$$ selling his homemade pasta, and it proved to be so popular that he opened this authentic trattoria. The kitchen still rolls out the dough for dishes gnocchi with gorgonzola. Other standouts include seafood risotto, shrimp linguine, and lobster ravioli. Save room for desserts like the homemade tiramisu or the warm chocolate tart. The service is attentive, although sometimes distracting, as waiters walk around with ear pieces and handheld computers. The food more than makes up for all of this. ⊠*Atlantis World Casino, Rhine Rd. 106, Cupecoy* ☎*599/544–3938* ⊟*AE, MC, V* ☾*No lunch.*

$$–$$$$ ✕**Trattoria Pizza Pasta.** Tucked away on a quiet street near Casino Royale, this Italian eatery is extremely popular with locals. The menu includes favorites like penne Bolognese and eggplant Parmesan, but the real winners are the thin crust pizzas. The freshly brewed ice tea is great on a hot day. With its laid-back atmosphere and friendly staff, this is a good spot for large groups and families with small children. It can get quite loud, however. ⊠*Maho Shopping Plaza, Maho* ☎*599/545–4034* ⊟*No credit cards* ☾*No lunch Sun.*

1

SEAFOOD

$–$$ ✕**The Boathouse.** On the waterfront in Simpson Bay, this lively restaurant stays true to its nautical theme with life preservers and other sailing equipment decorating the walls. As you might guess, the menu leans toward seafood and includes dishes like coconut shrimp and red snapper stuffed with crabmeat. The steaks and burgers are also worth a try. The bar is a great place to catch live music throughout the week. ✉ *74 Airport Rd., Simpson Bay* ☎ *599/544–5409* ▭ *D, MC, V.*

STEAK

$$–$$$$ ✕**Los Gauchos Argentine Grill.** You might not expect to find
★ first-quality Argentine meat on an island in the Caribbean, but here it is. The restaurant, decorated with cow-print chairs, has some of the best beef in town. On Friday, there's an all-you can-eat barbecue ($21.95) accompanied by a steel-pan band. Less carnivorous types will find chicken, fish, and even vegetarian selections on the menu. Selections from Argentina are featured on the wine list. ✉ *Pelican Resort Club Marina, Simpson Bay* ☎ *599/544–4084* ▭ *D, MC, V.*

$$$ ✕**Rare.** If you're craving a hearty steak, Rare is the place to go. There's a window into the kitchen so you can watch as your meat is grilled to perfection. Chef Dino Jagtiani has put together a creative menu that includes everything from filet mignon to stone-crab claws. Don't pass up the delicious sides like truffled macaroni and cheese, chili-garlic fries, and Vidalia onion rings with rhubarb ketchup and wasabi hollandaise. Desserts like icebox cake or the chocolate pudding napoleon are definitely worth a try. ✉ *Atlantis World Casino, Rhine Rd. 106, Cupecoy* ☎ *599/545–5714* ▭ *AE, D, MC, V* ☉ *Close Sun. mid-Apr.–mid-Dec. No lunch.*

VEGETARIAN

¢–$ ✕**Top Carrot.** This vegetarian café and juice bar serves sandwiches, salads, and homemade pastries for breakfast and lunch. Get here early, as the place closed at 6 PM. Favorites include a pastry stuffed with pesto, avocado, red pepper, and feta cheese or a cauliflower, spinach, and tomato quiche. Other health-food specialties include homemade granola and yogurt. Adjacent to the restaurant is a small gift shop with Asian-inspired items plus books on eating healthily. ✉ *Airport Rd., near Simpson Bay Yacht Club, Simpson Bay* ☎ *599/544–3381* ▭ *MC, V* ☉ *Closed Sun. No dinner.*

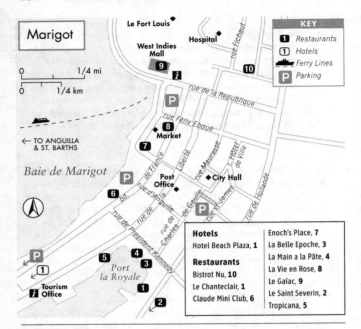

Marigot

KEY
- **1** Restaurants
- **1** Hotels
- Ferry Lines
- **P** Parking

0 ———— 1/4 mi
0 ———— 1/4 km

← TO ANGUILLA & ST. BARTHS

Baie de Marigot

Le Fort Louis
West Indies Mall
Hospital
rue de la République
rue Félix Eboué
Market
rue de France
Liberté
rue Maurasse
L. Hôtel de Ville
Post Office
City Hall
rue de la République
Port la Royale
bd. de Gaulle
rue de Anguille
rue de Chartres
rue de President Kennedy
rue de Hollande
rue st-James
Tourism Office

Hotels
Hotel Beach Plaza, **1**

Restaurants
Bistrot Nu, **10**
Le Chanteclair, **1**
Claude Mini Club, **6**

Enoch's Place, **7**
La Belle Epoche, **3**
La Main a la Pâte, **4**
La Vie en Rose, **8**
Le Gaïac, **9**
Le Saint Severin, **2**
Tropicana, **5**

FRENCH SIDE

ASIAN

$$ ✕**Thai Garden.** A longtime favorite, Thai Garden remains quite popular among locals. The decor evokes Asian with bamboo tables and chairs, golden Buddha statues, and crimson walls. Some of the Thai, Vietnamese, and Japanese dishes on the menu include crispy fried spring rolls, lemongrass soup, and an array of spicy curries. There's also a sushi and sashimi bar serving the catch of the day. The restaurant is on the road between Nettle Bay and Marigot, with several signs pointing the way. ⊠*68 Rte. de Terres Basses, Sandy Ground* ☎*590/87–88–44* ▤*MC, V* ⊘*Closed Sun. No lunch.*

CARIBBEAN

$$–$$$$ ✕**Claude Mini-Club.** An island institution, Claude Mini-Club has delighted patrons with its blend of creole and French food since 1969. The whole place is built tree-house style around the trunks of coconut palms, and the lofty perch means you have great views of Marigot Harbor. The chairs and tablecloths are a mélange of sunny yellows and oranges. The €40 dinner buffet on Wednesday and Saturday night is legendary. It includes more than 30 dishes, like conch soup, baked ham, blackened goose, and roast pig. Fresh snapper is one of the specialties on the à la carte menu. There's live music nightly. ⊠*Front de Mer, Marigot* ☎*590/87–50–69* ⊟*AE, MC, V* ☉*Closed Sun.*

$ ×**Enoch's Place.** The blue-and-white-stripe awning on a corner of the Marigot Market makes this place hard to miss. But Enoch's cooking is what draws the crowds. Specialties include garlic shrimp, fresh lobster, and rice and beans (like your St. Martin mother used to make). Try the salt fish and fried johnnycake—a great breakfast option. The food more than makes up for the lack of decor, and chances are you'll be counting the days until you can return. ⊠*Marigot Market, Front de Mer, Marigot* ☎*590/29–29–88* ⊟*No credit cards* ☉*Closed Sun. No dinner.*

$–$$$ ×**Le Ti Coin Creole.** A meal here is like dining with friends. Chef Carl Philips creates the atmosphere and succulent creole cuisine at this cozy spot, like chicken with tamarind sauce and pasta with peppers, onions, and hot sauce. He serves these goodies on the verandah of his mother's house. It's reasonably priced and friendly. What else do you need? ⊠*Grand Case Blvd., Grand Case* ☎*590/87–92–09* ⊟*MC, V.*

$$ ×**Paradise View.** For some of the best views of Orient Beach, ★ Pinel Island, and St. Barths, head to this place on Baie Orientale. Sit back with cocktails like the ti punch or Mango Madness while owner Claudette Davis regales you with stories about the island. Menu choices include everything from sandwiches and salads to ribs and seafood. There's also a good Sunday lunch buffet. ⊠*Hope Hill, Baie Orientale* ☎*590/29–45–37* ⊟*AE, MC, V* ☉*Closed Mon.*

★ Fodor'sChoice ×**Talk of the Town.** Although Grand Case is
¢–$ known for its upscale dining, you can also find a number of *lolos,* or roadside barbecue stands. One of the most popular is Talk of the Town. With plastic utensils and paper plates, it couldn't be more informal. The menu includes everything from succulent grilled ribs to stewed conch. Don't miss the johnnycakes and side dishes like plantains, curried rice, beans and coleslaw. The service is friendly, if a bit slow, but sit back with a beer and enjoy the experience. ⊠*Grand Case Blvd., Grand Case* ☎*No phone* ⊟*No credit cards.*

ECLECTIC

$$–$$$$ ✕**Kon Tiki.** Thatched roofs cover the booths at this happening beach bar and restaurant on beautiful Baie Orientale. The food here is great, ranging from casual dishes like burgers and sandwiches to more substantial fare like grilled tuna and mahimahi. There's one potential problem: nude bathers occasionally stroll by, making it somewhat difficult to concentrate on your meal. An added bonus: you can book a variety of water sports right at the restaurant. ⊠*5 Baie Orientale* ☎*590/87–43–27* ▭*MC, V* ⊘*No dinner.*

$–$$ ✕**La Belle Epoque.** A favorite among locals, this sometimes
★ frenzied little bistro is on the marina. Whether you stop for a drink or a meal, you'll soon discover that it's a prime venue for boat- and people-watching. The menu has a bit of everything, from pizza and pasta to lobster and seafood. There's also a good wine list. ⊠*Marina Royale, Marigot* ☎*590/87–87–70* ▭*AE, MC, V.*

$–$$$ ✕**La Main à La Pâte.** A great place to people-watch, this
★ restaurant sits on the waterfront at Marina Royale. One of the highlights on the globetrotting menu is the lobster-tail salad, a light concoction full of firm lobster meat and tomato sauce. La Palette Caraïbes, which includes three different fish, includes the tastiest tuna steak on the island. Be sure to try the passion pie with mango ice cream for dessert. The staff is friendly and knowledgeable. ⊠*Marina Royale, Marigot* ☎*590/87–71–19* ▭*D, MC, V.*

$$$–$$$$ ✕**Le Pressoir.** In a West Indian house painted ravishing shades
★ of yellow and blue, Le Pressoir has charm to spare. French and creole cuisine dominates the menu, so you'll find dishes like sea scallops in a mango butter sauce and rum-marinated foie gras. Don't miss the seafood special, which includes a first course of shrimp, scallops, and mussels and a second with four types of grilled fish. The name, by the way, comes from the historic salt press that sits opposite the restaurant. ⊠*30 blvd. de Grand Case, Grand Case* ☎*590/87–76–62* ▭*AE, MC, V* ⊘*Closed Sun. No lunch.*

$$$–$$$$ ✕**Le Tastevin.** In the heart of Grand Case, Le Tastevin is filled with flowers, plants, and coconut palms. The owners also founded the popular L'Auberge Gourmande across the street. The menu changes frequently, but you might find ambitious offerings like foie gras with figs, crab tartare with tomato, or beef with sauterne sauce. ⊠*86 blvd. de Grand Case, Grand Case* ☎*590/87–55–45* ⚲*Reservations essential* ▭*AE, MC, V* ⊘*Closed mid-Aug.–Sept.*

★ **Fodor'sChoice** ✕**Rainbow Café.** Refreshing sea breezes mean
$$$–$$$$ that these palm-shaded tables are always in demand. It

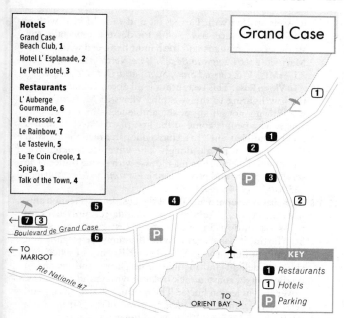

Hotels

Grand Case
Beach Club, **1**

Hotel L' Esplanade, **2**

Le Petit Hotel, **3**

Restaurants

L' Auberge
Gourmande, **6**

Le Pressoir, **2**

Le Rainbow, **7**

Le Tastevin, **5**

Le Te Coin Creole, **1**

Spiga, **3**

Talk of the Town, **4**

Grand Case

KEY

1 Restaurants

1 Hotels

P Parking

← TO
MARIGOT

TO
ORIENT BAY →

has great views of the bay, but the real reason people
come to this comfortable bistro is for the food. The menu
includes shrimp and scallop with an island-style chutney.
The friendly owners and staff make a meal here memo-
rable. Check out the upstairs lounge, which has a cigar
and pipe bar. ⊠*176 blvd. de Grand Case, Grand Case*
☎*590/87–55–80* ▭*AE, MC, V* ⊘*Closed Sun.*

FRENCH

$$–$$$$ ✕**Bistrot Nu.** It's hard to top the simple, unadorned fare and
reasonable prices you can find at this intimate restaurant
tucked in a Marigot alley. Traditional French and Creole
food—coq au vin, fish soup, snails—is served in a friendly,
intimate dining room. The prix-fixe menu is a very good
value. The place is popular, and the tables are routinely
packed until it closes at midnight. It can be difficult to park
here, so take your chances at finding a spot on the street—or
try a taxi. ⊠*Rue de Hollande, Marigot* ☎*590/87–97–09*
▭*MC, V* ⌕*Reservations essential* ⊘*Closed Sun.*

$$$–$$$$ ✕**La Cigale.** On the edge of Baie Nettlé, La Cigale has won-
derful views of the lagoon from its dining room and its
open-air patio. The restaurant stays true to its French
roots with dishes like bouillabaisse of frogs' legs and snails,

mussels stuffed with Parmesan, and rack of veal with a honey-citrus sauce. Save room for dessert, especially the strawberries, mangos and fresh mint flambéed with Grand Marnier. ✉ *101 Laguna Beach, Baie Nettlé* ☎599/87–90–23 ═MC, V ⊘ *Closed Sun., Sept., and Oct. No lunch.*

$$–$$$$ ✕**La Vie en Rose.** This restaurant is all about romance, from the low lighting to the sweeping views of Marigot's harbor. But it's not all about the ambience—the French cuisine is why people come in the first place. Favorite dishes include sautéed foie gras, smoked lobster medallions, and the escargot in phyllo dough. The wine list is extensive, and desserts include banana mousse with crème brûlée. The service is polite and professional. ✉ *Front de Mer, Marigot* ☎590/87–54–42 ═AE, MC, V.

$$–$$$ ✕**L'Auberge Gourmande.** One of the best-known restaurants in Grand Case, L'Auberge Gourmande certainly lives up to its reputation. In one of the oldest creole houses in St. Martin, it has elegant arches framing the elegant and charming dining room. Chef Didier Rochat's French cuisine is a delight and includes blue cheese and pecans in phyllo dough, roasted rack of lamb with garlic and herbs, dover sole in lemon butter. The restaurant also has a good selection of wines. ✉ *89 blvd. de Grand Case, Grand Case* ☎590/87–73–37 ═MC, V ⊘ *No lunch.*

$$–$$$ ✕**Le Chanteclair.** Award-winning chef Cecile Braud-Richard is the force behind this gem in Marigot's Marina Royale. The family-run restaurant serves French dishes with an inventive Caribbean twist. The menu features *assiettes degustations* (tasting plates) with a selection of the most popular appetizers; the *menu gastronomique special langouste,* is a set menu with a standout lobster dish. The desserts are just as creative, especially the *l'innommable au chocolat,* the "unnamable" desert made with chocolate and vanilla ice cream. ✉ *Marina Royale, Marigot* ☎590/87–94–60 ═MC, V ⊘ *Closed Sun., mid-Sept.–mid-Oct.*

$$$$ ✕**Le Gaïac.** Although you might wonder about this restaurant's location in the West Indies Mall, the terrace means you have great views of Marigot Bay. Meals at this French restaurant come with a hefty price tag, but many say that the food is well worth it. The setting is cozy and intimate. Must-try specialties include braised boneless lamb shoulder served with a creamy garlic sauce, pan-seared duck foie gras accompanied by slices of mango, and black risotto with lobster. The desserts include a chocolate fondant stuffed with bananas. ✉ *West Indies Mall, Marigot* ☎590/51–

St. Maarten vs. St. Martin

If this is your first trip to St. Maarten/St. Martin, you're probably wondering which side will better suit your needs. That's hard to say, because in some ways the difference between the two can seem as subtle as the hazy boundary line dividing them. But there are some major differences. St. Maarten, the Dutch side, has the casinos, more nightlife and bigger hotels. St. Martin, the French side, has no casinos, less nightlife, and hotels that are smaller and more intimate. Many have kitchenettes, and most include breakfast. Even though there are many very good restaurants on the Dutch side, the French side rules when it comes to gourmet dining. The biggest difference might be currency— the Netherlands Antilles guilder on the Dutch side, the euro on the French side. Of course, many estrablishments on both sides accept U.S. dollars.

97–66 ▱*AE, MC, V* ⊘*Closed Sun. and Sept.–mid-Oct. No lunch.*

$$–$$$ ×**Le Saint Severin.** Hidden away in a shopping area near
★ Marigot, Le Saint Severin is a well-kept secret. The simple bistro features cuisine from southwest France (foie gras terrine, grilled duck breast in caramelized shallot sauce, and cod fish tournedos wrapped in bacon), but there are also some dishes from Spain (the excellent paella). You can't go wrong with seafood, and various types are flown in from France Thursday to Sunday. Lunch is quite busy thanks to the wonderful couscous dishes. The staff is attentive and solicitous, treating customers like old friends. ▱*Les Portes de St. Martin, Bellevue* ☏*590/87–97–00* ▱*MC, V* ⊘*Closed Sun. and Mon.*

$$$–$$$$ ×**Le Santal.** Brooke Shields, Steven Tyler, and Diana Ross
★ are among the celebrities who have snagged a table at Le Santal. There are some oceanfront tables, although these are often reserved far in advance. The rest of the tables are nearly as good, with crisp white linens illuminated by flickering candles. Highlights of the award-winning menu include lacquered duckling marinated with honey and caramelized pineapple, chateaubriand with bearnaise sauce, and grilled whole snapper in a white wine sauce. Standouts on the dessert menu include the apple tartlet flambéed with apple brandy. ▱*40 rue Lady Fish, Sandy Ground* ☏*590/87–53–48* ▵*Reservations essential* ▱*AE, MC, V* ⊘*No lunch.*

$$$–$$$$ ✕**Mario's Bistro.** This romantic eatery earns raves for its won-
★ derful cuisine and the romantic ambience. Didier Gonnon
and Martyne Tardif are out front, while chef Mario Tardif
is in the kitchen creating dishes such as sautéed sea scal-
lops with crab mashed potatoes, baked mahimahi with a
macadamia nut crust, and rack of lamb with pesto and goat
cheese. The open-air, country French–style restaurant is on
the canal just after you cross the bridge from Sandy Ground.
⊠*At Sandy Ground Bridge, Sandy Ground* ☎*590/87–06–
36* ⚑*Reservations essential* ▤*MC, V* ⊘*Closed Sun. and
Aug.–Sept. No lunch.*

★ **Fodor'sChoice** ✕**Sol é Luna.** In a small creole house, this res-
$$–$$$ taurant couldn't be more charming. Take a table in the
dining room, on the balcony, or on one of the wraparound
terraces to enjoy the great views. Begin your meal with an
appetizer like the monkfish rolls or tuna carpaccio, then
move on to the lamb shank with date-ginger puree or the
filet mignon with mashed potatoes. Don't be surprised if
you see a proposal or two during your meal, as this is one
of the most romantic restaurants on the island. ⊠*61 Rte. de
Mont Vernon, French Cul de Sac* ☎*590/29–08–56* ▤*MC,
V* ⊘*Closed mid-June–early July and Sept.–early Oct.*

$$–$$$ ✕**Tropicana.** This bustling bistro at the Marina Royale has a
★ completely different vibe at lunch and at dinner. Salads are a
must for lunch, especially the salad niçoise with medallions
of crusted goat cheese. Dinner includes some exceptional
steak and seafood dishes. The wine list is quite extensive.
Desserts are tasty, and you'll never be disappointed with
old standbys like the crème brûlée. You can dine outside or
inside along the yacht-filled waterfront. ⊠*Marina Royale,
Marigot* ☎*590/87–79–07* ▤*D, MC, V.*

ITALIAN

$$–$$$ ✕**Spiga.** In a beautifully restored creole house, Spiga has
been a hit since it opened. There are not many tables, so
book ahead to ensure you can get one out on the terrace.
Chef Ciro Russo describes his cuisine a fusion of Italian
and Caribbean ingredients and cooking techniques. Look
for dishes like spinach tagliatelle with porcini mushrooms,
sun-dried tomato taglioni with lobster, shrimp, and crab.
Other standouts include garlic and ginger diver scallops and
roast pork tenderloin wrapped in smoked pancetta. Save
room for the lemon-ricotta cake and try the selection of
grappa. ⊠*4 Rte. de L'Esperance, Grand Case* ☎*590/524–
783* ▤*D, MC, V* ⊘*Closed mid-Sept.–late Oct. Closed Tues.
June–mid-Sept. No lunch Sun.*

WHERE TO STAY

Scattered up and down the beaches—particularly Simpson Bay and Maho Bay in St. Maarten and Baies Orientale and Nettle in St. Martin—and within the city limits of both Philipsburg and Marigot are a multitude of accommodations. They offer a variety of prices and tastes. Lodgings range from megaresorts like the Sonesta Maho Beach to condos and small inns. On the Dutch side many hotels cater to groups, and although that's also true to some extent on the French side, you can find a larger collection of intimate accommodations there. Time-shares have become extremely popular options, especially since most are available as short-term rentals. Keep in mind that off-season rates (April through the beginning of December) can be as little as half the high-season rates.

ABOUT THE HOTELS

Assume that hotels operate on the European Plan (EP—with no meals) unless we specify that they use either the Continental Plan (CP—with a continental breakfast), Breakfast Plan (BP—with full breakfast), or the Modified American Plan (MAP—with breakfast and dinner). Other hotels may offer the Full American Plan (FAP—including all meals but no drinks) or may be All-Inclusive (AI—with all meals, drinks, and most activities).

WHAT IT COSTS IN U.S. DOLLARS				
$$$$	$$$	$$	$	¢
HOTELS*				
over $350	$250–$350	$150–$250	$80–$150	under $80
HOTELS**				
over $450	$350–$450	$250–$350	$125–$250	under $125

*EP, BP, CP **AI, FAP, MAP; Hotel prices are for two people in a double room in high season, excluding taxes, service charges, and meal plans (except at all-inclusive hotels).

Hot Deals in High Season

The most expensive time to visit St. Maarten/St. Martin is the high season that runs from December to April. But this shouldn't deter bargain hunters. Finding good deals takes perseverance, patience, and flexibility. When you're booking a room, it never hurts to call the hotel directly and ask about special offers. Even the most upscale resorts offer discount rates for certain rooms and certain days of the week during high season. Packages with special themes like water sports or spas can also save you money. Check out deals where kids stay free, you get a free night when you book a certain number of nights, or you're treated to breakfast.

There's a lot of competition at the island's shops and boutiques. Try bargaining, especially in the jewelery stores. Maybe they won't give you a deal, but you won't find out unless you ask. The casinos are always giving something away—chips, drinks, limo service. At restaurants, the prix-fixe lunch or dinner is usually the better deal. On slower nights like Monday and Tuesday, many restaurants offer specials. Look for special offers at the local tourism board and in the local newspaper, the *Daily Herald*.

HOTELS

DUTCH SIDE

$$–$$$ 🏨 **Divi Little Bay Beach Resort.** Popular with tour groups worrying more about price than posh, this resort offers handsome sea views from the balconies of simple and comfortable rooms. The property borders a lovely, not very crowded beach that juts out into Little Bay. There are more than enough activities to keep you busy, including trips on the bay in the resort's own glass-bottom boat. It's also a quick trip to the heart of Philipsburg. **Pros:** Good location, lovely beach. **Cons:** Packed with package tour groups, hallways are dark. ⊠*Little Bay Rd., Box 961, Philipsburg* 🕾*599/542–2333 or 800/367–3484* ⊕*www.diviresorts. com* ⌨*224 rooms* ⚿*In-room: kitchen (some), refrigerator (some), VCR (some). In-hotel: 3 restaurants, bars, tennis court, pools, gym, spa, beachfront, diving, water sports, no elevator, children's programs (ages 3–12), laundry facilities, laundry service* ▤*AE, D, DC, MC, V* ⏧*EP.*

$$–$$$$ 🏨 **Holland House Beach Hotel.** An ideal location for shop fanatics and sun worshippers, this hotel faces the Front Street pedestrian mall; to the rear is the boardwalk and

a lovely stretch of Great Bay Beach. The open lobby provides easy access from street to beach, and has free Internet access. Rooms are basic but comfortable, with balconies and kitchenettes. Reasonably priced food is served at the open-air seaside restaurant. **Pros:** Excellent location, pleasant property. **Cons:** In a busy location, rooms are nothing fancy. ✉*43 Front St., Box 393, Philipsburg* ☎*599/542–2572* ⊕*www.hhbh.com* ➠*48 rooms, 6 suites* �б*In-room: safe, kitchen (some), refrigerator. In-hotel: restaurant, bar, beachfront, public Internet* ☐*AE, D, DC, MC, V* ⧖*EP.*

★ **Fodor'sChoice** ⊡**The Horny Toad.** This lovely guesthouse is widely
$–$$ considered the best on this side of the island. Its virtues are many: the stupendous view of Simpson Bay, the clean and comfortable rooms, the creative decor. But the one thing that keeps patrons coming back year after year is the hospitality of owner Betty Vaughn (ask her how the inn got its name). Treating guests like long-lost relatives, she is so welcoming that you simply can't resist her charms. Book early, because the Toad fills up fast. All rooms but one have air-conditioning. **Pros:** Cozy rooms, friendly vibe, beautiful beach is usually deserted. **Cons:** Rooms are very basic, need a car to get around. ✉*2 Vlaun Dr., Simpson Bay* ☎*599/545–4323 or 800/417–9361* ⊕*www.thehornytoadguesthouse.com* ➠*8 rooms* �б*In-room: no a/c (some), kitchen, no TV. In-hotel: beachfront, no elevator, laundry service, public Internet, public Wi-Fi, no kids under 7* ☐*AE, D, MC, V* ⧖*EP.*

$$–$$$$ ⊡**The Inn at Cupecoy.** Overlooking Cupecoy Beach, this cozy little inn oozes comfort and luxury. Rooms are furnished with zebra-skin rugs, antique chaise lounges, and four-poster king-size beds. Large bathrooms have marble vanities and travertine sinks. The complimentary continental breakfast is served poolside. The Market at Cupecoy supplies gourmet foods, baked goods, cheese, and wine, while the Citrus restaurant specializes in French cuisine. The entire inn can be rented out as a five-bedroom villa. **Pros:** Intimate feel, lovely furnishings, near nightlife. **Cons:** Service is hit or miss, atmosphere is too quiet for some. ✉*130 Lowlands, Cupecoy* ☎*599/545–4333* ➠*5 rooms* �б*In-room: DVD. In-hotel: restaurant, pool, beachfront, no elevator, concierge, airport shuttle* ☐*AE, D, MC, V* ⊘*Closed Aug. 20–Oct. 20* ⧖*CP.*

$$–$$$ ⊡**La Vista.** Hibiscus and bougainvillea line brick walkways
★ that connect the 32 wood-frame bungalows and beachfront suites of this intimate and friendly, family-owned resort perched at the foot of Pelican Key. The rooms are somewhat sparsely furnished and have small bathrooms, but have

balconies with awesome views. The beach is rocky, but good for snorkeling. **Pros:** Nice views, close to restaurants and bars. **Cons:** No-frills furnishings, not the best beach. ✉53 Billy Folly Rd., Pelican Key, Box 2086, Simpson Bay ☎599/544–3005 or 888/790–5264 ⊕www.lavistaresort. com ➷18 rooms, 32 suites &In-room: safe, kitchen (some). In-hotel: restaurant, pools, beachfront, no elevator, laundry facilities ⊟AE, D, MC, V ⊗EP.

$–$$$ ⊞**Mary's Boon Beach Plantation.** On a lovely stretch of Simp-★ son Bay, this attractive guesthouse has a shaded courtyard where guests can gather. Pilot Mary Pomeroy chose this site because of its proximity to the airport. (Ask someone to tell you about her life and her mysterious disappearance.) Indonesian-style furniture graces the lobby as well as the rooms. Accommodations have cathedral ceilings, enormous four-poster beds, and verandahs. You'll find an honor bar with free popcorn and a well-known restaurant with a menu that has not changed since the mid-1970s. **Pros:** Small and intimate, interesting history. **Cons:** Rooms are just average, noisy location, mosquitoes abound. ✉117 Simpson Bay Rd., Simpson Bay ☎599/545–7000 ⊕www.marysboon. com ➷37 rooms &In-room: kitchen (some), dial-up, Wi-Fi. In-hotel: restaurant, bars, pool, beachfront, no elevator, public Internet ⊟AE, D, MC, V ⊗EP.

$$–$$$$ ⊞**Oyster Bay Beach Resort.** Jutting out into Oyster Bay, this out-of-the-way condo resort sits on the shores of Dawn Beach. Rooms are spacious and tastefully decorated with bright colors. All have balconies that feature a fine view of St. Barths or the marina in Oyster Bay. The open-air lobby is as attractive as the free-form infinity pool. Besides the Jade restaurant, there's Beau Beau's, which features island dishes and dancing waitresses called—of course—the Beaubettes. There's a $5 per day charge for air-conditioning. **Pros:** Lots of activities, nightly entertainment, comfortable accommodations. **Cons:** Isolated location, need a car to get around. ✉10 Emerald Merit Rd., Oyster Pond ⟟Box 239, Philipsburg ☎599/543–6040 or 866/978–0212 ⊕www. oysterbaybeachresort.com ➷178 condos &In-room: safe, kitchen, VCR (some). In-hotel: 2 restaurants, bar, pool, gym, beachfront, bicycles, no elevator, laundry facilities, public Internet ⊟AE, D, MC, V ⊗EP.

$–$$ ⊞**Pasanggrahan Royal Inn.** Guests are treated like friends ★ of the family at this cozy inn. The oldest hotel on the island, it once served as the governor's mansion. Walls of the entranceway are lined with pictures of Dutch royalty. Specialty rooms have hand-carved furniture, four-poster beds with mosquito netting, and private balconies. Standard rooms have more of an island flair, with plantation-style furniture. The hotel's restaurant serves excellent meals for a reasonable price; the view looking out over Great Bay isn't bad, either. In case you're wondering, *pasanggrahan* means guesthouse in Indonesian. **Pros:** Well situated, really cozy, friendly staff. **Cons:** On the main drag, crowded beach, small parking lot. ⊠*15 Front St., Box 151, Philipsburg* ☎*599/542–3588 or 599/542–2743* ⊕*www.pasanhotel. com* ⇨*31 rooms* ⚹*In-room: safe, refrigerator. In-hotel: restaurant, bar, beachfront, no elevator, public Internet* ⊟*AE, D, MC, V* ⦿*EP.*

$$$–$$$$ ⊞**Princess Heights.** Sitting on a hill 900 feet above Oyster Bay, this property's spacious suites offer plenty of privacy. Each tastefully decorated apartment has one or two bedrooms, a kitchen whose side-by-side refrigerator comes stocked with complimentary beverages, marble bathrooms with whirlpool tubs, and a white-balustrade balcony with a smashing view of St. Barths. You also get daily maid service. If you send a grocery list, your kitchen will be stocked just prior to your arrival. There's a fee for the service, but it saves searching for a grocery store. The property is 4 mi (6 km) from Philipsburg. At this writing, 18 larger suites are scheduled to be completed sometime in 2008. **Pros:** Away from the crowds, friendly staff, every room has a gorgeous view. **Cons:** Numerous steps to climb, not easy to find, need a car to get around. ⊠*156 Oyster Pond Rd., Oyster Pond* ☎*599/543–6906 or 800/441–7227* ⊕*www.princessheights. com* ⇨*15 suites* ⚹*In-room: safe, kitchen, refrigerator, Wi-Fi. In-hotel: pool, gym, beachfront, no elevator, concierge, laundry service* ⊟*AE, MC, V* ⦿*EP.*

$ ⊞**Royal Turtle Inn.** This intimate hotel appeals to a wide range of people, from families with children to older travelers to gay couples. It has a great location about three minutes from the main beach. Rooms are nicely furnished, and have romantic touches like four-poster beds. Each has a view of the lagoon. A sundeck is one of the most popular spots on the nicely landscaped grounds. Breakfast at Turtle Pier Restaurant is included. **Pros:** Personalized service, intimate atmosphere. **Cons:** Not on the beach, faces a very busy street. ⊠*114 Airport Rd., Simpson Bay* ☎*599/545–2563* ⊕*www.theroyalturtle.com* ⇨*8 rooms* ⚹*In room: refrigerator, Wi-Fi. In hotel: pool* ⊟*MC, V* ⦿*BP.*

$$–$$$$ ⊞**Sonesta Great Bay Beach Resort & Casino.** Location, location, location. Away from the docks that are usually crawling with cruise ships, but only a 10-minute walk to downtown

Philipsburg, this resort is especially well positioned. It was closed for well over a year for total renovations. Gorgeous hues of oranges and yellows now accent the comfortable, Caribbean-style guest rooms. All have terraces with fine views. The circular marble lobby faces Great Bay and overlooks the cruise-ship pier on one side and mountains on the other. Its big plus is the white-sand beach, which is rarely crowded. **Pros:** Good location, nice beach, enough activities to keep you busy. **Cons:** Hallways have a hospital-like feel, often filled with groups. ⊠*19 Little Bay Rd., Great Bay* ⬧*Box 91, Philipsburg* ☎*599/542–2446 or 800/223–0757* ⬧*www.sonesta.com/greatbay* ⬧*210 rooms, 22 studios, 30 suites* ⬧*In-room: safe, Wi-Fi. In-hotel: 3 restaurants, bars, tennis court, pools, gym, spa, beachfront, water sports, children's programs (ages 4–12)* ☰*AE, D, DC, MC, V* ⭘*EP.*

$$–$$$$ 🖼**Sonesta Maho Beach Resort & Casino.** Las Vegas glitz and
⟳ glamour rule in the island's largest hotel on beautiful Maho Beach. Whatever your pleasure—sunning or swimming, sailing or shopping, dancing till dawn or pampering yourself in the spa—the island's largest resort also has the widest range of activities. Rooms have balconies with sea or garden views. Not only is its lobby the biggest in the Caribbean, but the resort has a casino, a theater, 5 clubs, 3 restaurants, and 40 shops. Seven other restaurants and an outlet mall surround the resort complex; there's no reason to stray farther. **Pros:** Huge facility, lots of shopping, nonstop nightlife. **Cons:** Internet connection needs upgrading, not the place for a quiet getaway. ⊠*1 Rhine Rd., Box 834, Maho Bay* ☎*599/545–2115, 800/223–0757, or 800/766–3782* ⬧*www.sonesta.com/mahobeach* ⬧*537 rooms* ⬧*In-room: safe, dial-up. In-hotel: 3 restaurants, bars, tennis courts, pools, gym, spa, beachfront, public Wi-Fi* ☰*AE, D, DC, MC, V* ⭘*EP.*

$$$–$$$$ 🖼**Westin St. Maarten, Dawn Beach Resort & Spa.** This glitzy new resort is making a splash—and it isn't because the island's largest freshwater pool is on the property. Two restaurants, four bars, a casino, nightclub, and a slew of activities make it so self-contained that you need never leave the property until you go home. Being a Westin property, it has spacious rooms with the chain's signature beds. Each contemporary-style room is partially carpeted and has a balcony with either an ocean or island view. Large bathrooms have romantic touches like dual showerheads. But what is most heavenly is the hotel's location. Dawn Beach is one of the most scenic spots on the island and *the* place

The Wedding Planner

1

Preparing for your big day is always stressful, even if you aren't planning an event that will take place on an island in the Caribbean. Wedding planners are there to make the process as painless as possible. Give them as little as two months lead time and they will push through the necessary paperwork, help choose the venue, and coordinate the entire event. Securing a minister, photographer, florist, caterer, and driver are all tasks taken off your shoulders. Unconventional events like clothing-optional or underwater weddings are no sweat for these pros. Fees vary according to services. The basic package, which includes securing all the necessary documents, is $940.

Another option is using service provided by your hotel. Larger resorts have on-site wedding coordinators who take care of everything. Small hotels also have wedding and honeymoon packages.

St. Maarten Marry Me.com (☎599/542–2214 or 599/553–8148 ⊕www.sint-maartenmarry-me.com) offers a full line of services for your wedding. The island-based company works with many of the hotels. **Weddings in St. Maarten** (☎599/557–5478 or 599/581–5843 ⊕www.stmaarten-beachweddings.com) offers A-to-Z wedding consulting services. Owner Jean Rich's motto is, "If you can dream it, I can do it."

to be at sunrise. The DJ at the trendy Opal nightclub keeps the dance floor hopping until 2 AM. **Pros:** On Dawn Beach, plenty of activities. **Cons:** Chain-hotel decor, lacks charm, a bit off the beaten track. ⊠144 Oyster Pond Rd., Oyster Pond ☎599/543–6700 ⊕www.westin.com/stmaarten ⊅311 rooms, 6 suites ⚫In-room: safe, refrigerator, Ethernet. In-hotel: restaurants, bars, gym, spa, children's program (ages 3–12) ▤AE, D, DC, MC, V ⚫EP.

FRENCH SIDE

Unless otherwise specified, breakfast is included with the room rate.

$$$–$$$$ **Alamanda Resort.** On the white-sand beach of Orient Bay, this hotel has a funky feel. Painted doors decorated with cutout boats, fish, and other oceany things lead to colonial-style suites with terraces that overlook the pool, beach, or the ocean. Two-level rooms also have private decks. Ala-

manda Café is surrounded by a fragrant tropical garden; the Kakao Beach restaurant looks out toward the ocean. A hotel card gives you access to activities and restaurants at any resort in the area. The staff at the 24-hour activity desk will be happy to arrange island activities. **Pros:** Pleasant property, friendly staff. **Cons:** Need a car to get around, can be difficult to find. ☒*Baie Orientale* ✆*BP 5166, Grand Case, 97071* ☎*590/52–87–40 or 800/622–7836* ⊕*www. alamanda-resort.com* ➪*42 rooms* ⚡*In-room: safe, kitchen. In-hotel: 2 restaurants, room service, tennis courts, pool, gym, water sports, no elevator, laundry service, public Internet* ⊟*AE, MC, V* ⦿*BP.*

$$–$$$ 🏨**Captain Oliver's Resort.** This cluster of pink bungalows are perched high on a hill above a lagoon. They're nothing fancy, but they do come with lots of lush landscape and a fine view of the Caribbean and St. Barths. Rooms are clean and simple, and have private verandahs. The restaurant has live music every Saturday. The reasonable price means people return again and again. **Pros:** Restaurant is reasonably priced, fishing trips leave from the hotel. **Cons:** Not on the beach, some crime in the neighborhood. ☒*Oyster Pond* ☎*590/87–40–26 or 888/790–5264* ⊕*www. captainolivers.com* ➪*50 suites* ⚡*In room: safe, refrigerator. In hotel: restaurant, bars, pool, public Internet* ⊟*AE, D, MC, V* ⊘*Closed Sept.–Oct.* ⦿*BP.*

$$–$$$$ 🏨**Club Orient Resort.** Let it all hang out at this clothing-optional hotel on Baie Orientale. There are plenty of activites, including a nude catamaran cruise (shoes, suntan lotion, and towel are suggested). Unlike many of the guests, the smaller suites are modest, with knotty pine walls, fully equipped kitchens, and front and back patios. A nice touch is the complimentary bottle of Bordeaux. For a bit of adventure, try a nude catamaran cruise (but wear sunscreen, of course). **Pros:** Nice location, on-site convenience store. **Cons:** A bit pricey, rooms are the bare minimum. ☒*1 Baie Orientale, Baie Orientale* ☎*590/87–33–85 or 800/690–0199* ⊕*www.cluborient.com* ➪*137 rooms* ⚡*In room: safe, Wi-Fi. In hotel: 2 restaurants, water sports, gym* ⊟*AE, D, MC, V* ⦿*EP.*

$$$–$$$$ 🏨**Esmeralda Resort.** The short path from Orient Bay is just
🕐 long enough to whisk you away from the crowds. Almost all of the upscale villas, which can be configured to meet the needs of different groups, have their own private pool. Caribbean-style rooms all have terraces and fully equipped kitchenettes. A 24-hour activities desk can arrange everything from snorkeling and tennis to car rental and baby-

sitting. The resort has two restaurants—Astrolabe for fine dining and Coco Beach for anything from sushi and burgers. To make your beach life easier, you receive a hotel card for activities at any resort in the area. **Pros:** Beachfront location, pretty pools, plenty of activities. **Cons:** Need a car to get around. ⌂*Box 5141, Baie Orientale, 97071* ☎*590/87–36–36 or 800/622–7836* ⊕*www.esmeralda-resort.com* ⇥*65 rooms* ☖*In-room: safe, kitchen (some), refrigerator. In-hotel: 2 restaurants, room service, tennis courts, pools, beachfront, water sports, no elevator, laundry service, public Internet* ⊟*AE, MC, V* ⓘ*EP.*

$$–$$$$ ▨ **Grand Case Beach Club.** The bottle of wine at check-in is
★ a nice touch. Then again, there are many nice things about this beachfront property, including a friendly staff and a spectacular view of Anguilla. Fully equipped kitchens have good-size refrigerators and granite counters; CD players are standard in every apartment. Room service is available from the Sunset Café. **Pros:** Comfortable rooms, walking distance to restaurants. **Cons:** Small beach. ✉*21 rue de Petit Plage, at north end of blvd. de Grand Case, Box 339, Grand Case,* ☎*590/87–51–87 or 800/344–3016* ⊕*www.grandcasebeachclub.com* ⇥*72 apartments* ☖*In-room: safe, kitchen, refrigerator, DVD. In-hotel: restaurant, bar, tennis court, beachfront, water sports, no elevator, laundry facilities, laundry service, public Internet* ⊟*AE, MC, V* ⓘ*CP.*

$$$$ ▨ **Green Cay Village.** Surrounded by 5 acres of lush green-
★ ery high above Baie Orientale, these villas are a perfect place for families or groups of friends who are looking for privacy and serenity. Each of the West Indian–style villas has its own pretty pool area. The interiors are quite spacious—the largest has three bedrooms, two baths, a living room, a full kitchen, and a dining patio. If you rent just the cheaper studios, you get a kitchenette and a large bedroom with a sitting area. Whichever you choose, the staff can arrange a cook to take care of all your meals. The beach and restaurants are a short walk away. Refrigerators come stocked with essentials like milk and eggs. There are also reserved parking spaces near the villa. **Pros:** Beautiful setting, near Baie Orientale, perfect for families. **Cons:** Need a car to get around, not on the beach. ✉*Parc de la Baie Orientale, Box 3006, Baie Orientale* ☎*590/87–38–63 or 866/592–4213* ⊕*www.greencayvillage.com* ⇥*16 villas* ☖*In-room: kitchen, refrigerator, VCR (some). In-hotel: tennis court, pools, no elevator, laundry service, airport shuttle* ⊟*AE, MC, V* ⓘ*CP.*

$$ ⌧**Hôtel Alizéa.** This Caribbean-style hotel sits on a hillside above Orient Bay. Rooms have either king-size or twin beds and a convertible sofa, so they're perfect for families. On the terrace is a fully equipped kitchen, dining table, and some lounge chairs. Though breakfast is served in the restaurant, you can also have it brought to your room. **Pros:** Incredible views, reasonable rates, walking distance to Baie Orientale. **Cons:** Basic rooms, not directly on the beach. ⊠*25 Mont Vernon BP 5131, Orient Beach* ☎*590/87–33–42* ⊕*www. alizeahotel.com* ⇨*18 rooms, 8 bungalows* ⌂*In room: kitchen. In hotel: restaurant* ⊟*AE, MC, V* ⦿*BP.*

$$–$$$$ ⌧**Hotel Beach Plaza.** What is most appealing about this hotel is its location on Baie de Marigot. Terraced rooms are simple but adequate—opt for one with an ocean view. The three-story atrium lobby is airy and attractive. The harbor side has a restaurant and freshwater pool with a poolside bar. The staff is quite accommodating. **Pros:** Great location, nice views. **Cons:** Traffic noise, small beach, few activities. ⊠*Baie de Marigot, Marigot* ☎*590/87–87–00* ⊕*www.hotelbeachplazaxm.com* ⇨*144 rooms* ⌂*In-room: safe. In-hotel: restaurant, room service, pool, diving, public Wi-Fi* ⦿*BP.*

$$–$$$$ ⌧**Hotel La Plantation.** Perched high above Orient Bay, this ★ colonial-style hotel is a charmer. French doors open to a wraparound verandah with an expansive view of Orient Bay. Each spacious villa is composed of a suite and two studios that can be rented together or separately. All are accented with yellow, green, and stenciled wall decorations. Mosquito nets hang over king-size beds, and good-size bathrooms have large showers and two sinks. Alongside the pool is the cozy Café Plantation, where complimentary breakfast is served. Monday's Lobster Night is a deliciously good deal. **Pros:** Relaxing atmosphere, eye-popping views. **Cons:** Small pool, beach is a 10-minute walk away. ⊠*C5 Parc de La Baie Orientale* ☎*590/29–58–00* ⊕*www. la-plantation.com* ⇨*17 suites, 34 studios* ⌂*In-room: safe, kitchen (some), refrigerator. In-hotel: restaurant, tennis courts, pool, gym, no elevator* ⊘*Closed Sept.–mid-Oct.* ⊟*AE, MC, V* ⦿*BP.*

$$$–$$$$ ⌧**Hôtel Le Marquis.** If you crave spectacular vistas and intimate surroundings, this might be the place. Contemporary Caribbean decor in the spacious rooms means a splash of bright colors, marble bathrooms, and a private terrace with a hammock. If you wish, arrange for spa treatments in your room. A nice touch is the fresh fruit assortment waiting for you in your room. There's a complimentary airport transfer. **Pros:** Romantic honeymoon destination, doting staff, facilities for people with disabilities. **Cons:** Not on the beach, no restaurant. ✉*Pigeon Pea Hill, Anse Marcel* ☎*590/29–42–30* ⊕*www.hotel-marquis.com* 🛏*17 rooms* ⚐*In room: safe, refrigerator, DVD (some). In hotel: bar, gym, spa, no elevator* ⊟*AE, MC, V* ❑*BP.*

$$$–$$$$ 🏨**Hôtel L'Esplanade Caraïbes.** Guests often return to this
★ Mediterranean-style hotel for its quiet elegance and excellent service. When you arrive, you'll find your suite stocked with a welcome basket filled with a baguette, cookies, and other goodies. All the suites at this hilltop abode have beamed ceilings, teak furnishings, and smashing views of the bay and the village of Grand Case from the patios. Two curved stone staircases lead to the gardens and pool. A path down the hillside leads to the fabulous restaurants of Grand Case and the beach. **Pros:** Lovely property, family-friendly feel. **Cons:** Lots of stairs to climb, not on the beach. ✍*Box 5007, Grand Case, 97150* ☎*590/87–06–55 or 866/596–8365* ⊕*www.lesplanade.com* 🛏*24 units* ⚐*In-room: safe, kitchen, refrigerator. In-hotel: pools, no elevator, laundry service* ⊟*AE, MC, V* ❑*EP.*

★ **Fodor's**Choice 🏨**La Samanna.** A long stretch of white-sand
$$$$ beach borders this dazzling resort. This is the kind of ultra-chic retreat where you can arrange for a curtained beach cabana equipped with its own television—-for just $200 per day. Rooms are smartly designed with tiled or marble floors, mahogany and teak furnishings, and high-tech toys like DVD players and plasma TVs. A few of the suites have private rooftop sundecks. What separates this hotel from the rest of the island's properties is its high level of service—for example, the management will buy you lunch if you happen to check-in before your room is ready. The hotel offers a wide array of activities, including one-on-one Pilates instruction and yoga at the state-of-the-art workout facility. The Elysées Spa is surrounded by a lush private garden and waterfall. Many treatment rooms include a private outdoor area with a shower. In the main dining room, the menu combines Asian, French, and creole influences. Each course can be paired with a selection of more than 450 different wines from the hotel's award-winning cellar. For cocktails, there's an authentic Moroccan bar. **Pros:** The most luxurious hotel on the island, service is unparalleled, beach is drop dead gorgeous. **Cons:** Very pricey. ✉*Baie Longue* ✍*Box 4077, Marigot, 97064* ☎*590/87–64–00 or 800/854–2252* ⊕*www.lasamanna.orient-express.com* 🛏*27 rooms, 54 suites* ⚐*In-room: safe, kitchen (some),*

refrigerator (some), VCR (some). In-hotel: 2 restaurants, bar, tennis courts, pool, gym, spa, beachfront, water sports, no elevator, public Wi-Fi ⊟AE, MC, V ⊘Closed Sept. and Oct. ⊚BP.

$$$–$$$$ ⊠**Le Domaine Hotel.** At the end of its charming, open-air lobby, Le Domaine give ways to a tropical garden with a covered path to the sea. All of the spacious, Caribbean-style rooms have lattice-trimmed balconies facing the greenery. Accented in yellow and turquoise, each of the rooms has rounded bathtubs (no showers except for the suites), flat-screen TVs, and in-room safes that can accommodate laptops. A waterfall drops into the attractive pool, and nearby are a gazebo and a hot tub. At La Veranda restaurant, French cuisine is the specialty of chef Philippe Dorange. Therapies from the Caribbean and beyond are on the menu at the Ti Paradis Spa. To reach the hotel, head north at French Cul de Sac. **Pros:** Lovely gardens, beachfront setting. **Cons:** Closed six months a year, very pricey, need a car to get around. ⊠*Anse Marcel, 97150* 🕾*590/52–34–52* ⊕*www.hotel-le-domaine.com* ⊅*120 rooms, 18 suites* ⬩*In-room: safe, kitchen (some). In-hotel: restaurant, room service, bar, pool, gym, spa, beachfront, laundry service, public Internet, airport shuttle* ⊟*AE, DC, MC, V* ⊘*Closed June–Nov.* ⊚*BP.*

$$–$$$$ ⊠**Le Flamboyant.** The Caribbean-style architecture of this ♺ hotel's indoor-outdoor lobby is quite inviting. Rooms are comfortably furnished with carved wood and rattan pieces. Each has a terrace that faces either the garden or the lagoon and is equipped with an outdoor kitchenette. A nightly shuttle to the casinos on the Dutch side is a plus, as are the many recreational activities, including tennis on a lighted tennis court, kayaking and snorkeling in Baie Nettlé, and water aerobics. Meal plans are available. **Pros:** Close to Marigot. **Cons:** Quite pricey for what you get. ⊠*Rte. des Terres Basses, Baie Nettlé* 🕾*590/87–60–00* ⊕*www.hmc-hotels.com* ⊅*200 suites* ⬩*In-room: safe, kitchen. In-hotel: restaurant, bar, pools, gym, beachfront, no elevator* ⊟*AE, DC, MC, V* ⊘*Closed early Sept.–mid-Oct.* ⊚*EP.*

$$$–$$$$ ⊠**Le Petit Hotel.** Surrounded by some of the best restaurants in the Caribbean, this tiny beachfront hotel oozes charm. A Mediterranean staircase leads to its nine spacious rooms and a one-bedroom suite. Each of the rooms has some high-tech touches, such as CD and DVD players and flat-screen TV. Baskets are provided at the self-serve buffet breakfast of croissants, coffee, and freshly squeezed juices; you can then carry these yummies back to your private terrace.

Because the hotel has no pool, you're invited to use the pool at nearby Hôtel L'Esplanade Caraïbes. **Pros:** Walking distance to everything in Grand Case, friendly staff. **Cons:** Many stairs to climb, no pool. ⊠*248 blvd. de Grand Case, Grand Case* ☎*590/29–09–65* ⊕*www.lepetithotel.com* ↝*9 rooms, 1 suite* ⌂*In-room: safe, kitchen. In-hotel: beachfront, no elevator* ▭*AE, MC, V* ⓘ*CP.*

$–$$$$ 🖵**Mercure Simson Beach Saint-Martin.** Once dull and dreary, ☾ rooms have been totally transformed by a color scheme of cheery oranges and yellows. Rooms have three single beds or a single and a double, except for loft rooms that sleep two upstairs and two more on the fold-out couch downstairs. Superior rooms are the only ones that face the ocean. Other rooms have a lagoon, pool, or garden view. Bathrooms are small but adequate. All-inclusive plans are available. **Pros:** Lush grounds, shuttle service to casinos. **Cons:** Small bathrooms, pricey for what you get. ⊠*Baie Nettle BP 172,* ☎*590/87–54–54* ⊕*www.accorhotels.com* ↝*168 rooms, 1 suite* ⌂*In-room: refrigerator, safe. In-hotel: beachfront, pool, tennis court, water sports, public Wi-Fi* ▭*AE, MC, V* ⓘ*BP.*

RADISSON ST. MARTIN RESORT & SPA The former Le Méridien resort in Anse Marcel has undergone an $80-million facelift and will emerge as the **Radisson St. Martin Resort & Spa** (⊠*BP 581 Marcel Cove, Anse Marsel* ☎*590/ 87–67–09 or 888/201–1718* ⊕*www.radisson.com/stmartin*) sometime in late summer 2008. Because the hotel, which will have 189 rooms and 63 suites, was still under construction when this book was being researched, it could not be reviewed.

TIME-SHARE RENTALS

Time-share properties are scattered around the island, mostly on the Dutch side. There's no reason to buy a share, as these condos are rented out whenever the owners are not in residence. If you stay in one, be prepared for a sales pitch. Most rent by the night, but there's often substantial savings if you secure a weekly rate. Not all offer daily maid service, so make sure to ask before you book.

$$ 🖵**Atrium.** Lush tropical foliage in the glassed-in lobby— ☾ hence the name—makes a great first impression. All the spacious suites and studios open to the lobby, and have lagoon or ocean views. They're equipped with kitchenettes with microwaves, refrigerators, and ice-makers. With plenty of activities for kids, this property is the perfect place for families. **Pros:** Family-friendly environment, short walk to restaurants. **Cons:** Rooms lack private balconies, neighborhood is crowded. ⊠*6 Billy Folly Rd., Pelican Reef* ☎*800/929–0744 or 599/544–2126* ⊕*www.festivaresorts. com/atrium.php* ⬐*85 rooms* ⚭*In-room: kitchen, refrigerator, Ethernet. In hotel: tennis court, pools, gym, laundry facilities, public Wi-Fi* ⊟*AE, MC, V* ⏍*EP.*

$$$–$$$$ ▦**Belair Beach.** This time-share rental has an unbeatable location on Little Bay Beach, one of St. Maarten's nicest and least crowded stretches of sand. The accommodations, all of them suites, include living and dining areas, fully equipped kitchens, and terraces. For a fee, Jody's Place, an on-site convenience store, will fill your refrigerator before you arrive. Grab a light meal at the beachfront Gingerbread Café. The staff can arrange car rentals and island activities. **Pros:** Close to Philipsburg, away from the crowds. **Cons:** No full-service restaurant, rooms are a bit dated. ⊠*Little Bay Beach Rd., Little Bay Beach* ☎*599/542–366* ⊕*www. belairbeach.com* ⬐*72 suites* ⚭*In room: safe. In hotel: pool, beachfront, water sports, public Internet* ⊟*MC, V* ⏍*EP.*

$$–$$$ ▦ **Flamingo Beach Resort.** There are so many activities at ☙ this resort that you might not return to your room before bedtime. That would be a shame, as the accommodations have lovely balconies overlooking Simpson Bay. Wicker furniture and bright colors keep things inside feeling cheery. Bedrooms have king-size beds, and there are sofabeds in the living rooms. Kitchens are fully equipped. **Pros:** Close to a variety of restaurants and nightlife options. **Cons:** Area gets crowded, small beach. ⊠*6 Billy Folly Rd.* ☎*599/544– 3900 or 800/438–2929* ⊕*www.diamondresortsgetaway. com* ⬐*206 units* ⚭*In-room: safe, kitchen. In hotel: restaurant, tennis courts, pool, beachfront, water sports, laundry service* ⊟*AE, D, MC, V* ⏍*EP.*

$$–$$$$ ▦**Pelican Resort Club.** Tucked away on Pelican Key, this ☙ resort has a lot going for it. First of all, it borders both the bay and the ocean, giving you a front-row seat for island sunsets from your terrace. The spacious suites are tastefully decorated with Caribbean-style furniture and fully equipped kitchens. Most have sleeper sofas, making them just right for families. Kids can enjoy the pool or playground while grown-ups head to the on-site spa. **Pros:** Family-friendly destination, near nightlife options. **Cons:** Maid service only weekly, crowded area. ⊠*Billy Folly Rd. 7, Pelican Key, Simpson Bay* ☎*877/736–4586 or 599/544–2503* ⊕*www.*

pelicanresort.com ⇌*342 units* ⚲*In room: safe, kitchens. In hotel: 2 restaurants, bars, tennis courts, pools, beachfront, spa, public Internet* ⊟*AE, V* ⦿*EP.*

$–$$$ 🏨**Princess Port de Plaisance Resort.** The resort has everything you'd expect—and more. During the day, laze around at the pool, pamper yourself at the state-of-the-art spa, work out with a trainer at the fitness center, or head out for some water sports. If you're living too much of the high life, visit the anti-aging clinic. In the evening, the giant Princess Casino has live entertainment. There are several restaurants, including the Courtside Café and it's health-conscious menu. (Don't worry, not everything on the menu is good for you.) Spacious suites offer garden or pool views. Each has a fully equipped kitchen. **Pros:** Huge casino, children under 18 stay free. **Cons:** Not on the beach, needs refurbishing. ⊠*Union Rd., Cole Bay* ☎*599/544–4311 or 866/786–2278* ⦿*www.princessportdeplaisance.com* ⇌*88 units* ⚲*In room: safe, kitchen. In hotel: 2 restaurants, bar, tennis courts, pool, gym, spa, public Internet* ⊟*AE, D, MC, V* ⦿*EP.*

$$–$$$ 🏨**Royal Islander Club la Terrasse.** The Royal Islander Club
♻ la Plage is right across the street, so this smaller property shares many of the amenities. Suites have fine vistas, either of the garden, the pool, or the ocean. Furnished with rattan furniture, each of the tile-floor units has a fully equipped kitchen and marble-topped bathroom. There's weekly maid service, but you can arrange daily service for an extra fee. **Pros:** In a hip area, near restaurants and bars. **Cons:** Not on the beach, rooms are hard to book. ⊠*1 Rhine Rd., Maho Bay* ☎*599/545–2388* ⦿*www.royalislander.com* ⇌*67 units* ⚲*In room: kitchen, Wi-Fi. In hotel: 2 restaurants, pool* ⊟*AE, D, MC, V* ⊙*Closed 1st 2 wks in Sept.* ⦿*EP.*

$$$–$$$$ 🏨 **Royal Palm Beach.** Step out onto your balcony for a sweep-
♻ ing view of the ocean and the large swimming pools that shimmy up to it. Caribbean-style furnishings and soothing pastels grace the two-bedroom suites. The living room also has a sleeper sofa, so larger families have plenty of space. (The three bathrooms are nice, too). One nice touch is room service—an unusual amenity for time-shares. There are also resort-style services, like babysitting and a concierge. **Pros:** Great room service, near restaurants and bars. **Cons:** No small units available, on a busy street. ⊠*Airport Rd., Simpson Bay* ☎*599/544–3912 or 800/438–2929* ⦿*www. diamondresortsgetaway.com* ⇌*140 units* ⚲*In room: kitchens. In hotel: restaurant, room service, bar, gym, water sports, public Internet* ⊟*AE, D, MC, V* ⦿*EP.*

$ ☷ **Sea Palace.** This eye-popping shade of pink is hard to miss. The funky lobby has a glass-brick reception desk. Balconied rooms boast views of the cruise ships sailing into Great Bay. The wicker furniture is accented with flowery fabrics. Each unit has a fully equipped kitchenette. **Pros:** In the heart of Philipsburg, walking distance to shopping. **Cons:** Area crowded when cruise ships dock, not much for kids. ✉*147 Front St., Philipsburg* ☎*599/542–2411 or 599/542–2700* ⊕*www.seapalace.net* ⤶*32 units* ⚒*In room: kitchen. In hotel: restaurant, beachfront* ▭*MC, V* ⍟*EP.*

$$$–$$$$ ☷ **Towers at Mullet Bay.** The main building sits alongside powdery Mullet Bay Beach, which some consider among the island's best. This is the island's only lodging with a golf course, although it's not well maintained. Accommodations are pleasant, with either patios or terraces. The kitchens have nice touches like refrigerators big enough for a family and dishwashers to handle the cleaning. **Pros:** Close to restaurants and shops, on a gorgeous beach. **Cons:** Disappointing golf course. ✉*28 Rhine Rd., Mullet Bay* ☎*599/545–3069 or 800/235–5889* ⊕*www.towersatmulletbay.com* ⤶*81 units* ⚒*In-room: kitchens, Wi-Fi. In-hotel: golf course, pool, gym, laundry service* ▭*AE, MC, V.*

$$–$$$ ☷ **Wyndham Sapphire Beach Hotel & Resort.** A picturesque beach, paths through lush gardens, and a short walk to restaurants, shops, and nightlife—what more could you want? Well, maybe a room with a balcony overlooking Simpson Bay Lagoon or the Caribbean Sea. Those on the ocean side have private hot tubs on their balconies, making the view even more memorable. The accommodations have island-style furnishings, fully equipped kitchens, and bathrooms with Italian marble. **Pros:** American-style breakfast, good rates for longer stays. **Cons:** Meager gym. ✉*9 Rhine Rd., Cupecoy* ☎*599/545–2179 or 877/999–3223* ⊕*www.sbcwi.com* ⤶*150 units* ⚒*In room: kitchen, Wi-Fi. In hotel: restaurant, pool, beachfront, gym, spa, laundry service* ▭*AE, D, MC, V* ⍟*BP.*

PRIVATE VILLAS

Villas are a great lodging option, especially for families who don't need to keep the kids occupied or groups of friends who just like hanging out together. Since these are for the most part freestanding houses, their greatest advantage is privacy. These properties are scattered through the island, often in gated communities or on secluded roads. Some have bare-bones furnishings, while others are over-the-top luxurious, with gyms, theaters, game rooms, and several different pools. There are private chefs, gardeners, maids, and other staffers to care for both the villa and its occupants.

Villas are secured through rental companies. They offer properties with weekly prices that range from reasonable to more than many people make in a year. Check around, as prices for the same property varies from agent to agent. Rental companies usually provide airport transfers and concierge service, and for an extra fee will even stock your refrigerator.

VILLAS RENTAL AGENTS

On the French side of the island, **Caribbean Villas by Blue Escape** (✉ *2414 Exposition Blvd., Suite B120, Austin, TX* ☎ *512/472–8832 or 800/556–4801* ⊕ *http://blueescapes. com*) rents villas in Terres Basses, not far from Marigot.

Carimo (✉ *23 rue du Général de Gaulle, Box 220, Marigot* ☎ *590/87–57–58 or 866/978–5297* ⊕ *www.carimo.com*) rents villas in the tony Terres Basses area as well as Simpson Bay and Baie Longue.

French Caribbean International (✉ *5662 Calle Real, Suite 333, Santa Barbara, CA* ☎ *805/967–9850 or 800/322–2223* ⊕ *www.frenchcaribbean.com*) offers rental properties on the French side of the island.

Island Hideaways (✉ *3843 Highland Oaks Dr., Fairfax, VA* ☎ *800/832–2302 or 703/378–7840* ⊕ *www.islandhideaways.com*), the island's oldest rental company, rents villas on both sides.

Island Properties (✉ *62 Welfare Rd., Simpson Bay, St. Maarten* ☎ *599/544–4580 or 866/978–5852* ⊕ *www.islandpropertiesonline.com*) has properties scattered around the island.

Jennifer's Vacation Villas (✉ *Plaza Del Lago, Simpson Bay Yacht Club, St. Maarten* ☎ *631/546–7345 or 011/599–54–43107* ⊕ *www.jennifersvacationvillas.com*) rents villas on both sides of the island.

Romac Southeby's International Realty (✉ *54 Simpson Bay Rd., St. Maarten* ☎ *599/544–2924 or 877/537–9282* ⊕ *www.romacsothebysrealty.com*) rents luxury villas, many in gated communities.

Condo Rentals

CLOSE UP

Condo rentals are another lodging option. They appeal to travelers who aren't interested in the the one-size-fits-all activities offered by the resorts. Condos are much cheaper than villas, but you get many of the same amenities, including kitchens where you can cook your own meals. To rent a condo, contact the rental company or the individual owner.

CyberRentals (⊠ *3801 S. Capital of Texas Hwy., Austin, Texas* ☎ *800/942–6725* or *512/684–1098* ⊕ *www.cyberrentals.com*) is a listing service. To rent a condo, you contact the owner directly.

The Cliff at Cupecoy Beach (⊠ *Rhine Rd., Cupecoy Beach* ☎ *866/978–5839 and 599/546–6633* ⊕ *www.cliffsxm.com*) rents condos at a beautiful property very close to Maho's nightlife.

Jennifer's Vacation Villas (⊠ *Plaza Del Lago, Simpson Bay Yacht Club, St. Maarten* ☎ *631/546–7345* or *011/599–54–43107* ⊕ *www.jennifersvacationvillas.com*) rents condos near Simpson Bay Beach.

Sint Maarten Condos (⊠ *22 Poema La., Hot Springs Village, AK* ☎ *501/915–8003* ⊕ *www.stmaartencondos.com*) rents condos on Pelican Key.

Villas of Distinction (⊠ *951 Transport Way, Petaluma, CA* ☎ *800/289–0900* ⊕ *www.villasofdistinction.com*) is one of the oldest villa-rental companies on the French side of the island.

WIMCO (⊡ *Box 1461, Newport, RI 02840* ☎ *401/849–8012* or *866/449–1553* ⊕ *www.wimco.com*) has more hotel, villa, apartment, and condo listings in the Caribbean than just about anyone else.

DUTCH SIDE

$$$$ 🖾 **Villa Bella Vita.** From this villa entryway you gaze down into a stark white living room—a view every bit as dramatic as the once outdoors. This place has everything: a workout room with an adjoining outdoor spa, a game room, plus a theater room with a projection TV and a pull-down screen. Each bedroom is different with walk-in closets, flat screen TVs and its own unique fragrance. Large bathrooms showers have multiple shower heads and custom toiletries. Extra amenities include a Jet Ski available for guest use and free worldwide phone calls. **Pros:** Free long-distance, every amenity you can imagine. **Cons:** A short ride to the beach, sometimes shown to prospective renters while it's occupied.

✉6 Opal Rd., Pelican Key ⊕www.jennifersvacationvillas. com/villabellavita.html ⇌7 bedrooms, 8½ baths ⚷safe, dishwasher, DVD, VCR, Wi-Fi, daily maid service, fully staffed, on-site security, water toys, laundry facilities ☲AE, MC, V ⌽EP.

$$$$ ⌑**Villa Le Cliff.** This community has such a friendly feel that you wouldn't think twice about going next door to borrow a cup of sugar. The villas' spacious rooms have handsome beamed ceilings and attractive furnishings. Chefs will appreciate the fully equipped kitchen with its Viking range. From many spots around the villa you'll enjoy amazing vistas. Take a seat at dawn and watch the sun rise over St. Barths. If you need extra space, there's a fourth bedroom with a separate entrance for an additional price. **Pros:** Master bedroom on its own level, nice fixtures in bathrooms. **Cons:** A 10-minute walk to the beach. ✉Dawn Beach Estates, Oyster Bay ⊕www.romacsothebysrealty.com ⇌3 bedrooms, 3 bathrooms ⚷DVD, twice weekly maid service, pool, laundry facilities ☲MC, V ⌽EP.

$$$$ ⌑**Villa Roma.** Two statues guard the entrance to this whitewashed villa. Inside, a narrow flight of stairs leads down to sumptuous living quarters. The owner has made sure the place is completely up-to-date, so it has every electronic gizmo you've ever wanted (and some you didn't know had been invented, such as the 100-disc DVD player). There's an 85-inch plasma television in the common area, and more modest 50-inch versions in each bedroom. The beam-ceilinged great room is lovely, but the trade breezes will make you want to spend all of your time on the pool terrace, in the hot tub, or on the expansive roof-top deck. **Pros:** Near water taxi service, amenties to spare. **Cons:** In a crowded neighborhood, giant satellite dish does not add to the scenery. ✉Aqua Marina, Cupecoy ⊕www.sothebysrealty.com ⇌3 bedrooms, 3½ baths ⚷safe, dishwasher, DVD, VCR, Wi-Fi, weekly maid service, on-site security, hot tub, pool, gym, water toys, laundry facilities ☲MC, V ⌽EP.

$$$$ ⌑**Villa Selah.** This bright yellow house sits high on a hill amid a verdant landscape. Simply furnished, it has a comfortable living area where people tend to gather. Every room has a great view. The master bedroom has cathedral ceilings, a private terrace, and a bathroom with its own hot tub. **Pros:** Reasonably priced, lovely location, good for families. **Cons:** Not on the beach, a bit isolated, stairs to climb. ✉54 Limpet Rd., Oyster Pond ⊕www.islandpropertiesonline.com ⇌3 *bedrooms, 2½ baths △dishwasher, DVD, VCR, Wi-Fi, daily maid service, hot tub, laundry facilities* ⊟*MC, V* ◉*EP.*

FRENCH SIDE

$$$$ ▦**Amber.** Because this villa sits high above Baie Rouge, you can be anywhere on its wraparound terrace and enjoy fine views of the Caribbean. The contemporary living room has glass doors that you can fling open for a different perspective on the ocean. Two of the four bedrooms have king-size beds; the third has two singles, and the fourth bedroom has one single. Adjoining bathrooms are quite attractive, with dark tile walls and floors. The fully equipped kitchen has a central island that can accommodate more than one cook. The rental company stocks the refrigerator with the basics—milk, bread, eggs, butter, orange juice, coffee—so you don't have to go shopping the first day you arrive. **Pros:** Great views, good for families with children. **Cons:** Fourth bedroom is small. ⊠*Terres Basses* ⊕*www.blue escapes.com* ↝*4 bedrooms, 4 bathrooms* △*safe, dishwasher, Wi-Fi, daily maid service, on-site security, laundry facilities* ⊟*AE, MC, V* ◉*EP.*

$$$$ ▦**Beau Rivage.** After a dip in pool, you can take a break from the sun under this villa's gorgeous gazebo. Located two steps from Baie Rouge, you can be in the ocean in no time. The living room, with vaulted ceilings and sleek contemporary furniture, has glass doors that open onto views of Anguilla. The kitchen is equipped with everything a chef could ask for. Bedrooms are roomy, with king-size beds. **Pros:** Beachfront property, perfect for large families. **Cons:** Beachfront property doesn't come cheap. ⊠*Terre Basses* ⊕*www.islandhideaways.com* ↝*3 bedrooms, 3½ baths* △*dishwasher, VCR, Wi-Fi, daily maid service, pool, beachfront* ⊟*AE, D, MC, V* ◉*EP.*

$$$$ ▦**La Savanne.** This Spanish colonial-style home is perched on a hillside facing beautiful Baie Longue. Its layout makes it a good fit for large families or several couples traveling together. The master bedroom suite is by itself upstairs, giving it added privacy. Three of the bedrooms have king-size beds, while the fourth has a queen. A covered terrace with dining and sitting areas overlooks the pool and gazebo. The living room, furnished with contemporary pieces, has plenty of high-tech gadgets. The cheerful white kitchen has granite countertops and is equipped with everything you need to make a big meal. **Pros:** Lovely views, plenty of privacy, good for a family. **Cons:** Master suite has an especially low ceiling. ⊠*Terres Basses* ⊕*www.stmartinluxuryvillas.com*

1

➥*4 bedrooms, 4 bathrooms* ⚬*Dishwasher, DVD, VCR, on-site security, pool, laundry facilities, no-smoking* ▭*No credit cards* ⊙*EP.*

🏠**Le Jardin de la Mer.** This Moorish-style building with graceful pillars and arched doorways is a stunning contrast to the blue waters of Plum Bay Beach. If the whitewashed villa makes you think of a celebrity's island getaway, it's because this is the former home of Harry Belafonte. The freeform swimming pool is flanked by a terrace and a covered verandah—just the place to kick back with a cocktail and watch the sunset. In the beam-ceilinged living room you'll find contemporary furnishings and high-tech touches like a plasma TV, DVD player, and an impressive sound system. Four large bedrooms have king-size beds and bathrooms with double-sink vanities. One of the bathrooms has both an indoor and an outdoor shower. The gourmet kitchen includes a custom-made stove and barbeque grill. **Pros:** Gorgeous design, impressive outdoor space, beachfront setting. **Cons:** Beachfront property doesn't come cheap, some bedrooms are small. ✉*Plum Bay Beach* ⊕*www.stmartin-luxuryvillas.com* ➥*4 bedrooms, 4 baths* ⚬*dishwasher, safe, daily maid service, pool, beachfront, pool, laundry facilities, no-smoking* ▭*No credit cards* ⊙*EP.*

☺ 🏠**Villa La Nina.** From the flower-bordered terrace, you can see the tranquil Baie Longue in the distance. A red-tiled gazebo allows you to sit alongside the pool without worrying about getting too much sun. This small, but comfortable, French-style villa is decorated in restrained shades of yellow and blue. The open-air kitchen and its breakfast bar overlook the pretty pool (shared with another villa). **Pros:** Well suited for a small family. **Cons:** Not on the beach, one bedroom has twin beds. ✉*Terres Basses* ⊕*www.wimco.com* ➥*2 bedrooms, 2 baths* ⚬*safe, dishwasher, DVD, VCR, daily maid service, fully staffed, pool, laundry facilities, no-smoking* ▭*AE, MC, V* ⊙*EP.*

🏠**Villa Mirabelle.** On a hillside overlooking Simpson Bay sits this charming villa. Rooms have vaulted ceilings and views of the gardens or the lagoon. The gourmet kitchen is stocked with everything you need. The living area makes you want to grab a book and curl up on one of its couches. Each of the three bedrooms has a king-size bed. All open onto the covered terrace leading down to the pool and the ocean. **Pros:** Easy walk to Baie Rouge, short drive to Marigot. **Cons:** Children under 11 require a hefty security deposit. ✉*Simpson Bay Lagoon* ⊕*www.wimco.com* ➥*3 bedrooms, 3 baths* ⚬*Dishwasher safe, DVD, Wi-Fi, daily* maid service, generator, pool, laundry facilities, no-smoking ⊟AE, MC, V ⊗Closed mid-Dec.–early Jan. ⓘⓄEP.

NIGHTLIFE

★ St. Maarten has lots of evening and late-night action, the vast majority of which is on the Dutch side of the island. To find out what's doing on the island, pick up *St. Maarten Nights, St. Maarten Quick Pick Guide,* or *St. Maarten Events,* all of which are distributed free in the tourist office and hotels. The glossy *Discover St. Martin/St. Maarten* magazine, also free, has articles on island history and on the newest shops, discos, and restaurants. Or buy a copy of Thursday's *Daily Herald* newspaper, which lists all the week's entertainment.

BARS

DUTCH SIDE

On the Dutch side, **Axum Café** (⊠*7L Front St., Philipsburg* ☎*599/52–0547*), a 1960s-style coffee shop, offers cultural activities as well as live jazz and reggae. It's open daily, 11:30 AM until the wee hours.

Bamboo Bernies (⊠*Caravanserai Resort, 2 Beacon Rd., Simpson Bay* ☎*599/545–3622*), is an indoor-outdoor tiki bar with a different theme every night.

The open-air **Bliss** (⊠*Caravanserai Resort, Simpson Bay* ☎*599/545–3996*) plays techno music.

Buccaneer Bar (⊠*Behind Atrium Hotel, Simpson Bay* ☎*599/ 544–5876*) is the place to enjoy a BBC (Bailey's banana colada) and slice of pizza.

Cheri's Café (⊠*Airport Rd., Simpson Bay* ☎*599/545–3361*), across from Maho Beach Resort & Casino, features Sweet Chocolate, a lively band that will get your toes tapping and your tush twisting.

The casual **Cliffhanger Beach Bar** (⊠*Cupecoy Beach* ☎*599/ 552–9440*) is the perfect place to chill out, have a drink, and watch the sunset.

The **Ocean Lounge** (⊠*Holland House Hotel, 43 Front St., Philipsburg* ☎*599/542–2572*) is the quintessential people-watching venue. Sip a guavaberry colada and point your chair toward the boardwalk.

The **Red Piano** (⌧*Hollywood Casino, Simpson Bay* ☎*599/ 544–6008*) has live music and tasty cocktails.

Starting each night at 8, the pianist at **Soprano's** (⌧*Sonesta Maho Beach Resort, Maho Beach* ☎*599/522–7088*) takes requests for oldies, romantic favorites, or smooth jazz.

Sunset Beach Bar (⌧*2 Beacon Hill, Beacon Hill* ☎*599/545– 3998*) has a relaxed, anything-goes atmosphere. Enjoy live music Wednesday through Sunday as you watch planes from the airport next door fly directly over your head.

Lady C (⌧*Simpson Bay* ☎*599/544–4710*), a 70-year-old sailboat, is transformed into a floating party bar. It sits in Simpson Bay Lagoon, making it very convenient for the yachties.

At **Pineapple Pete** (⌧*Airport Rd., Simpson Bay* ☎*599/544– 6030*) you can groove to live music or visit the game room for a couple of rounds or pool.

FRENCH SIDE

On the French side, **Kali's Beach Bar** (⌧*Friars Bay* ☎*690/49– 06–81*) is a happening spot with live music until mid-night. On Friday night, the big attraction is the huge beach bonfire.

CASINOS

The island's casinos—all 14 of them—are found only on the Dutch side. All have craps, blackjack, roulette, and slot machines. You must be 18 years or older to gamble. Dress is casual (but excludes bathing suits or skimpy beachwear). Most are found in hotels, but there are also some independents.

With some of the best restaurants on the island, **Atlantis World Casino** (⌧*106 Rhine Rd., Cupecoy* ☎*599/545–4601*) is a popular destination even for those who don't gamble. It has more than 500 slot machines and gaming tables offering roulette, baccarat, three-card poker, Texas hold-'em poker, and Omaha high poker.

Beach Plaza Casino (⌧*Front St., Philipsburg* ☎*599/543– 2031*), located in the heart of the shopping area, has more than 180 slots and multigame machines with the latest in touch-screen technology. Because of its location, it is popular with cruise ship passengers.

One of the island's largest gambling joints, **Casino Royale** (⊠*Maho Beach Resort & Casino, Maho Bay* ☎*599/545–2602*) is in bustling Maho, near plenty of restaurants, bars, and clubs.

Coliseum Casino (⊠*Front St., Philipsburg* ☎*599/543–2101*) is popular with fans of slots, blackjack, poker, or roulette.

Dawn Beach Casino (⊠*Westin St. Maarten, 144 Oyster Pond Rd., Oyster Pond* ☎*599/543–6700*) is big and glitzy. If you ever get tired of the endless array of slot machines and gaming tables, beautiful Dawn Beach is just outside the door.

Diamond Casino (⊠*1 Front St., Philipsburg* ☎*599/543–2583*) has 250 slot machines plus the usual tables offering games like blackjack, roulette, and three-card poker. The casino is in the heart of Philipsburg.

The **Dolphin Casino** (⊠*Caravanserai Resort, Simpson Bay* ☎*599/545–4601*), near the airport, has a giant slot machine at the entrance.

In the lobby of the Great Bay Beach Hotel, **Golden Casino** (⊠*Great Bay Beach Hotel, Little Bay Rd., Great Bay* ☎*599/542–2446*) is on the small side. But fans say the 84 slots machines and tables with Caribbean poker, blackjack and roulette are more than enough.

Hollywood Casino (⊠*Pelican Resort, Pelican Key, Simpson Bay* ☎*599/544–4463*) has an upbeat theme and a nice late-night buffet.

Jump-Up Casino (⊠*1 Emmaplein, Philipsburg* ☎*599/542–0862*) is near the cruise-ship pier, so it attracts lots of day-trippers.

Paradise Plaza Casino (⊠*Airport Rd., Simpson Bay* ☎*599/543–4721*) has 250 slots and multigame machines. Betting on sporting events is a big thing here, which explains the 20 televisions tuned to whatever game happens to be on at the time.

One of the island's largest gaming halls, **Princess Casino** (⊠*Port de Plaisance, Union Rd., Cole Bay* ☎*599/544–4311*), has a wide array of restaurants and entertainment options. **Rouge et Noir Casino** (⊠*Front St., Philipsburg* ☎*599/542–2952*) is small but busy, catering mostly to cruise-ship passengers.

Tropicana Casino (⊠*Welfare Rd., Cole Bay* ☎*599/544–5654*) offers slot machines and games like poker, blackjack, and roulette, as well as live entertainment and a nightly buffet.

DANCE CLUBS

DUTCH SIDE

On the Dutch side, **Greenhouse** (⊠*Front St., Philipsburg* ☎*599/542–2941*) plays soca, merengue, zouk, and salsa, and has a two-for-one happy hour that lasts all night Tuesday.

Q-Club (⊠*Sonesta Maho Beach Resort, Maho Bay* ☎*599/ 545–2632*) is a popular disco at the Casino Royale with music for everyone.

FRENCH SIDE

On the French side, **Boo Boo Jam** (⊠*Orient Bay* ☎*590/87– 03–13*) is a jumping joint with a mix of calypso, meringue, salsa, and other beats.

La Chapelle (⊠*Orient Bay* ☎*590/52–38–90*) is a sports bar that transforms itself into a disco at night.

BEACHES

Warm surf and a gentle breeze can be found at the island's 37 beaches, and every one of them is open to the public. What could be better? Each is unique: some bustling and some bare, some refined and some rocky, some good for snorkeling and some good for sunning. Whatever you fancy in the beach landscape department, you can find it here, including a clothing-optional one at the south end of Baie Orientale. If you plan on keeping your valuables, it's a good idea to leave them at the hotel.

DUTCH SIDE

Cupecoy Beach. This picturesque area of sandstone cliffs, white sand, and shoreline caves is actually a series of beaches that come and go according to the whims of the sea. Though the surf can be rough, it's popular with gay locals and visitors. It's near the Dutch-French border. ⊠*Cupecoy, between Baie Longue and Mullet Bay.*

★ **Dawn Beach.** True to its name, Dawn Beach is the place to be at sunrise. On the Atlantic side of Oyster Pond, just south of the French border, this is a first-class beach for sunning and snorkeling. It's not usually crowded, and there are several good restaurants nearby. To find it, follow the signs for either Mr. Busby's or Scavenger's restaurant. ✉*South of Oyster Pond*.

Great Bay. This is probably the easiest beach to find because it curves around Philipsburg. A bustling, white-sand beach, Great Bay is just behind Front Street. Here you'll find boutiques, eateries, and a pleasant boardwalk. Because of the cruise ships and the salt pond, it's not the best place for swimming. If you must get wet, do it west of Captain Hodge Pier. ✉*Philipsburg*.

Guana Bay. If you're looking for seclusion, you'll find it here. There are no umbrellas, no lounge chairs, and a beach shack with no regular service. What this bay does have is a long expanse of soft sand. The surf is strong, making this beach a popular surfer hangout. It's definitely not recommended for kids. It's five minutes northeast of Philipsburg. Turn on Guana Bay Road, which is behind Great Bay Salt Pond. ✉*Upper Prince's Quarter*.

Little Bay. Although it's popular with snorkelers and divers as well as kayakers and boating enthusiasts, Little Bay isn't as crowded as many other beaches. Maybe it's because the sand is somewhat gravelly. What it does have is panoramic views of St. Eustatius, Philipsburg, the cruise-ship terminal, Saba, and St. Kitts. The beach is west of Fort Amsterdam and accessible via the Divi Little Bay Resort. ✉*Little Bay Rd*.

Mullet Bay Beach. Many believe that this mile-long, powdery white-sand beach near the medical school is the island's best. Swimmers like it because the water is usually calm. When the swell is up, the surfers hit the beach. It's also the place to listen for the "whispering pebbles" as the waves wash up. ✉*Mullet Bay, south of Cupecoy*.

Simpson Bay Beach. This secluded, half-moon stretch of white-sand beach on the island's Caribbean side is a hidden gem. It's mostly surrounded by private residences. There are no big resorts, no jet skiers, no food concessions, and no crowds. It's just you, the sand, and the water. Southeast of the airport, follow the signs to Mary's Boon and the Horny Toad guesthouses. ✉*Simpson Bay*.

Anse Heureuse. Not many people know about this romantic, hidden gem. Happy Bay has powdery sand, palm trees, and stunning views of Anguilla. The snorkeling is also good. To get here, turn left on the dead-end road to Baie de Friars. The beach itself is a 10- to 15-minute walk from the last beach bar at Baie de Friars. Hike up the hill and down a bushy trail for about ½ km (¼ mi). ⊠ *Happy Bay.*

★ **Baie de Friars.** This white stretch of sand has a couple of simple good-food restaurants, calm waters, and a lovely view of Anguilla. The shack with the yellow, red, and green picnic tables belong to Kali's Beach Bar, where every Friday night people come for music, dancing, and a huge bonfire. To get to the beach take National Road 7 from Marigot, go toward Grand Case to the Morne Valois hill, and turn left on the dead-end road. ⊠ *Baie de Friar.*

Baie de Grand Case. A stripe of a beach, this sandy shoreline borders Grand Case, a charming little hamlet with gingerbread-style architecture. The sea is calm, water sports are available, and if the heat becomes too much, you can have a bite to eat at one of the *lolos* (barbecue huts). ⊠ *Grand Case.*

Baie Longue. Though it extends over the French Lowlands, from the cliff at La Samanna to La Pointe des Canniers, the island's longest beach has no facilities or vendors. It's the perfect place for a romantic walk. To get here, take National Road 7 south of Marigot. The entrance marked LA SAMANNA is the first entrance to the beach. ⊠ *Baie Longue.*

★ Fodor'sChoice **Baie Orientale.** Many consider this the island's most beautiful beach, but its satiny white sand, underwater marine reserve, variety of water sports, beach bars, and hotels also make it one of the most crowded. The conservative north end is more family-oriented, while the liberal south end is clothing-optional and eventually becomes full-on nudie territory. To get to Baie Orientale from Marigot, take National Road 7 past Grand Case, past the Aéroport de L'Espérance. ⊠ *Baie Orientale.*

Baie Rouge. Home to a couple of beach bars, Baie Rouge, in the French Lowlands, means Red Bay. It got its name from the lightly tinted, soft sand that borders the shoreline. It's thought to have the best snorkeling beaches on the island. You can swim the crystal waters along the point and explore a swim-through cave. The beach is fairly popular with gay men. Baie Rouge is five minutes from Marigot, off Route 7 at the Nettlé Bay turnoff. ⊠*Baie Rouge.*

☼ **Ilet Pinel.** A protected nature reserve, this kid-friendly island is a five-minute ferry ride from French Cul de Sac ($6 per person round-trip). The water is clear and shallow, and the shore is sheltered. If you like snorkeling, don your gear and paddle along both sides of the coasts of this pencil-shape speck in the ocean. Off the pier you'll see live lobsters just waiting to become someone's lunch at the isle's two restaurants. A small boutique sells wraps, hats, and T-shirts. Because of its popularity, Ilet Pinel is often crowded. ⊠*Ilet Pinel.*

☼ **Le Galion.** A coral reef borders this quiet beach. The water is calm, clear, and quite shallow, so it's a perfect place to let the kiddies wade. Kiteboarders and windsurfers like the tradewinds. In addition to chairs and umbrellas, kayaks, paddle boats, and snorkeling gear are for rent at the shop. To get to Le Galion, follow the signs to the Butterfly Farm and continue toward the water. ⊠*Quartier d'Orle.*

SPORTS & THE OUTDOORS

BIKING

Biking is a great way to see the island. Beginner intermediate cyclists can ride the coastal trails from Cay Bay to Fort Amsterdam or Mullet Beach. More serious bikers can cruise the Bellevue Trail from Port de Plaisance to Marigot. Bring your bathing suit—along the way you can stop at Baie Rouge or Baie des Prunes for a dip. The bike trails to Fort Louis offer fabulous views. The most challenging ride is up Pic du Paradis. If you would feel better tackling this route with a guide, ask at one of the bike shops.

DUTCH SIDE

Go Scoot (⊠*20 Airport Rd., Simpson Bay* ☎*599/545–4553*) has well-maintained bikes and helpful clerks. **TriSport** (⊠*Airport Rd. 14B, Simpson Bay* ☎*599/545–4384* ⊕*www. trisportsxm.com*) rents bikes that come with helmets, water bottle, locks, and repair kits. Rates are $22 per day and $110 per week.

A Day in St. Eustatius

Unless you're a diver or a history buff, chances are you have never heard of St. Eustatius, or Statia. So many ships once crowded its harbor that it was tagged the Emporium of the Western World. That abruptly changed in 1776. With an 11-gun salute to the American *Andrew Doria*, Statia became the first country to recognize U.S. independence. Great Britain retaliated by economically devastating the island.

Fort Oranje, from where famous shots came, is a history buff favorite. In Oranjestad, it has protected the island beginning in 1636. Its courtyard houses the original Dutch Reformed Church (1776). Holen Dalim, one of the oldest synagogues in the Caribbean (1738), is on Synagogepad (Synagogue Path).

The island's interior is gorgeous. For hikers, the Quill is the challenge. The long and windy trail to the top of the 1,968-foot crater is lined with wild orchids, frilly ferns, elephant ears, and various other kinds of flora. Beaches, on the other hand, hold little attraction. There's no real sandy spot on the Caribbean shore, and the beaches on the Atlantic side are too rough for swimming.

Statia is a pleasant change. No matter how much time you spend on the island, locals will wave or beep at you in recognition. You never feel like a stranger. For more information contact the **Statia Tourist Office** (☎599/318-2433 ⊕*www.statiatourism.com*).

FRENCH SIDE

Loterie Farm (⊠*Rte. de Pic du Paradis* ☎590/87–86–16 or 590/57–28–55) arranges mountain biking tours around Pic du Paradis. **Rent A Scoot** (⊠*Baie Nettle., St. Martin* ☎590/87–20–59 ⊕*www.l2r-rentascoot.com*) rents bikes for €10 per day or €60 per week.

BOATING & SAILING

The island is surrounded by water, so why not get out and enjoy it? The water and winds are perfect for skimming the surf. It'll cost you around $1,000 per day to rent a 28- to 40-foot powerboat, considerably less for smaller boats or small sailboats.

DUTCH SIDE

Lagoon Sailboat Rental (✉*Airport Rd., near Uncle Harry's, Simpson Bay* ☎*599/557-0714* ⊕*www.lagoonsailboatrental. com*) has 20-foot day sailers for rent within Simpson Bay Lagoon for $150 per day, with a half day for $110. Either explore on your own or rent a skipper to navigate the calm, sheltered waters around Simpson Bay Yacht Club and miles of coastline on both the French and Dutch sides of the islands. **Random Wind** (☎*599/544-5148 or 599/557-5742* ⊕*www.randomwind.com*) offers half- and full-day sailing and snorkeling trips on a 54-foot clipper. Charter prices depend on the size of the group and whether lunch is served, but the regularly scheduled Paradise Daysail costs $95 per person. Departures are on the Dutch side, from Ric's Place at Simpson Bay are at 9 AM Tuesday through Friday. Sailing experience is not necessary for the **St. Maarten 12-Metre Challenge** (✉*Bobby's Marina, Philipsburg* ☎*599/542-0045* ⊕*www.12metre.com*), one of the island's most popular activities. Participants compete on 68-foot racing yachts, including Dennis Connor's *Stars and Stripes* (the actual boat that won the America's Cup in 1987) and the *Canada II*. Anyone can help the crew grind winches, trim sails, and punch the stopwatch, or you can just sit back and watch everyone else work. The thrill of it is priceless, but book well in advance; this is the most popular shore excursion offered by cruise ships in the Caribbean.

FRENCH SIDE

The **Moorings** (✉*Captain Oliver's Marina, Oyster Pond* ☎*590/87-32-55 or 888/952-8420* ⊕*www.moorings. com*) has a fleet of Beneteau yachts as well as bareboat and crewed catamarans for those who opt for a sailing vacation.

FISHING

You can angle for yellowtail snapper, grouper, marlin, tuna, and wahoo on deep-sea excursions. Costs range from $150 per person for a half day to $250 for a full day. Prices usually include bait and tackle, instruction for novices, and refreshments. Ask about licensing and insurance.

DUTCH SIDE

Lee's Deepsea Fishing (✉*Welfare Rd. 82, Simpson Bay* ☎*599/544-4233 or 599/544-4234* ⊕*www.leesfish.com*) organizes excursions, and when you return, Lee's Roadside Grill will cook your tuna, wahoo, or whatever else you catch and keep. **Rudy's Deep Sea Fishing** (⊠*14 Airport Rd., Simpson Bay* ☎*599/545–2177 or 599/522–7120* ⊕*www.rudysdeepseafishing.com*) has been around for years and is one of the more experienced sport-angling outfits.

FRENCH SIDE

Big Sailfish Too (⊠*Anse Marcel* ☎*690/27–40–90*) is your best bet on the French side of the island.

GOLF

St. Maarten is not a golf destination. Although **Mullet Bay Golf Course** (⊠*Airport Rd., north of airport* ☎*599/545–2801*), on the Dutch side, is an 18-hole course, it's the island's *only* one. Though lately it has been better tended, it's still not in the best of shape and many feel it's not worth the cost.

HORSEBACK RIDING

Island stables offer riding packages for everyone from novices to experts. The usual 90-minute ride along the beach costs €50 to $70 for group rides and €70 to $90 for private treks. Reservations are necessary. You can arrange rides directly or through most hotels.

DUTCH SIDE

On the Dutch side contact **Lucky Stables** (⊠*Traybay Dr. 2, Cay Bay* ☎*599/544–5255 or 599/555–7246*), which offers mountain- and beach-trail rides, including a romantic champagne night ride. Rides start at $45.

FRENCH SIDE

Bayside Riding Club (⊠*Galion Beach Rd., Baie Orientale* ☎*590/87–36–64 or 599/557–6822* ⊕*www.baysideriding club.com*), on the French side, is a long-established outfit that can accommodate all levels of riders.

KAYAKING

Kayaking is becoming very popular and is almost always offered at the many water-sports operations on both the Dutch and the French sides. Rental starts at about $15 per hour.

DUTCH SIDE

On the Dutch side, **Blue Bubbles** (⊠ *Westin St. Maarten Dawn Beach Resort & Spa, Oyster Pond* ☎599/542–2333 ⊕*www.bluebubblessxm.com*) offers lagoon paddles and snorkeling tours by kayak. **TriSport** (⊠*Airport Rd. 14B, Simpson Bay* ☎599/545–4384 ⊕*www.trisportsxm.com*) organizes similar kayaking and snorkeling excursions.

FRENCH SIDE

On the French side, kayaks are available at **Kauak Tour** (⊠*French Cul de Sac* ☎599/557–0112 or 690/47–76–72). Near Le Galion Beach, **Wind Adventures** (⊠*Orient Bay* ☎590/29–41–57 ⊕*www.wind-adventures.com*) offers kayaking.

PARASAILING

DUTCH SIDE

On the Dutch side, **Westport Water Sports** (⊠*Simpson Bay* ☎599/544–2557), at Kim Sha Beach, has Jet Skis for rent and offers parasailing excursions. Fees are $50 for single fly and $90 for double fly. **Blue Bubbles** (⊠ *Westin St. Maarten Dawn Beach Resort & Spa, Oyster Pond* ☎599/542–2333 ⊕*www.bluebubblessxm.com*) offers parasailing, jet skiing, and other water-sports adventures.

FRENCH SIDE

On the French side, **Kontiki Watersports** (⊠*Northern beach entrance, Baie Orientale* ☎590/87–46–89) offers parasailing for $40 per half hour on Baie Orientale, giving you aerial views of Green Key, Tintamarre, Ilet Pinel, and St. Barths. You can also rent Jet Skis for $45 for a half hour.

SCUBA DIVING

The water temperature here is rarely below 70°F (21°C). Visibility is often excellent, averaging about 100 feet to 120 feet. The island has more than 40 good dive sites, from wrecks to rocky labyrinths. Beginners and night divers will get a kick out of tugboat *Annie,* which lies in 25 feet to 30 feet of water in Simpson Bay. Right outside of Philipsburg, 55 feet under the water, is the HMS *Proselyte,* once explored by Jacques Cousteau. Although it sank in 1801, the boat's cannons and coral-encrusted anchors are still visible.

Off the north coast, in the protected and mostly current-free Grand Case Bay, is **Creole Rock.** The water here ranges in depth from 10 feet to 25 feet, and visibility is excellent. Other sites off the north coast include **Ilet Pinel,** with its good shallow diving; **Green Key,** with its vibrant barrier reef; and **Tintamarre,** with its sheltered coves and geologic faults. On average, one-tank dives start at $51; two-tank dives are about $95. Certification courses start at about $400.

DUTCH SIDE

On the Dutch side, the following shops are full-service outfitters and SSI (Scuba Schools International) and/or PADI certified.

Blue Bubbles (⊠*Dawn Beach Resort, Oyster Pond* ☎*599/542–2333* ⊕*www.bluebubblessxm.com*) has several locations, including two in Great Bay. The company offers both scuba diving and snuba (which offers a scuba-like experience while you are tethered to a breathing tank above the water), not to mention a wide variety of other water sports and excursions. Snuba is available to younger kids (8 and above) who aren't certified divers. **Dive Safaris** (⊠*Bobby's Marina, Yrausquin Blvd., Philipsburg* ☎*599/544–9001 or 599/545–2401* ⊕*www.divestmaarten.com*) has a shark-awareness dive where participants can watch professional feeders give reef sharks a little nosh. **Ocean Explorers Dive Shop** (⊠*113 Welfare Rd., Simpson Bay* ☎*599/544–5252* ⊕*www.stmaartendiving.com*) is St. Maarten's oldest dive shop, and offers different types of certification courses.

FRENCH SIDE

On the French side, **Blue Ocean** (⊠*Sandy Ground Rd., Baie Nettlé* ☎*590/87–89–73* ⊕*www.blueocean.ws*) is a PADI-certified dive center. **Octoplus** (⊠*Blvd. de Grand Case, Grand Case* ☎*590/87–20–62* ⊕*www.octoplus-dive.com*) offers diving certification courses and all-inclusive dive packages. At Grand Case Beach Club, **O2 Limits** (⊠*Blvd. de Grand Case, Grand Case* ☎*690/50–04–00*) offers a variety of dives.

SEA EXCURSIONS

DUTCH SIDE

You can take day cruises to Prickly Pear Cay, off Anguilla, aboard the *Lambada,* or sunset and dinner cruises on the 65-foot sail catamaran *Tango* with **Aqua Marina Adventures** (☎*599/544–2640 or 599/544–2621* ⊕*www. stmaarten-activities.com*). The 50-foot catamaran **Bluebeard II** (⊠*Simpson Bay* ☎*599/577–5935* ⊕*www.blue beardcharters.com*) sails around Anguilla's south and

CLOSE UP

A Day in Saba

Erupting out of the Caribbean, that 5-square-mi rock is called Saba (pronounced say-ba). The 14-minute flight from St. Martin has you landing on the world's smallest commercial runway—bordered on three sides by 100-foot cliffs. Arrive by boat and you will not see a beach. The sand on this island comes and goes at the whim of the sea.

Hire a cab to navigate "The Road" and its 14 hairpin turns. The thoroughfare, under construction for 25 years, leads to the island towns of Windwardside, Hells Gate, and the Bottom (a funny name for a place that is about halfway up the mountain). Gingerbread-like cottages hang off the hillsides, making this island feel like a step back in time.

The Road may be a thrill ride, but most people visit Saba to do some hiking, diving, and relaxing. Its most famous trek is up the 1,064 steps to the summit of 2,855-foot Mt. Scenery. Goats occupy the snakelike Sulphur Mine Trail, which winds around to an abandoned mine and a colony of bats. Extraordinary underwater wonders attract divers. Saba National Marine Park, which circles the island, has a labyrinth formed by an old lava flow and various tunnels and caves filled with colorful fish.

The isle is renowned for its 151-proof rum, Saba Spice. The rum, along with lace and hand-blown glass are the most popular souvenirs. For more information, contact **Saba Tourist Office** (☎599/416–2231 ⊕www.sabatourism.com).

northwest coasts to Prickly Pear Cay, where there are excellent coral reefs for snorkeling and powdery white sands for sunning. For low-impact sunset and dinner cruises, try the catamaran **Celine** (⊠*Skip Jack's Restaurant, Simpson Bay* ☎*599/545–3961 or 599/552–1535* ⊕*www.sailstmaarten.com*). The sleek 76-foot catamaran **Golden Eagle** (☎*599/542–3323* ⊕*www.sailingsxm.com*) takes day-sailors to outlying islets and reefs for snorkeling and partying.

FRENCH SIDE

A cross between a submarine and a glass-bottom boat, the 34-passenger **Seaworld Explorer** (⊠*Blvd. de Grand Case, Grand Case* ☎*599/542–4078* ⊕*www.atlantisadventures. com*), a semi-submarine, crawls along the water's surface from Grand Case to Creole Rock; while submerged in a lower chamber, passengers view marine life and coral

Family Fun

CLOSE UP

When it comes to family vacations, many people choose St. Maarten/St. Martin because of the wide range of activities and outdoor excursions that will keep kids busy regardless of which side of the island you are staying on. Since the island is so small, you're rarely more than a half-hour drive from either Phillipsburg or Marigot (or any place in between).

Aqua Marina Adventures *see* ⇒ **Bayside Riding Club** *see* ⇒ **Blue Bubbles** *see* ⇒ **Butterfly Farm** *see* ⇒ **Lord Sheffield** *see* ⇒ Zip lines and suspended bridges are found on the "Little Tarzan" trail at the **Loterie Farm** (*see* ⇒ Exploring St. Maarten/St. Martin). The semi-submersible **Seaworld Explorer** (*see* ⇒ Sea Excursions) will make you feel a bit like Jacques Cousteau.

through large windows. Divers jump off the boat and feed the fish and eels.

SNORKELING

Some of the best snorkeling on the Dutch side can be found around the rocks below Fort Amsterdam off Little Bay Beach, in the west end of Maho Bay, off Pelican Key, and around the reefs off Oyster Pond Beach. On the French side, the area around Orient Bay—including Caye Verte, Ilet Pinel, and Tintamarre—is especially lovely and is officially classified and protected as a regional underwater nature reserve. Sea creatures also congregate around Creole Rock at the point of Grand Case Bay. The average cost of an afternoon snorkeling trip is about $45 per person.

DUTCH SIDE

Aqua Mania Adventures (⊠*Pelican Marina, Simpson Bay* ☎*590/544–2640 or 599/544–2621* ⊕*www.stmaarten-activities.com*) offers snorkeling and diving trips, motorized and nonmotorized equipment, and a variety of cruises. The newest activity, called "rock 'n roll safaris," lets participants not only snorkel, but navigate their own motorized rafts. **Blue Bubbles** (⊠*Dawn Beach Resort, Oyster Pond* ☎*599/542–2333* ⊕*www.bluebubblessxm.com*) offers both boat and shore snorkel excursions. **Eagle Tours** (⊠*Bobby's Marina, Philipsburg* ☎*599/542–3323* ⊕*www.sailingsxm.com*) combines sailing, snorkeling, and lunch aboard a 76-foot catamaran. St. Maarten's version of a pirate adventure is a snorkeling cruise on the **Lord Sheffield** (⊠*Great Bay Marina* ☎*599/552–0875*).

On the French side, **Blue Ocean** (⊠*Sandy Ground Rd., Baie Nettlé* ☎*590/87–89–73* ⊕*www.blueocean.ws*) offers snorkeling trips. Arrange equipment rentals and snorkeling trips through **Kontiki Watersports** (⊠*Northern beach entrance, Baie Orientale* ☎*590/87–46–89*).

SPAS

In the last few years, spas have become very "in." Most hotels worth their salt have a spa, usually a very luxurious one. Newer hotels compete to see who can offer the most amenties. Here are a few that you might want to check out during your island visit.

★ Fodor'sChoice **Christian Dior Spa.** The oceanfront setting is undeniably dramatic. There are no ho-hum treatments either. The Intense Youthfulness Treatment starts with a 30-minute back massage, then continues with facial cleansing therapy and a shiatsu head massage. The two-hour Harmonizing Body Massage combines several techniques such as reflexology and shiatsu. Guests have all-day use of the pool, steam room, and sauna. A full line of Dior products are available for purchase. The spa is open weekdays 9 to 6 and Saturday 9 to 4. (⊠*The Cliff at Cupecoy Beach, Rhine Rd., Cupecoy* ☎*599/546–6620*)

Good Life Spa. This pleasant facility has aloe vera treatments (to combat sunburn) and a wide range of scrubs and wraps. There's also a fitness center. It's open weekdays 8 to 8, Saturday 8 to 6, and Sunday 10 to 6. (⊠*Sonesta Maho Beach Resort, 1 Rhine Rd., Maho* ☎*599/545–2540 or 599/545–2356* ⊕*www.thegoodlifespa.com*)

Hibiscus Spa. This attractive facility offers the usual menu of facials, body treatment, and massages. The Hibiscus Expert Facial is formulated to benefit your skin type. It's open daily 8 to 7. (⊠*Westin St. Maarten Dawn Beach Resort & Spa, 144 Oyster Pond Rd., Oyster Pond* ☎*599/543–6700* ⊕*www.westin.com/stmaarten*)

★ Fodor'sChoice **The Spa.** Enter via the "Traditional Path," a dimly-lighted hallway with black marble stepping stones. A huge hydrotherapy pool has seating that resembles lounge chairs. It has a waterfall jet for back treatments and several other jets for the rest of the body. A dozen different kinds of massages are available, including one treatment that is done on the floor. The specialty, a customized couple's massage, is administered in the Yin Yang Room. Besides the massage tables, this room has a huge oval aromatherapy tub. Couples can spend another 90 minutes in the room after the treatment is finished. Champagne and flowers are optional. The spa is open Monday to Saturday 9:30 to 8. (⊠ *La Terrasse Maho Village, Rhine Rd., Maho* ☎ *599/545–2808* ⊕ *www.thespasintmaarten.com*)

FRENCH SIDE

★ Fodor'sChoice **Elysées Spa.** Surrounded by tropical plants and a cascading waterfall, The setting is heavenly. Treatment rooms have private walled gardens with outdoor showers. One of the signature treatments is the 90-minute moxa massage, which combines heated herbal sticks on pressure points with a vigorous massage. The spa's other exceptional therapy is the 90-minute Massage of Seven Chakras (referring to the supposed energy zones that run from the base of the spine to the crown of the head). This therapy uses gentle pressure on the head, back, and arms. There are a wide range of other massages, wraps, and polishes available. The spa is open daily 9 to 8. (⊠ *Baie Longue* ☎ *590/87–64–00 or 800/854–2252* ⊕ *www.lasamanna.orient-express.com*)

Larimar Spa. The cool, welcoming aloe and mint towel is a nice welcoming touch. This full-service facility offers a choice of massage, exfoliation, and body treatments. The fitness center has classes and personal trainers. It's open daily 9 to 7. (⊠ *Radisson St. Martin Resort & Spa, BP 581 Marcel Cove, Anse Marsel* ☎ *0590/87–67–09 or 888/201–1718* ⊕ *www.radisson.com*)

WATERSKIING

Expect to pay $50 per half hour for waterskiing, $40 to $45 per half hour for jet skiing. On the French side, **Kontiki Watersports** (⊠ *Northern beach entrance, Baie Orientale* ☎ *590/87–46–89*) rents windsurfing boards, takes waterskiers out, and provides instruction.

WINDSURFING

The best windsurfing is on Galion Bay on the French side. From November to May, trade winds can average 15 knots. **Club Nathalie Simon** (⊠ *Northern beach entrance, Baie Orientale* ☎ *590/29–41–57* ⊕ *www.wind-adventures.*

com) offers rentals and lessons in both windsurfing and kite surfing. One-hour lessons are about €40. **Windy Reef** (⊠*Galion Beach, past Butterfly Farm* ☎590/87–08–37 ⊕*www.windyreef.fr*) has offered windsurfing lessons and rentals since 1991.

SHOPPING

It's true that the island sparkles with its myriad outdoor activities—diving, snorkeling, sailing, swimming, and sunning—but shopaholics are drawn to the sparkle within the jewelry stores. The huge array of such stores is almost unrivaled in the Caribbean. In addition, duty-free shops offer substantial savings—about 15% to 30% below U.S. and Canadian prices—on cameras, watches, liquor, cigars, and designer clothing. It's no wonder that each year 500 cruise ships make Philipsburg a port of call. On both sides of the island, be alert for idlers. They can snatch unwatched purses.

Prices are in dollars on the Dutch side, in euros on the French side. As for bargains, there are more to be had on the Dutch side.

AREAS

Philipsburg's **Front Street** has reinvented itself. Now it's mall-like, with redbrick walk and streets, palm trees lining the sleek boutiques, jewelry stores, souvenir shops, outdoor restaurants, and the old reliables—including McDonald's and Burger King. Here and there a school or a church appears to remind visitors there's more to the island than shopping. Back Street is where you'll find the **Philipsburg Market Place,** an open-air market where you can haggle for bargains on items such as handicrafts, souvenirs, and cover-ups. **Old Street,** near the end of Front Street, has stores, boutiques, and open-air cafés offering French crepes, rich chocolates, and island mementos. You can find an outlet mall amid the more upscale shops at the **Maho** shopping plaza. The **Plaza del Lago** at the Simpson Bay Yacht Club complex has an excellent choice of restaurants as well as shops.

On the French side, wrought-iron balconies, colorful awnings, and gingerbread trim decorate Marigot's smart shops, tiny boutiques, and bistros in the **Marina Royale** complex and on the main streets, **Rue de la Liberté** and **Rue de la**

République. Also in Marigot is the pricey **West Indies Mall** and the **Plaza Caraïbes,** which house designer shops.

SPECIALTY STORES

ART GALLERIES

Maybe it's the vibrant colors, the gorgeous sunlight, or the scenic beauty that stimulates the creative juices of the many artists on the island. It must be something special, because there are a great many artists and and galleries their work.

DUTCH SIDE

On the Dutch side of the Island, **Art Gallery Le Saint Geran** (⊠*117 Front St., Philipsburg* ☎*599/542–1023*) has a collection of more than 250 original works. There's also a selection of sculptures and ceramics.

Ruby Bute (⊠*8 Plantz Rd., Ebenezer Estate* ☎*599/548– 3080*) has painted portraits of islanders for more than 50 years.

Tessa Urbanowicz (⊠*117 Front St., Philipsburg* ☎*599/542– 1023*) uses pewter, gold, and rhodium to create unique jewelry designs. Her work can also be seen at the Art Gallery Le Saint Feran.

FRENCH SIDE

On the French side, the paintings of **Antoine Chapon** (⊠*Terrasses de Cul-de-Sac, Baie Orientale* ☎*590/87–40–87*) reflect the peaceful atmosphere of the Caribbean. Many of his works are of the island.

Contemporary Caribbean artists are showcased at **Atelier des Tropismes** (⊠*107 Grand Case Blvd., Grand Case* ☎*590/ 29–10–60*).

Céramiques d'art Marie Moine (⊠*76 rue de la Flibuste, Oyster Pond* ☎*590/29–53–76*) sells ceramics that are unique and affordable.

Dona Bryhiel Art Gallery (⊠*Oyster Pond* ☎*590/87–43–93*), before the turnoff to Captain Oliver's Marina, deals mostly in modern figurative paintings by the owner. She will delight you with stories of her life and the paintings, which are steeped in romantic French and Caribbean traditions.

The modern works of **Francis Eck** (⊠*48 rue due Soleil Bevant, Concordia* ☎*590/87–12–32*) are painted in vibrant oils.

Galerie Camaïeu (✉*8 rue de Kennedy, Marigot* ☎*590/87–25–78*) sells both originals and copies of works by Caribbean artists.

Gingerbread Galerie (✉*Marina Royale, Marigot* ☎*590/87–73–21*) specializes in Haitian art.

Josiane Casaubon (✉*274 Parc de la Baie Orientale, Baie Orientale* ☎*590/87–33–66*) displays paintings every afternoon or by appointment.

Minguet Art Gallery (✉*Rambaud Hill* ☎*590/87–76–06*), between Marigot and Grand Case, is managed by the daughter of the late artist Alexandre Minguet. The gallery carries original paintings, lithographs, posters, and postcards depicting island flora and landscapes by Minguet, as well as original works by Robert Dago and Loic BarBotin.

Roland Richardson Gallery (✉*6 rue de la République, Marigot* ☎*590/87–32–24*) sells oil and watercolor paintings by well-known local artist Roland Richardson. The gallery, with a garden studio in the rear, is worth visiting even if you don't intend to buy a painting, and you may meet the artist himself or his stepmother.

DUTY-FREE SHOPS

Most of the island's duty-free shops have branches on both the Dutch and French sides.

Carat (✉*16 rue de la République, Marigot* ☎*590/87–73–40* ✉*73 Front St., Philipsburg* ☎*599/542–2180*) sells china and jewelry.

Cartier Boutique (✉*35 Front St., Philipsburg* ☎*599/543–7700* ✉*Rue de Général de Gaulle, Marigot* ☎*590/52–40–02*) has a lovely collection of fine jewelery.

David Yurman (✉*26 Front St., Philipsburg* ☎*599/542–5204* ✉*8 rue du Général de Gaulle, Marigot* ☎*590/52–24–80*) creates unique designs with gemstones and sterling silver.

Lipstick (✉*Plaza Caraïbes, Rue du Kennedy, Marigot* ☎*590/87–73–24* ✉*31 Front St., Philipsburg* ☎*599/542–6051*) has an enormous selection of perfume and cosmetics.

Little Europe (✉*80 Front St., Philipsburg* ☎*599/542–4371* ✉*1 rue du Général de Gaulle, Marigot* ☎*590/87–92–64*) sells fine jewelry, crystal, and china.

Little Switzerland (⊠*52 Front St., Philipsburg* ☎*599/542–3530* ⊠*Harbor Point Village, Pointe Blanche* ☎*599/542–7785* ⊠*Westin St. Maarten, Dawn Beach* ☎*599/643–6451*) sells watches, fine crystal, china, perfume, and jewelry.

Manek's (⊠*Rue de la République, Marigot* ☎*590/87–54–91*) sells, on two floors, luggage, perfume, jewelry, Cuban cigars, duty-free liquors, and tobacco products.

Oro Diamante (⊠*62-B Front St., Philipsburg* ☎*599/543–0342*) carries loose diamonds, jewelry, watches, perfume, and cosmetics.

HANDICRAFTS

DUTCH SIDE

Visitors to the Dutch side of the island come for free samples at the **Guavaberry Emporium** (⊠*8–10 Front St., Philipsburg* ☎*599/542–2965*), the small factory where the Sint Maarten Guavaberry Company makes its guavaberry liqueur. You'll find myriad versions, including one made with jalapeño peppers. Check out the hand-painted bottles.

The **Shipwreck Shop** (⊠*15 and 34 Front St., Philipsburg* ☎*599/542–5358* ⊕*www.shipwreckshops.com*) stocks a little of everything: colorful hammocks, handmade jewelry, and lots of the local guavaberry liqueur.

FRENCH SIDE

On the French side, **Dalila** (⊠*Zac de Bellevue, Marigot* ☎*590/87–22–06*) is the place to find interesting knickknacks and exotic wood carvings for your home.

CIGARS

The **Cigar Emporium** (⊠*66 Front St., Philipsburg* ☎*599/542–2787*) has the island's largest selection of Dominican and Cuban cigars, along with lots of other tobacco items.

CLOTHING

For fashionistas who insist on the upscale best, St. Maarten/St. Martin has designer shops that won't disappoint.

DUTCH SIDE

Most shops on the Dutch side are clustered around Front Street in Philipsburg.

Coach (⊠*52 Front St., Philipsburg* ☎*599/542–2523*) stocks its famous "C" purses and leather goods.

Liz Claiborne (⊠*48A Front St., Philipsburg* ☎*599/543–0380*) sells women's clothes.

Furla (✉*13 Front St., Philipsburg* ☎*599/542–9958*) is the place for very "in" purses.

Polo Ralph Lauren (✉*31 Front St., Philipsburg* ☎*599/543–0196*) has men's and women's sportswear.

Tommy Hilfiger (✉*28 Front St., Philipsburg* ☎*599/542–6315*) has sportswear in the designer's trademark colors.

FRENCH SIDE
On the French side, many shops are found in the West Indies Mall and Plaza Caraïbes in Marigot.

Hermès (✉*Rue du Général de Gaulle, Marigot* ☎*590/87–28–48*) stocks the famous scarves along with other selections of the famous designer's apparel.

Hugo Boss (✉*Rue du Général de Gaulle, Marigot* ☎*590/87–81–28*) sells the famous designer's men's clothing.

Lacoste (✉*West Indies Mall, Marigot* ☎*590/52–84–84*) has everything with the alligator logo.

Longchamp (✉*Général de Gaulle, Marigot* ☎*590/87–92–76*) is the local outpost for the chic French leather goods designer.

Max Mara (✉*6 rue du Kennedy, Marigot* ☎*590/52–99–75*) offers trendy Italian casual togs.

CRYSTAL & CHINA
The Dutch Delft Blue Gallery (✉*37 Front St., Philipsburg* ☎*599/542–5204*) is famous for it blue-and-white porcelain pieces.

Lalique (✉*13 Sint Rose Arcade, Front St., Philipsburg* ☎*599/542–0763*) has a fine collection of French crystal.

St. Barthélemy

WORD OF MOUTH

"The best dinner we had on St. Barths was the pâte, baguettte, brie, and wine that we bought at a French deli and ate at sunset on a totally deserted beach! So romantic!"

—chicgeek

"Don't miss Saline beach! The water is pure turquoise blue and white sand beach—looks like the South Pacific."

—Ashley

Updated
by Elise
Meyer

STEPPING ONTO THE VILLA PATIO, I watch the sun rise over the volcanic mountain, glittering on the cobalt sea, and bathing the hills in a golden light. I stretch lazily, detecting the aroma of freshly brewed coffee. Should breakfast be an almond croissant? Or should we just have the ethereal brioche we discovered yesterday? I decide that a walk to the boulangerie is in order, especially in light of that new bikini. Ahhh, another perfect day in paradise. I make a mental note to book another Thai massage for Friday and grab my sunglasses. Is there any way this could be any better?

St. Barthélemy blends the respective essences of the Caribbean and France in perfect proportions. A sophisticated but unstudied approach to relaxation and respite prevails: you can spend the day on a beach, try on the latest French fashions, and watch the sunset while nibbling tapas over Gustavia Harbor, then choose from nearly 100 excellent restaurants for an elegant evening meal. You can putter around the island, scuba dive, windsurf on a quiet cove, or just admire the lovely views.

A mere 8 square mi (21 square km), St. Barths is a hilly island, with many sheltered inlets providing visitors with many opportunities to try out picturesque, quiet beaches. The town of Gustavia wraps itself neatly around a lilliputian harbor lined with impressive yachts and rustic fishing boats. Red-roofed bungalows dot the hillsides. Beaches run the gamut from calm to "surfable," from deserted to packed. The cuisine is tops in the Caribbean, part of the French *savoir vivre* that prevails throughout the island.

Longtime visitors speak wistfully of the old, quiet St. Barths. Development has quickened the pace of life here, that's true, but the island hasn't yet been overbuilt, and a 1982 ordinance limited new tourist lodgings to 12 rooms. The largest hotel—the Guanahani—has fewer than 100 rooms; the island's other rooms are divided among some 40 small hotels and guesthouses. About half the island's visitors stay in private villas. The tiny planes that arrive with regularity still land at the tidy airport only during daylight hours. And although "nightlife" usually means a leisurely dinner and a stargazing walk on the beach, something of a renaissance is under way, and a couple of hot new clubs might give you a reason to pack a pair of dancing shoes.

Christopher Columbus discovered the island—called "Ouanalao" by its native Carib Indians—in 1493; he named it for his brother Bartholomé. The first group of French colonists arrived in 1648, drawn by the ideal location on the West Indian Trade Route, but they were wiped out by the Caribs, who dominated the area. Another small group from Normandy and Brittany arrived in 1694. This time the settlers prospered—with the help of French buccaneers, who took advantage of the island's strategic location and protected harbor. In 1784 the French traded the island to King Gustav III of Sweden in exchange for port rights in Göteborg. The king dubbed the capital Gustavia, laid out and paved streets, built three forts, and turned the community into a prosperous free port. The island thrived as a shipping and commercial center until the 19th century, when earthquakes, fires, and hurricanes brought financial ruin. Many residents fled for newer lands of opportunity, and Oscar II of Sweden decided to return the island to France. After briefly considering selling it to America, the French took possession of Saint-Barthélemy again on August 10, 1877.

Today the island is still a free port and is part of an overseas department of France. Arid, hilly, and rocky, St. Barths was unsuited to sugar production and thus never developed an extensive slave base. Most of the 3,000 current residents are descendants of the tough Norman and Breton settlers of three centuries ago. They are feisty, industrious, and friendly—but insular. However, you will find many new, young French arrivals, predominantly from northwestern France and Provence, who speak English well.

EXPLORING ST. BARTHÉLEMY

With a little practice, negotiating St. Barths' narrow, steep roads soon becomes fun. Free maps are everywhere, roads are well marked, and painted signs will point you where the tourist office has annotated maps with walking tours that highlight sights of interest. Starting in December 2005, some of the parking congestion on the island was alleviated by the **St-Barth Shuttle,** a fleet of four air-conditioned minibuses with high-season round-trip routes between Gustavia, Flamands, Lorient, and Grand Cul de Sac. The round-trip ticket costs €10.

Numbers in the margin correspond to points of interest on the St. Barthélemy map.

ᗕ **Corossol.** The island's French-provincial origins are most evident in this two-street fishing village with a little rocky

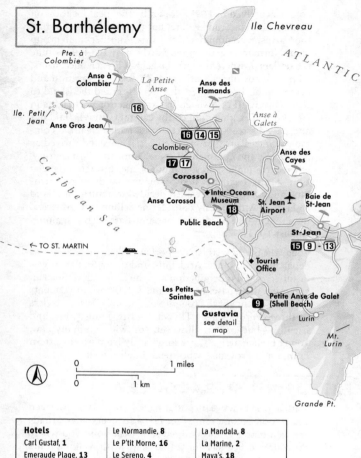

St. Barthélemy

Ile Chevreau

ATLANTIC

Pte. à Colombier

Anse à Colombier

La Petite Anse

Anse des Flamands

Ile. Petit Jean

Anse Gros Jean

16

Anse à Galets

Colombier

16 **14** **15**

Anse des Cayes

17 **17**

Corossol

Anse Corossol

◆ Inter-Oceans Museum

St. Jean Airport

Baie de St-Jean

18

Public Beach

St-Jean

15 **9** - **13**

Caribbean Sea

← TO ST. MARTIN

◆ Tourist Office

Les Petits Saints

Petite Anse de Galet (Shell Beach)

9

Lurin

Gustavia see detail map

Mt. Lurin

0   1 miles

0   1 km

Grande Pt.

Hotels

Carl Gustaf, **1**

Emeraude Plage, **13**

Eden Rock, **10**

François Plantation, **17**

Hôtel Guanahani, **5**

Hôtel Baie des Anges, **15**

Hôtel La Banane, **6**

Hôtel le Village St-Jean, **12**

Hôtel St-Barth Ile de France, **14**

Les Mouettes, **7**

Les Îlets de la Plage, **11**

Le Normandie, **8**

Le P'tit Morne, **16**

Le Sereno, **4**

Le Toiny, **3**

Le Tom Beach Hôtel, **9**

Salines Garden Cottages, **2**

Restaurants

Do Brazil, **9**

Eddy's, **4**

François Plantation, **17**

Le Cesar, **15**

Le Gaïac, **12**

La Langouste, **16**

La Mandala, **8**

La Marine, **2**

Maya's, **18**

O' Corner, **6**

PaCri, **11**

Pipiri Palace, **5**

Le Repaire, **7**

Restaurant des Pêcheurs, **13**

Le Sapotillier, **3**

Le Tamarin, **10**

Le Ti St. Barth, **14**

Wall House, **1**

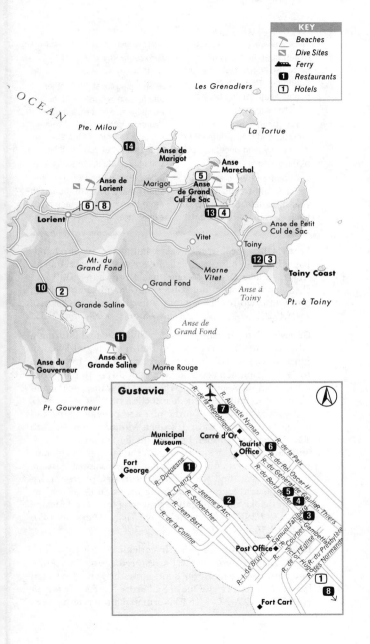

KEY
- Beaches
- Dive Sites
- Ferry
- **1** Restaurants
- **1** Hotels

OCEAN

Les Grenadiers

La Tortue

Pte. Milou

14

Anse de Marigot

Anse Marechal

5

Marigot

Anse de Grand Cul de Sac

Anse de Lorient

6 **8**

13 **4**

Lorient

Vitet

Anse de Petit Cul de Sac

Toiny

Mt. du Grand Fond

Morne Vitet

12 **3**

Toiny Coast

Grand Fond

Anse à Toiny

10 **2**

Grande Saline

Anse de Grand Fond

Pt. à Toiny

11

Anse de Grande Saline

Morne Rouge

Anse du Gouverneur

Pt. Gouverneur

Gustavia

R. de la République

R. Auguste Nyman

7

Municipal Museum

Carré d'Or

Tourist Office

6

R. de la Paix

R. du Rol Oscar II.

R. du Général de Gaulle

R. Thiers

R. du Bord de Mer

Fort George

1

R. Duquesne

R. Chanzy

R. Jeanne d'Arc

R. Schoelcher

2

5

4

R. Samuel Fahlberg

3

R. Jean Bart

R. de la Colline

Post Office ◆

R. Courbet

R. Victor Hugo

R. de l'Église

R. Gambetta

R. du Presbytère

R. des Normandie

R. t. de Bruyn

1

8

Fort Cart

CLOSE UP

St. Barths Best Bets

Beautiful St. Barths is like a bit of the French Riviera in the Caribbean. There's a reason people keep coming back despite the expense.

■ The island is active, sexy, hedonistic, and hip, with plenty of attractive young people as part of the scenery.

■ If food and wine are your true loves, then you'll find your bliss here. Such an excellent selection of restaurants is exceedingly rare in the Caribbean.

■ Shopping for stylish clothes and fashion accessories is better nowhere else in the Caribbean. You may not find a lot of true bargains because of the strength of the euro, but you will think you've died and gone to Paris.

■ Windsurfing and other water sports make going to the beach more than just a sun-tanning experience.

beach. Older local women weave lantana straw into handbags, baskets, hats, and delicate strings of birds. Ingenu Magras's **Inter Oceans Museum** has more than 9,000 seashells and an intriguing collection of sand samples from around the world. You can buy souvenir shells. ✉*Corossol* ☎*0590/27–62–97* 🖼*€3* ⏲*Tues.–Sun. 9–12:30 and 2–5.*

Gustavia. You can easily explore all of Gustavia during a two-hour stroll. Street signs in both French and Swedish illustrate the island's history. Most shops close from noon to 2, so plan lunch accordingly. A good spot to park your car is rue de la République, where catamarans, yachts, and sailboats are moored. The **tourist office** (☎*0590/27–87–27* ✉*odtsb@wanadoo.fr*) on the pier can provide maps and a wealth of information. It's open Monday from 8:30 to 12:30, Tuesday through Friday from 8 to noon and 2 to 5, and Saturday from 9 to noon. On the far side of the harbor known as La Pointe is the charming **Municipal Museum,** where you can find watercolors, portraits, photographs, and historic documents detailing the island's history as well as displays of the island's flowers, plants, and marine life. ☎*599/29–71–55* 🖼*€2* ⏲*Mon., Tues., Thurs., and Fri. 8:30–12:30 and 2:30–6, Sat. 9–12:30.*

Lorient. Site of the first French settlement, Lorient is one of the island's two parishes; a restored church, a school, and a post office mark the spot. Note the gaily decorated graves in the cemetery. One of St. Barths' secrets is **Le Manoir** (☎*0590/27–79–27*), a 1610 Norman manor, now a guesthouse, which was painstakingly shipped from France and reconstructed in Lorient in 1984. Look for the entrance by the Ligne St. Barths building.

St-Jean. The half-mile-long crescent of sand at St-Jean is the island's most popular beach. Windsurfers skim along the water here, catching the strong trade winds. A popular activity is watching and photographing the hair-raising airplane landings. You'll also find some of the best shopping on the island here, as well as several restaurants.

Toiny coast. Over the hills beyond Grand Cul de Sac is this much-photographed coastline. Stone fences crisscross the steep slopes of Morne Vitet, one of many small mountains on St. Barths, along a rocky shore that resembles the rugged coast of Normandy. It's one island beach that's been nicknamed the "washing machine" because of its turbulent surf. Even expert swimmers should beware of the strong undertow here; swimming is generally not recommended.

WHERE TO EAT

Dining on St. Barths compares favorably to almost anywhere in the world. Varied and exquisite cuisine, a French flair in the decorations, sensational wine, and attentive service make for a wonderful epicurean experience. St. Barths' style is expressed in more than 80 charming restaurants, from beachfront grills to serious establishments serving five-course meals. On most menus, freshly caught local seafood mingles on the plate with top-quality provisions that arrive regularly from Paris.

Most restaurants offer a chalkboard full of daily specials that are usually a good bet. But even the pickiest eaters will find something on every menu. The weakness of the dollar means that if you're not careful, you could easily spend $150 per person each day on meals. On top of this, restaurant prices have escalated in the last year or two due to fuel surcharges. However, you can dine superbly at a number of the island's better restaurants without breaking the bank, if you watch your wine selections, share appetizers or desserts, and pick up snacks and picnic meals from one of the well-stocked markets. Or, follow the locals to small *crêperies,* cafés, sandwich shops, and pizzerias in the main shopping areas. Lunch is usually less costly than dinner.

ABOUT THE RESTAURANTS

Reservations are strongly recommended and, in high season, essential. However, except during Christmas–New Year's it's not usually necessary to book far in advance. A day's—or even a few hours'—notice is usually sufficient. If you enter a restaurant without a reservation, you may not be seated, even if there are empty tables. Restaurant owners on St. Barths take great pride in their service as well as in their food, and they would rather turn you away than slight you on an understaffed evening. At the end of the meal, as in France, you must request the bill. Until you do, you can feel free to linger at the table and enjoy the complimentary vanilla rum that's likely to appear.

Check restaurant bills carefully. A service charge (*service compris*) is always added by law, but you should leave the server 5% to 10% extra in cash. You'll usually come out ahead if you charge restaurant meals on a credit card in euros instead of paying with American currency, as your credit card will offer a better exchange rate than the restaurant. Many restaurants serve locally caught lobster (*langouste*); priced by weight, it's usually the most expensive item on a menu and, depending on its size and the restaurant, will range in price from $40 to $60. In menu prices below, it has been left out of the range.

WHAT IT COSTS IN EURS				
$$$$	$$$	$$	$	¢
RESTAURANTS				
over €30	€20–€30	€12–€20	€8–€12	under €8

Restaurant prices are for a main course at dinner and include a 15% service charge.

WHAT TO WEAR

A bathing suit and pareu (sarong) are acceptable at beachside lunch spots. Most top it off with a T-shirt or tank top. Jackets are never required and rarely worn, but people dress fashionably for dinner. Casual chic is the idea; women wear whatever is hip, current, and sexy. You can't go wrong in a tank dress or a hippie-chic skirt and top. Nice shorts (not beachy ones) at the dinner table may label a man *américain,* but many locals have adopted the habit, and nobody cares much. Pack a light sweater or shawl for an after-dinner beach stroll.

ASIAN FUSION

$$–$$$$ ✕ **Eddy's.** By local standards, dinner in the pretty, open-
★ air, tropical garden here is reasonably priced. The cook-
ing is French-creole-Asian. Fish specialties, especially the
sushi tuna sampler, are fresh and delicious, and there are
always plenty of notable daily specials. Just remember some
mosquito repellent for your ankles. ✉*Rue du Centenaire*
☎*0590/27–54–17* ⚄*Reservations not accepted* ☰*AE, MC,
V* ⊘*Closed Sun. No lunch.*

$$–$$$$ ✕ **La Mandala.** Owner Boubou has a couple of popular restaurants on the island, all of which are cute, fun, and
have of-the-moment menus and friendly staff. This one
offers tasty Thai-influenced food on a sweeping terrace
over Gustavia Harbor. The sushi bar is a huge hit with the
celebrities that flock here. It's also great for a sunset cocktail. Try the vegetable-curry spring rolls, fish tempura with
kimchee sauce, Peking-style duck, or the Thai-scented sea
bass steamed in foil. Save room for the apple donuts with
Szechwan pepper-and-coriander syrup. ✉*Rue de la Sous-
Préfecture, Gustavia* ☎*0590/27–96–96* ☰*AE, MC, V.*

CARIBBEAN

$$$–$$$$ ✕ **Pipiri Palace.** Tucked into a tropical garden, this popular
★ in-town restaurant known for its barbecued ribs, beef fil-
let, and rack of lamb is consistently one of our absolute
favorites. Fish-market specialties like red snapper cooked
in a banana leaf or grilled tuna are good here, as are grilled
duck with mushroom sauce and a skewered surf-and-turf
with a green curry sauce. The blackboard lists daily spe-
cials that are usually a great choice, like a salad of tomato,
mango, and basil. Pierrot, the friendly owner, is sure to
take good care of you. ✉*Rue Général-de-Gaulle, Gus-
tavia* ☎*0590/27–53–20* ⚄*Reservations essential* ☰*MC,
V* ⊘*Closed mid-June–July.*

ECLECTIC

$$$–$$$$ ✕ **Do Brazil.** At this cozy restaurant nestled at the cliff side
of Gustavia's Shell Beach, you'll be able to sample more
of restaurateur Boubou's fusion creations. The menu is
more French-Thai than Brazilian, although at dinner there
are usually a couple of Brazilian specialties. The decor is
vaguely jungle-chic—romantic at night, lively at lunch. The
€42 menu is a good deal. Grilled sandwiches at the snack
bar on the beachfront level are the perfect lunch. For din-
ner, choose between varied salads, raw fish, hand-chopped

steak tartare, and a variety of fresh-caught grilled fish. The service has been known to be a little relaxed. ⊠*Shell Beach, Gustavia* ☎*0590/29–06–66* ⚓*Reservations essential* ▭*AE, MC, V.*

$$$$ ✕**Maya's.** New Englander Randy Gurly and his French–chef
★ wife, Maya, provide a warm welcome and a very pleasant dinner on their cheerful dock decorated with big, round tables and crayon-color canvas chairs, all overlooking Gustavia Harbor. A market-inspired menu of good, simply prepared and garnished dishes like mahimahi in creole sauce, shrimp scampi, pepper-marinated beef fillet changes daily, assuring the ongoing popularity of a restaurant that seems to be on everyone's list of favorites. ⊠*Public, Gustavia* ☎*0590/27–75–73* ⚓*Reservations essential* ▭*AE, MC, V.*

$$–$$$ ✕**Le Repaire.** This friendly brasserie overlooks Gustavia's
★ harbor and is a popular spot from its early-morning opening at 7 AM to its late-night closing at midnight. Its flexible hours are great if you arrive mid-afternoon and need a good snack before dinner. Grab a cappuccino, pull a captain's chair to the streetside rail, and watch the pretty girls. The menu ranges from cheeseburgers, which are served only at lunch along with the island's best fries, to simply grilled fish and meat. The composed salads always please. Wonderful ice-cream sundaes round out the menu. Try your hand at the billiards table or show up on weekends for live music. ⊠*Quai de la République, Gustavia* ☎*0590/ 27–72–48* ▭*MC, V.*

$$$–$$$$ ✕**Le Ti St. Barth Caribbean Tavern.** Chef-owner Carole Gruson
★ captures the funky, sexy spirit of the island in her wildly popular hilltop hot spot. We always come here to dance to great music with the attractive crowd lingering at the bar, lounge at one of the pillow-strewn banquettes, or chat on the torch-lighted terrace. By the time your appetizers arrive, you'll be best friends with the next table. The menu includes Thai beef salad, lobster ceviche, rare grilled tuna with Chinese noodles, and the best beef on the island. Provocatively named desserts, such as Nymph Thighs (airy lemon cake with vanilla custard) and Daddy's Balls (passion fruit sorbet and ice cream) end the meal on a fun note. Around this time someone is sure to be dancing on top of the tables. There's an extensive wine list. The famously raucous full-moon parties are legendary. ⊠*Pointe Milou* ☎*0590/27–97–71* ⚓*Reservations essential* ▭*MC, V.*

$$–$$$ ✕**Wall House.** The food can be really good—and the service
★ is always friendly—at this restaurant on the far side of

2

Gustavia harbor. The menu has been changed to emphasize the dishes that Frank, the amiable chef, does best, and the quality of everything continues to rise. Some of the best choices are specialties cooked on the elaborate gas rotisserie, including spit-roasted grouper, stuffed saddle of lamb, or five-spice honey pineapple duck. The pesto gnocchi are out of this world. Local businesspeople crowd the restaurant for the bargain prix-fixe lunch menu. The daily €29 dinner menu is a pretty good deal, too. An old-fashioned dessert trolley showcases some really yummy sweets. ⊠*La Pointe, Gustavia* ☎*0590/27–71–83* ⌖*Reservations essential* ⊟*AE, MC, V* ⊙*Closed Sept. and Oct.*

FRENCH

$$–$$$ ✕**Le Cesar.** This brand-new restaurant next to Hôtel le Village St-Jean features excellent, locally caught seafood ably prepared by the former chef of Le Marine. You can have mussels any day, or good grilled meats with a wide choice of vegetable side dishes. There's a €10 children's menu. The mango *tarte tatin* is a treat. ⊠*Les Hauts de Saint-Jean* ☎*0590/27–70–67* ⌖*Reservations essential* ⊟*AE, MC, V.*

★ Fodor'sChoice ✕**François Plantation.** This St. Barths favorite has **$$$$** been wonderfully reincarnated with sexy new decor, including pretty white drapery, and ethnographic black-and-white photos on the walls. Fresh Caribbean produce and seafood combine with European provisions like foie gras, artisanal cheeses, black truffles, and rare spices. First-rate presentation and exceptional service add to (the admittedly costly) delight. Definitely sample the exquisite desserts, such as cucumber-mojito-lemon pound cake. ⊠*François Plantation, Colombier* ☎*0590/29–80–22* ⌖*Reservations essential* ⊟*AE, MC, V* ⊙*Closed Sept. and Oct. No lunch.*

$$$$ ✕**Le Gaïac.** If you're in the mood to dress up, this is the ★ elegant, sophisticated restaurant at which to do it. Everything is taken very seriously here. Starched napery and impeccable service complement the blue bay view. Lunch includes chilled, spicy mango soup, salads, and grilled seafood. The dinner menu showcases really serious food: beef fillet with a tamarind glaze and tempura vegetables, coconut-crusted saddle of lamb, lime-infused halibut with banana, and black truffle veal chop cooked in a sea-salt crust: are you salivating? Table-side crêpes suzette are de rigueur, but then again, who could resist lime, orange, or berry soufflé? There's a €43 buffet brunch on Sunday.

✉ *Le Toiny, Anse à Toiny* ☎ *0590/29–77–47* ▭ *AE, DC, MC, V* ⊘ *Closed Sept.–mid-Oct.*

$$$–$$$$ ✕ **La Marine.** This St. Barths harborside classic is run by Carole Gruson, who has created a spiffy decor to match and meld into her hot next-door nightclub, Le Yacht Club. The traditional Thursday- and Friday-night mussels are always a hit, along with lots of other seafood choices. The Caribbean "B.B.Q. night" features all- you-can-eat grilled spiny lobster. It's a good choice for lunch, too. ✉ *Rue Jeanne d'Arc, Gustavia* ☎ *0590/27–68–91* ▭ *AE, MC, V.*

$$–$$$ ✕ **O'Corner.** New on the St. Barths restaurant scene in 2007, O'Corner has received favorable early reports on its cool art deco design, live music, and tasty fresh food offered in small, medium, and large sizes. The music is loud, and the crowd is hip. The real party starts after 11 each evening. It's all under the watchful eye of Hervé Chovet from the former St. Barths Beach Hotel. A mix of salads, stir-fries, grilled meats, and lots of veggie options makes this a great choice for a crowd. There's a plasma TV in the bar. ✉ *Rue du Roi Oscar II, Gustavia* ☎ *0590/51–00–05* ▭ *AE, MC, V.*

$$$–$$$$ ✕ **Le Sapotillier.** The romantic brick walls, hand-painted
★ wooden chairs, exquisite white-linen tablecloths, and vivid creole paintings evoke an old-style private island home. The service reminds us of dinner in the "best" homes, but this is not the cooking of your *maman.* Classic French food like rack of lamb, dover sole *meuniere.* and roasted Bresse chicken with potato gratin anchors the menu. Caramelized foie gras with cinnamon spiced pear and *sangria* is not to be missed. The sumptuous chocolate mousse and raspberry soufflé are longtime favorites. ✉ *Rue du Centenaire, Gustavia* ☎ *0590/27–60–28* ⚓ *Reservations essential* ▭ *MC, V* ⊘ *Closed mid-May–late Oct. No lunch.*

$$$–$$$$ ✕ **Le Tamarin.** A leisurely lunch here en route to Grand Saline
★ beach is a St. Barths *must.* Delicious French cuisine by Maxime Deschamps, formerly of Le Toiny, is served at this sophisticated open-air restaurant. Artistic salads tempt at lunch, especially the one garnished with foie gras. Dinner options include Moroccan-style lamb glazed with mango, along with plenty of daily specials. ✉ *Salines* ☎ *0590/27–72–12* ▭ *AE, MC, V* ⊘ *Closed Mon.*

ITALIAN

$$$–$$$$ ✕**PaCrì.** An adorable, young husband-and-wife team (she is
★   the chef) serve delicious, huge portions of housemade pasta,
wood-oven-fired pizza (at lunch), and authentic Italian main
courses, like Pugliese mahimahi, succulent meatballs, and
sautéed veal *saltimbocca* on a breezy open terrace right
near Saline Beach. The menu changes daily. Don't miss the
softball-size hunk of the best artisanal mozzarella you've
ever had, flown in from Italy and garnished with prosciutto
or tomato and basil. The eggplant Parmesan appetizer is
delicious and more than enough for a meal. Unusual des-
serts like lemon profiteroles are definitely worth the calo-
ries. Gorgeous waitstaff of both sexes add to the general
air of voluptuousness. ⊠*Rte. de Saline* ☎*0590/29–35–63*
⌂*Reservations essential* ▤*AE, MC, V.*

SEAFOOD

$$–$$$ ✕**La Langouste.** This tiny beachside restaurant in the pool-
courtyard of Hôtel Baie des Anges is run by Anny, the
hotel's amiable, ever-present proprietor. It lives up to its
name by serving fantastic, fresh-grilled lobster at a price
that is somewhat gentler than at most other island venues.
Simple, well-prepared fish, pastas, and an assortment of
refreshing cold soups are also available. Be sure to try the
warm goat cheese in pastry served on a green salad. ⊠*Hôtel
Baie des Anges, Flamands Beach* ☎*0590/27–63–61* ⌂*Res-
ervations essential* ▤*MC, V* ⊗*Closed May–Oct.*

$$–$$$$ ✕**Restaurant des Pêcheurs.** From fresh, morning beachside
★   brioche to a final evening drink in the sexy lounge, you can
dine all day in this soaring thatch pavilion that is the epit-
ome of chic. The restaurant at Le Sereno, like the Christian
Liaigre–designed resort, is serenity itself. Each menu item
is a miniature work of art, beautifully arranged and ami-
ably served. Each day there is a different €44 three-course
menu. "Authentic" two-course *Bouillabaisse à l'ancienne,*
the famous French seafood stew, is served every Friday,
and the chef even gives a class in its preparation, but the
menu also lists daily oceanic arrivals from Marseille, and
Quiberon on France's Atlantic coast: roasted, salt-crusted,
or grilled to perfection. This, and sand between your toes,
is heaven. ⊠*Grand Cul-de-Sac* ⌂*Reservations essential*
▤*AE, D, MC, V.*

WHERE TO STAY

There's no denying that hotel rooms and villas on St. Barths carry high prices, and the current weakness of the dollar makes for a costly respite. You're paying primarily for the privilege of staying on the island, and even at $800 a night the bedrooms tend to be small. Still, if you're flexible—in terms of timing and in your choice of lodgings—you can enjoy a holiday in St. Barths and still afford to send the kids to college.

ABOUT THE HOTELS

The most expensive season falls during the holidays (mid-December to early January), when hotels are booked far in advance, usually require a 10- or 14-day stay, and can be double the high-season rates. A 5% government Tourism Tax on room prices (excluding breakfast) went into effect in 2008.

Assume that hotels operate on the European Plan (EP—with no meals) unless we specify that they use either the Continental Plan (CP—with a continental breakfast), Breakfast Plan (BP—with full breakfast), or the Modified American Plan (MAP—with breakfast and dinner). Other hotels may offer the Full American Plan (FAP—including all meals but no drinks) or may be All-Inclusive (AI—with all meals, drinks, and most activities).

WHAT IT COSTS IN EUROS				
$$$$	$$$	$$	$	¢
HOTELS*				
over €350	€250–€350	€150–€250	€80–€150	under €80
HOTELS**				
over €450	€350–€450	€250–€350	€125–€250	under €125

*EP, BP, CP **AI, FAP, MAP; Hotel prices are per night for a double room in high season, excluding taxes, service charges, and meal plans.

CLOSE UP

Bliss & More

Visitors to St. Barths can enjoy more than the comforts of home by taking advantage of any of the myriad spa and beauty treatments that are now available on the island. Two major hotels, the Isle de France and the Guanahani, have beautiful, comprehensive, on-site spas for their guests. Depending on availability, other visitors to the island can also book services. In addition, scores of independent therapists will come to your hotel room or villa and provide any therapeutic discipline you can think of, including yoga, Thai massage, shiatsu, reflexology, and even manicures, pedicures, and hairdressing. You can find current therapists listed in the local guide, *Ti Gourmet*, or at the Tourist Office in Gustavia.

VILLAS & CONDOMINIUMS

On St. Barths, the term "villa" is used to describe anything from a small cottage to a luxurious, modern estate. Today almost half of St. Barths' accommodations are in villas, and we recommend considering this option, especially if you're traveling with friends or family. An advantage to Americans is that villa rates are usually quoted and confirmed in dollars, thus bypassing unfavorable euro fluctuations. Most villas have a small private swimming pool and maid service daily except Sunday. They are well furnished with linens, kitchen utensils, and such electronic playthings as CD and DVD players, satellite TV, and broadband Internet. In-season rates range from $1,400 to $40,000 a week. Most villa-rental companies are based in the United States and have extensive Web sites that allow you to see pictures of the place you're renting; their local offices oversee maintenance and housekeeping and provide concierge services to clients. Just be aware that there are few beachfront villas, so if you have your heart set on "toes in the sand" and a cute waiter delivering your kir royale, stick with the hotels or villas operated by hotel properties.

St. Barth Properties, Inc. (☎*508/528–7727 or 800/421–3396* 🖷*508/528–7789* ⊕*www.stbarth.com*), owned by American Peg Walsh—a regular on St. Barths since 1986—represents more than 120 properties here and can guide you to the perfect place to stay. Weekly peak-season rates range from $1,400 to $40,000 depending on the property's size, location, and amenities. The excellent Web site offers virtual tours of most of the villas and even details of availability. An office in Gustavia can take care of any problems you may have and offers some concierge-type services.

Marla (☎0590/27–62–02 ⊕*www.marlavillas.com*) is a local St. Barth villa-rental company that represents more than 100 villas, many that are not listed with other companies.

Wimco (☎800/932–3222 ☐401/847–6290 ⊕*www.wimco. com*), which is based in Rhode Island, oversees book-ings for more than 230 properties on St. Barths—they're represented on the island by SiBarth. Rents range from $2,000 to $10,000 for two- and three-bedroom villas; larger villas rent for $7,000 per week and up. Properties can be previewed and reserved on Wimco's Web site (which occasionally lists last-minute specials), or you can obtain a catalog by mail. The company will arrange for babysitters, massages, chefs, and other in-villa services for clients, as well as private air charters.

HOTELS

When it comes to booking a hotel on St. Barths, the reserva-tion manager can be your best ally. Rooms within a prop-erty can vary greatly. It's well worth the price of a phone call or the time investment of an e-mail correspondence to make a personal connection, which can mean much in arrang-ing a room that meets your needs or preferences. Details of accessibility, views, recent redecorating, meal options, and special package rates are topics open for discussion. Most quoted hotel rates are per room, not per person, and include service charges and airport transfers.

$$$$ ▣**Carl Gustaf.** This sophisticated hotel right in Gustavia
★   received a welcome overhaul in 2006, and its new incar-nation is the last word in luxury. Each apartment-suite is lavishly decorated and equipped with every modern con-venience: iPod-clock radios, multiple flat-screen TVs, and complete minikitchens with a Häagen-Dazs–stocked refrig-erator-freezer, and an espresso machine. You even have a computer and printer in the room! The hotel is a good option if you don't want to do much driving—it's within walking distance of everything in town if you don't mind climbing the hill. One- and two-bedroom suites with pri-vate decks and black-and-gold tile plunge pools spill down a hill overlooking quaint Gustavia Harbor. Summer rates and special Internet and honeymoon packages are offered. The Carl Gustaf restaurant, known for its classic French

cuisine, is spectacular for sunset cocktails and dinner over the twinkle of the harbor lights. **Pros:** Luxurious decor, in-town location, loads of in-room gadgets. **Cons:** It's not very "beachy," outdoor space limited to your private plunge pool. ⊠ *Rue des Normands, Box 700, Gustavia* ☎ *0590/29–79–00* 🖷 *0590/27–82–37* ⊕ *www.hotelcarlgustaf.com* 🛏 *14 suites* ⌕ *In-room: kitchen, refrigerator, VCR (some), DVD (some), Ethernet. In-hotel: restaurant, bar, pool, gym, no elevator* ⊟ *AE, MC, V* ⊠ *CP.*

★ **Fodor**Choice ⊞ **Eden Rock.** St. Barths' first hotel opened in
$$$$ the 1950s on the craggy bluff that splits Baie de St-Jean. Extensive renovations and an expansion in 2005 raised it into the top category of St. Barth properties. Each of the hotel's 29 unique rooms, suites, and villas is tastefully decorated and luxuriously appointed with plasma satellite TV and high-speed Internet. New, large bathrooms have either deep soaking tubs or walk-in showers; all have loads of fluffy towels and Bulgari suds. The six beachfront villas built on the property are magnificent and sleep up to four, with full kitchens and beautifully appointed modern living areas. Stunning bay views and great service are uniform. In 2008 the resort added three enormous (two- and three-bedroom) super-deluxe villas, each with two private pools, an art gallery, butler service, private cinema, and use of a Mini Cooper. The breakfast buffet, included in the rate, is terrific, and the on-site restaurants are first-rate and deserving of a visit. **Pros:** Chic clientele, beach setting, can walk to shopping and restaurants. **Cons:** Some suites are noisy because of proximity to street. ⊠ *Baie de St-Jean, 97133* ☎ *0590/29–79–99, 877/563–7015 in U.S.* 🖷 *0590/27–88–37* ⊕ *www.edenrockhotel.com* 🛏 *29 rooms, 3 villas* ⌕ *In-room: refrigerator, Ethernet. In-hotel: 2 restaurants, bars, pool, water sports, no elevator* ⊟ *AE, MC, V* ⊠ *BP.*

$$$-$$$$ ⊞ **Emeraude Plage.** Right on the beach of Baie de St-Jean,
★ this petite resort consists of small but immaculate bungalows and villas with fully equipped outdoor kitchenettes on small patios; nice bathrooms add to the comfort. At this writing, the reception area and units in the D and F bungalows have been completely renovated in the modern, clean, white-and-brown color scheme that has become the St. Barth "look"; now there are flat-screen TVs, and, on the patios, new white kitchens. A new beach pavilion serves breakfast, lunch, and drinks. Check for ongoing renovations when you inquire about reservations—the higher priced suites are the renovated ones. The complex is con-

venient to nearby restaurants and shops. The beachfront two-bedroom villas are something of a bargain, especially off-season. **Pros:** Beachfront and in-town location, good value, cool kitchens on each porch. **Cons:** Smallish rooms. ⊠*Baie de St-Jean, 97133* ☎*0590/27–64–78* ⧉*0590/27–83–08* ⊕*www.emeraudeplage.com* ⇘*21 bungalows, 4 suites, 2 cottages, 1 villa* ᓀ*In-room: safe, kitchen. In-hotel: bar, beachfront, no elevator, laundry service, public Internet* ⊟*MC, V* ⊘*Closed Sept.–Oct.* ⦿*EP.*

★ **Fodor'sChoice** ▣ **François Plantation.** A colonial-era graciousness
$$$$ pervades this intimate, exquisite hillside complex of West Indian–style cottages. The rooms have queen-size mahogany four-poster beds and colorful fabrics. Two larger rooms can accommodate an extra bed. The vanishing-edge pool sits atop a very steep hill with magnificent views from its pretty deck. The charming and sophisticated new management are retaining the wonderful, old-St. Barth qualities of the property, including the remarkable gardens, while making necessary improvements. Year-round, the prices are gentle for the island, but the off-season packages, which even include a car, are a real bargain. Villa Plantation, a new one-bedroom house with a private pool, is lovely and quite reasonable, with amazing views. **Pros:** Beautiful gardens, countryside location, wonderful restaurant. **Cons:** Rooms are small, steep hills between cottages, pool, and main area, need a car to get to beach and town. ⊠*Colombier, 97133* ☎*0590/29–80–22* ⧉*800/207–8071* ⊕*www.francois-plantation.com* ⇘*12 rooms, 1 villa* ᓀ*In-room: safe, refrigerator, dial-up. In-hotel: restaurant, pool, no elevator* ⊟*AE, MC, V* ⊘*Closed Sept. and Oct.* ⦿*CP.*

$$$$ ▣ **Hôtel Baie des Anges.** Everyone is treated like family at this
ᛒ casual retreat. Ten clean, fresh, and nicely decorated—if somewhat plain—rooms are right on serene Flamands Beach; each has a kitchenette and private terrace. There's also a small pool. The food at La Langouste, the hotel's restaurant, is tasty and reasonably priced. The proprietor also manages a four-bedroom, three-bath villa a bit farther up the hill. **Pros:** On St. Barth's longest beach, family-friendly. **Cons:** Rooms are basic. ⊠*Flamands, 97095* ☎*0590/27–63–61* ⧉*0590/27–83–44* ⊕*www.hotelbaiedesanges.fr* ⇘*10 rooms* ᓀ*In-room: safe, kitchen. In-hotel: restaurant, pool, beachfront* ⊟*AE, MC, V* ⦿*EP.*

$$$$ ▣ **Hôtel Guanahani & Spa.** The only full-service resort on the
ᛒ island has lovely rooms and suites (14 of which have private
★ pools) and impeccable personalized service, not to mention one of the only children's programs (though it's more of a

nursery). Rooms, all of which have large bathrooms with Clarins toiletries, were redecorated in 2006 in a hip and attractive grape-and-kiwi color scheme; at the same time, a stunningly serene Clarins Spa and Frederic Fekkai hair salon were added. Units vary in price, privacy, view, and distance from activities, so make your preferences known. The Wellness Suite, which is at the top of the property, can serve as your own hedonistic domain after the spa closes at night. Flat-screen TVs, iPod docks, and DVDs are new in all rooms, as is the sometimes dodgy, resort-wide Wi-Fi service; the well-equipped gym is newly expanded, and a renovated tennis court boasts an Astroturf surface. Also here are two well-regarded restaurants, poolside L'Indigo and sophisticated Bartolomeo, which has a lounge with music. **Pros:** Fantastic spa, beachside sports, family-friendly. **Cons:** Lots of cats, steep walk to beach. ✉ *Grand Cul de Sac, 97133* ☎ *0590/27–66–60* 📠 *0590/27–70–70* 🌐 *www.leguanahani.com* ⇨ *34 rooms, 33 suites, 1 3-bedroom villa* ♨ *In-room: DVD, Wi-Fi. In-hotel: 2 restaurants, room service, bar, tennis courts, pools, water sports, no elevator, children's programs (ages 2–12)* ▭ *AE, MC, V* 🍽 *CP.*

$$$$ **Hôtel La Banane.** Redone in 2006, the nine spacious pavilion-rooms with euro-style contemporary furnishings have yummy names like Watermelon, Pineapple, Grape, and Pomegranate that describe the bright color accents that counterpoint the white interiors. Private baths have every upscale amenity. The hotel's location behind a small shopping center may either be construed as a bother or a convenience, but Lorient Beach is a two-minute walk away. Breakfast is served around the palm-shaded pool. K'fe Massaï, the African-theme restaurant, is very popular. **Pros:** Short walk to beach, friendly and social atmosphere at pool areas, great baths. **Cons:** Rooms are small, location of entrance through parking lot is not attractive. ✉ *Quartier Lorient, 97133* ☎ *0590/52–03–00* 📠 *0590/27–68–44* 🌐 *www.labanane.com* ⇨ *9 rooms* ♨ *In-room: DVD, dial-up. In-hotel: restaurant, bar, pools, no elevator* ▭ *AE, MC, V* ⊗ *Closed Sept.–Oct. 15* 🍽 *CP.*

$$–$$$$ ★ **Hôtel le Village St-Jean.** For two generations, the Charneau family has offered friendly service and reasonable rates at its small hotel, making guests feel like a part of the family. Handsome, spacious, and comfortable, if not particularly trendy-chic, the airy stone-and-redwood cottages have high ceilings, sturdy furniture, modern baths, open-air kitchenettes, and lovely terraces with hammocks; one has a Jacuzzi. You get the advantages of a villa and the services of a hotel

here. The regular rooms have refrigerators, and most have king-size beds. In addition, there are three lovely villas of various sizes. Regulars are invited to store beach equipment. The location is great—you can walk to the beach and town from here—and most rooms and cottages have gorgeous views. See if Room 12, 15, or 10, perched on the edge of the hillside, is available when you book. A lounge with a plasma TV and Internet access is a popular gathering spot. Rooms (but not cottages) include continental breakfast in the rates. Cottages have kitchens; very reasonable summer rates for cottages include a car. **Pros:** Great value, convenient location, wonderful management. **Cons:** Somewhat old-fashioned, can be noisy. ⌂*Box 623, Baie de St-Jean, 97133* ☎*0590/27–61–39 or 800/651–8366* 🖷*0590/27–77–96* ⊕*www.villagestjeanhotel.com* ⌨*5 rooms, 20 cottages, 1 3-bedroom villa, 2 2-bedroom villas* ♿*In-room: kitchen (some), no TV. In-hotel: restaurant, bar, pool, no elevator* ▭*AE, MC, V* ⦿*EP.*

★ **Fodor's**Choice ▣**Hôtel St-Barth Isle de France.** An obsessively
$$$$ attentive management team ensures that this intimate, casually refined resort keeps remains among the very best accommodations in St. Barths—if the entire Caribbean. It's not hard to understand why the property boasts a 72% high-season return rate—it just keeps improving each season. A technology upgrade in 2007 added a reception-area computer for guests and broadband to rooms, which are huge and luxuriously outfitted, all with modern four-posters, French fabrics, and fine art, plus superb marble baths (all with a tub or Jacuzzi tub, both rare on the island). The beachside La Case de l'Isle restaurant serves nouvelle cuisine. The spa is by Molton Brown. The beautiful white-sand beach couldn't be more pristine. Good off-season and honeymoon packages help to keep the rates in check. **Pros:** Fabulous beach location, terrific management, great spa. **Cons:** Garden rooms—though large—can be dark, some complaints that the beds are hard. ⌂*Baie des Flamands, 97098* ☎*0590/27–61–81* 🖷*0590/27–86–83* ⊕*www.isle-de-france.com* ⌨*12 rooms, 5 suites, 13 bungalows, 1 2-bedroom villa* ♿*In-room: refrigerator, DVD, Ethernet. In-hotel: restaurant, room service, bar, tennis court, pools, gym, spa, public Internet* ▭*MC, V* ⦿*CP* ☉*Closed Sept.—mid-Oct.*

$$$$ ▣**Les Îlets de la Plage.** On the far side of the airport, tucked
★ away at the far corner of Baie de St-Jean, these well-priced, comfortably furnished island-style one-, two-, and three-bedroom bungalows (four right on the beach, seven up a

2

small hill) have small kitchens, pleasant open-air sitting areas, and comfortable bathrooms. This is a good choice if you want to be right on the beach with the space and convenience of a villa but the feel of a small resort. Crisp white linens and upholstery, lovely verandahs, and daily deliveries of fresh bread from a nearby bakery add to the pleasantness of the surroundings, though only the bedrooms are air-conditioned. **Pros:** Beach location, apartment conveniences, front porches. **Cons:** No a/c except in guest rooms, right next to the airport. ⊠*Plage de St-Jean,* ☎*0590/27–88–57* ▤*0590/27–88–58* ⊕*www.lesilets.com* ⤳*11 bungalows* ⚮*In-room: safe, kitchen, dial-up. In-hotel: pool, gym, beachfront, no elevator, concierge* ▤*AE, MC, V* ☉*Closed Sept.–Nov. 1* ⫮*EP.*

$-$$ ▦**Les Mouettes.** This guesthouse offers clean, simply furnished, and economical bungalows that open directly onto the beach. They're also quite close to the road, which can be either convenient for a quick shopping excursion or bothersome on account of the noise. Each air-conditioned bungalow has a bathroom with a shower only, a kitchenette, a patio, one or two double beds making this place a good bet for families or young visitors on a budget. **Pros:** Right on the beach, family-friendly. **Cons:** Rooms are basic, right near the road. ⊠*Lorient Beach, 97133* ☎*0590/27–77–91* ▤*0590/27–68–19* ⊕*www.st-barths.com/hotel-les-mouettes* ⤳*7 bungalows* ⚮*In-room: kitchen. In-hotel: beachfront, no elevator* ▤*No credit cards* ⫮*EP.*

$-$$ ▦**Le Normandie.** Wendy and Dennis Carlton, longtime St. Barth visitors, have renovated this eight-room inn in a Euro-meets-nautical theme, reflecting the eponymous art deco ocean liner. The rooms are small but stylish and will appeal to young visitors who will appreciate the in-town location, and clubby atmosphere of the tiny pool garden where breakfast and afternoon wine is served. Another thing is sure—there's nothing to compare at this price on the island. And, it's a two-minute walk to the beach. **Pros:** Youthful, house-party atmosphere, friendly. **Cons:** Tiny rooms. ⊠*Quartier Lorient* ☎*0590/27–61–66* ⊕*www.normandiehotelstbarts.com* ⤳*8 rooms* ⚮*In-room: Wi-Fi. In-hotel: bar, pool, no elevator* ▤*AE, MC, V* ⫮*CP.*

$$ ▦**Le P'tit Morne.** Each of the modestly furnished but freshly decorated and painted mountainside studios has a private balcony with panoramic views of the coastline. The small kitchenettes are adequate for creating picnic lunches and other light meals. The snack bar serves breakfast. It's relatively isolated here, however, and the beach is a 10-minute

drive away, but the young and friendly management is eager to help you enjoy your stay. There are weeklong packages that include a car, or a dive package. **Pros:** Reasonable rates, great area for hiking. **Cons:** Rooms are basic, remote location. ⌂ *Box 14, Colombier, 97133* ☎ *0590/52–95–50* 🖷 *0590/27–84–63* ⊕ *www.timorne.com* ⇆ *14 rooms* ⚑ *In-room: kitchen. In-hotel: pool, no elevator* ▤ *AE, MC, V* ⊚ *CP.*

$–$$ 🏠 **Salines Garden Cottages.** Budget-conscious beach lovers need look no further than these small garden cottages, a short stroll from what is arguably St. Barth's best beach. Each of the five studios is named for favorite places of the owners: Pavones, Padang, Waikiki, Cap Ferrat, and Essaouira. There's a small but pleasant pool set in the garden, and each studio unit has a private terrace. Three have full kitchenettes. You can choose to join the impromptu house party of the owners and residents, or just stay to yourself. **Pros:** Only property walkable to Salines Beach, quiet, reasonable rates. **Cons:** Far from town, not very private, no phones in rooms. ✉ *Salines* ☎ *0590/51–04–44* 🖷 *0590/27–64–65* ⊕ *www.salinesgarden.com* ⇆ *5 cottages* ⚑ *In-room: kitchen (some), Wi-Fi. In-hotel: bar, pool, no elevator, public Wi-Fi* ⊘ *Closed mid-Aug.–mid-Oct.* ⊚ *CP.*

★ **Fodor'sChoice** 🏨 **Le Sereno.** A St. Barth classic on a beauti-
$$$$ ful stretch of beach was reborn as an ultrachic retreat in 2005 (designed by superhot Parisian architect Christian Liaigre). Cutting-edge modern decor and techno amenities create a spare but luxurious, Zen-like serenity. The suites are huge by St. Barth standards and have spacious living areas and private sundecks. Large bathrooms, some with "steeping tubs," have roomy showers and vessel sinks of solid black granite. Other perks include cloud-soft linens and robes from Porthault, Parisian Ex Voto toiletries, high-speed Internet, plasma TVs, and iPod docks (for your own device or their fully loaded ones to borrow). Bedlike poolside lounges for two set the romantic tone for the hip all-day party. **Pros:** Beach location, super chic comfort, fun atmosphere. **Cons:** No a/c in the bathrooms, lots of construction planned for this part of the island over next few years. ✉ *B.P. 19 Grand-Cul-de-Sac,* ☎ *0590/29–83–00* 🖷 *0580/27–75–47* ⊕ *www.lesereno.com* ⇆ *37 suites and villas* ⚑ *In-room: safe, refrigerator, DVD, Wi-Fi. In-hotel: restaurant, room service, bar, pool, gym, no elevator, laundry service* ▤ *AE, MC, V* ⊚ *EP.*

$$$$ 🏨 **Le Toiny.** When perfection is more important than price,
★ choose Le Toiny's romantic villas with mahogany furniture,

2

yards of colored toile, and heated private pools. Rooms have every convenience of home: lush bathrooms, fully equipped kitchenettes, and either a stair-stepper or stationary bike. High-tech amenities include several flat-screen LCD TVs, stereos, fax machines, and Bang & Olufsen phones. Each suite has an outdoor shower. Breakfast comes to your terrace each morning, and in-villa spa services can be provided as well. If ever you want to leave your villa, Sunday brunch and haute cuisine can be had at the alfresco Le Gaiac overlooking the Italian-tile pool. New owners are adding a walking trail to the private beach with a seaside saltwater pool. Two of the villas are handicap accessible. **Pros:** Extremely private, luxurious rooms, flawless service. **Cons:** Not on the beach, at least half an hour drive from town. ⊠*Anse de Toiny, 97133* ☎*0590/27–88–88* ☎*0590/27–89–30* ⊕*www.letoiny.com* ⇝*14 1-bedroom villas, 1 3-bedroom villa* ⌂*In-room: safe, refrigerator, DVD, Wi-Fi. In-hotel: restaurant, bar, pool, no elevator, laundry service* ☰*AE, DC, MC, V* ⊙*Closed Sept.–late Oct.* ⏚*CP.*

$$$$ ⛱**Le Tom Beach Hôtel.** This chic but casual boutique hotel right on busy St. Jean beach is fun for social types. A garden winds around the brightly painted suites, over the pool via a small footbridge, into the hopping, open-air restaurant La Plage. The nonstop house party often spills out onto the terraces and lasts into the wee hours. Big, plantation-style rooms have high ceilings, cozy draped beds, nice baths, a TV with DVD player, direct-dial phones, and patios. Oceanfront suites are the most expensive, but all the rooms are clean and cozy, and were refurbished in 2007 with a romantic white, rose, and lavender color scheme. **Pros:** Party central at beach, restaurant, and pool, in-town location. **Cons:** Trendy social scene is not for everybody, especially light sleepers. ⊠*Plage St-Jean, 97133* ☎*0590/27–53–13* ☎*0590/27–53–15* ⊕*www.st-barths.com/tom-beach-hotel* ⇝*12 rooms* ⌂*In-room: safe, refrigerator, DVD. In-hotel: restaurant, bar, pool, beachfront, no elevator, public Internet* ☰*AE, MC, V* ⏚*CP.*

NIGHTLIFE

"In" clubs change from season to season, so you might ask around for the hot spot of the moment. There's more nightlife than ever in recent memory, and a late (10 PM or later) reservation at one of the club-restaurants will eventually become a front-row seat at a party.

Bar de l'Oubli (⊠*Rue du Roi Oscar II, Gustavia* ☎*0590/27–70–06*) is where young locals gather for drinks.

Carl Gustaf (⊠*Rue des Normands, Gustavia* ☎*0590/27–82–83*) lures a more sedate crowd, namely those in search of quiet conversation and sunset watching.

Le Feeling (⊠*Lurin* ☎*0590/52–84–09*) is a cabaret and disco in the Lurin Hills that has special theme nights on Thursday. It opens nightly at midnight for a cabaret show.

Le Nikki Beach (⊠*St-Jean* ☎*0590/27–64–64*) rocks on weekends during lunch, when the scantily clad young and beautiful lounge on the white canvas banquettes.

Le Repaire (⊠*Rue de la République, Gustavia* ☎*0590/27–72–48*) lures a crowd for cocktail hour and its pool table.

Le Santa Fé (⊠*Lurin* ☎*0590/27–61–04*), in the Lurin Hills, features a rowdy crowd, billiards, and satellite TV sports.

Le Sélect (⊠*Rue du Centenaire, Gustavia* ☎*0590/27–86–87*) is St. Barths' original hangout, commemorated by Jimmy Buffett's "Cheeseburger in Paradise." The boisterous garden is where the barefoot boating set gathers for a brew.

At this writing the hot spot was **Le Yacht Club** (⊠*Rue Jeanne d'Arc, Gustavia* ☎*0690/49–23–33*); although ads call it a private club, you can probably get in anyway.

BEACHES

There are many *anses* (coves) and nearly 20 *plages* (beaches) scattered around the island, each with a distinctive personality and each open to the general public. Even in season you can find a nearly empty beach. Topless sunbathing is common, but nudism is forbidden—although both Grande Saline and Gouverneur are de facto nude beaches. Bear in mind that the rocky beaches around Anse à Toiny are not swimmable.

Anse à Colombier. The beach here is the least accessible, thus the most private, on the island; to reach it you must take either a rocky footpath from Petite Anse or brave the 30-minute climb down (and back up) a steep, cactus-bordered—though clearly marked—trail from the top of the mountain behind the beach. Appropriate footgear is a must, and you should know that once you get to the beach, the only shade is a rock cave. Boaters favor this beach and cove for its calm anchorage. ⊠*Anse à Colombier*.

Anse des Flamands. This is the most beautiful of the hotel beaches—a roomy strip of silken sand. Visitors love to come here for lunch and then spend the afternoon sunning, taking a long beach walk and a swim in the turquoise water. From the beach, you can take a brisk hike to the top of the now-extinct volcano believed to have given birth to St. Barths. ⊠*Anse des Flamands*.

★ **Anse du Gouverneur.** Because it's so secluded, nude sunbathing is popular here; the beach is truly beautiful, with blissful swimming and views of St. Kitts, Saba, and St. Eustatius. Venture here at the end of the day, and watch the sun set behind the hills. The road here from Gustavia also offers spectacular vistas. Legend has it that pirates' treasure is buried in the vicinity. ⊠*Anse du Gouverneur*.

Anse de Grand Cul de Sac. The shallow, reef-protected beach is especially nice for small children, fly-fishermen, kayakers, and windsurfers; it has excellent lunch spots, water-sports rentals, and lots of the amusing pelicanlike frigate birds that dive-bomb the water fishing for their lunch. ⊠*Grand Cul de Sac*.

★ **Fodor'sChoice** **Anse de Grande Saline.** Secluded, with its sandy ocean bottom, this is just about everyone's favorite beach and great for swimmers, too. Without any major development, it's an ideal Caribbean strand, though it can be a bit windy here, so you can enjoy yourself more if you go on a calm day. In spite of the prohibition, young and old alike go nude. The beach is a 10-minute walk up a rocky dune trail, so be sure to wear sneakers or water shoes. The big salt ponds here are no longer in use, and the place looks a little desolate. ⊠*Grande Saline*.

Anse de Lorient. This beach is popular with St. Barths families and surfers, who like its rolling waves. Be aware of the level of the tide, which can come in very fast. Hikers and avid surfers like the walk over the hill to Point Milou in the late afternoon sun when the waves roll in. ⊠*Lorient*.

Baie de St-Jean. Like a mini–Côte d'Azur—beachside bistros, bungalow hotels, bronzed bodies, windsurfing, and lots of day-trippers—the reef-protected strip is divided by Eden Rock promontory, and there's good snorkeling west of the rock. ⊠*Baie de St-Jean*.

SPORTS & THE OUTDOORS

BOATING & SAILING

St. Barths is a popular yachting and sailing center, thanks to its location midway between Antigua and St. Thomas. Gustavia's harbor, 13 to 16 feet deep, has mooring and docking facilities for 40 yachts. There are also good anchorages available at Public, Corossol, and Colombier. You can charter sailing and motorboats in Gustavia Harbor for as little as a half day. Stop at the Tourist Office in Gustavia for an up-to-the-minute list of recommended charter companies.

Marine Service (⊠ *Gustavia* ☎ *0590/27–70–34* ⊕ *www. st-barths.com/marine.service*) offers full-day outings, either on a 42- or 46-foot catamaran, to the uninhabited Île Fourchue for swimming, snorkeling, cocktails, and lunch. The cost is $100 per person; an unskippered motor rental runs about $260 a day.

Yellow Submarine (⊠ *Ferry Dock, Gustavia* ☎ *0590/52–40–51* ⊕ *www.yellow-submarine.fr*) takes you "six feet under" (the surface of the sea) for a close-up view of St. Barth's coral reefs through large glass portholes. Once a week you can go at night. It costs €40 for adults and €12 for kids under 12. Trips depart hourly starting at 9 AM.

DIVING & SNORKELING

Several dive shops arrange scuba excursions to local sites. Depending on weather conditions, you may dive at **Pain de Sucre, Coco Island,** or toward nearby **Saba.** There's also an underwater shipwreck to explore, plus sharks, rays, sea tortoises, coral, and the usual varieties of colorful fish. The waters on the island's leeward side are the calmest. For the uncertified who still want to see what the island's waters hold, there's an accessible shallow reef right off the beach at Anse de Cayes if you have your own mask and fins.

Most of the waters surrounding St. Barths are protected in the island's **Réserve Marine de St-Barth** (⊠ *Gustavia* ☎ *0590/27–88–18*), which also provides information at its office in Gustavia. The diving here isn't nearly as rich as in the more dive-centered destinations like Saba and St. Eustatius, but the options aren't bad either, and none of the smaller islands offer the ambience of St. Barths.

Plongée Caraïbe (☎☎*0590/27–55–94*) is recommended for its up-to-the-minute equipment and dive boat.

Splash (✉*Gustavia* ☎*0690/56–90–24*) does scuba, snorkeling, and fishing, too.

Marine Service operates the only five-star, PADI-certified diving center on the island, called **West Indies Dive** (☎*0590/27–70–34* ⊕*www.westindiesdive.com*). Scuba trips, packages, resort dives, night dives, and certifications start at $90, including gear.

FISHING

Most fishing is done in the waters north of Lorient, Flamands, and Corossol. Popular catches are tuna, marlin, wahoo, and barracuda. There's an annual St. Barths Open Fishing Tournament, organized by Ocean Must, in mid-July.

Marine Service (✉*Gustavia* ☎*0590/27–70–34* ⊕*www.st-barths. com/marine.service*) arranges ocean-fishing excursions.

Océan Must Marina (✉*Gustavia* ☎*0590/27–62–25*) arranges deep-sea fishing expeditions as well as bareboat and staffed boat charters.

GOLF

Very well-heeled golf fanatics will be quite pleased with **Fly & Golf** (☎*0690/30–58–73* ⊕*www.flygolf.net*), which debuted in 2003. PGA pro and former champion Emmanuel Dussart will arrange tee times and flights from St. Barths to one of the excellent golf courses on Anguilla, St. Thomas, Nevis, or another nearby island. The maximum number of golfers per trip is three. Call about pricing; if you have to think about it, you probably can't afford it.

Golf in Paradise (✉*Petit Cul-de-Sac Pond* ☎*0690/37–46–45*) is a driving range on the water, with a video-golf simulator, and lessons. The company also arranges trips to golf courses on other islands.

HORSEBACK RIDING

Two-hour horseback trail-ride excursions in the morning or the afternoon led by Coralie Fournier are about $40 per person at **St. Barth Equitation** (✉*Ranch des Flamands, Anse des Flamands* ☎*0690/39–87–01*). Instruction is also available.

SHOPPING

★ Fodor'sChoice   St. Barths is a duty-free port, and with its sophisticated crowd of visitors, shopping in the island's 200-plus boutiques is a definite delight, especially for beachwear, accessories, jewelry, and casual wear. It would be no overstatement to say that shopping for fashionable clothing, accessories, and decorative items for the home is better in St. Barths than anywhere else in the Caribbean. New shops open all the time, so there's always something new to discover. Stores often close for lunch from noon to 2, and many on Wednesday afternoon as well, but they are open until about 7 in the evening. A popular afternoon pastime is strolling about the two major shopping areas in Gustavia and St-Jean.

AREAS

In Gustavia, boutiques line the three major shopping streets. Quai de la République, nicknamed rue du Couturier, which is right on the harbor, rivals New York's Madison Avenue or Paris's avenue Montaigne for high-end designer retail, including brand-new shops for **Dior, Louis Vuitton, Tod's, Bulgari, Cartier, Chopard,** and **Hermès.** These shops often carry items that are not available in the United States. The Carré d'Or plaza is great fun to explore. Shops are also clustered in **La Savane Commercial Center** (across from the airport), **La Villa Créole** (in St-Jean), and **Espace Neptune** (on the road to Lorient). It's worth working your way from one end to the other at these shopping complexes—just to see or, perhaps, be seen. Boutiques in all three areas carry the latest in French and Italian sportswear and some haute couture. You probably are not going to find any bargains as long as the euro remains high, but you might be able to snag that *pochette* that is sold out stateside, and in any case, you'll have a lot of fun hunting around.

SPECIALTY STORES

BOOKS

Funny Face Bookstore (⊠*Quai de la République, Gustavia* ☎*0590/29–60–14*) is a full-service bookstore with hundreds of English titles for adults and kids, plus armchairs, coffee, and Internet access.

CLOTHING

Shopping for up-to-the-minute fashions is as much a part of a visit to St. Barths as going to the beach. Shops change all the time, both in ownership and in the lines that are carried. Current listings are just a general guide. The best advice is simply to go for a long stroll and check out all the shops on the way. The following list is of shops that have an interesting variety of current and fun items, but it's by no means an exhaustive one.

Black Swan (⊠*Le Carré d'Or, Gustavia* ☎*0590/27–65–16* ⊠*La Villa Créole, St-Jean*) has an unparalleled selection of bathing suits. The wide range of styles and sizes is appreciated.

Boutique Lacoste (⊠*Rue Du Bord de Mer, Gustavia* ☎*0590/27–66–90*) has a huge selection of the once-again-chic alligator-logo wear, as well as a shop next door with a complete selection of the Petit Bateau line of T-shirts popular with teens.

Cachemire Crème (⊠*Rue du Bord du Mer, Gustavia* ☎*0590/52–48–42*) stocks, as the name suggests, deliciously fine cashmere in unusual styles and a whole tiny line for very lucky children.

Right next door to Cachemire Crème, **Cafe Coton** (⊠*Rue du Bord du Mer, Gustavia* ☎*0590/52–48–42*) is a great shop for men, especially for long-sleeve linen shirts in a rainbow of colors and Egyptian cotton dress shirts.

Calypso (⊠*Le Carré d'Or, Gustavia* ☎*0590/27–69–74*) carries resort wear for women by Balenciaga, Lucien Pellat-Finet, and Chloé.

Dovani (⊠*Rue de la République, Gustavia* ☎*0590/29–84–77*) has elegant leather goods and Baccarat jewelry.

Fans of Longchamp handbags and leather goods will find a good selection at about 20% off stateside prices at **Elysée Caraïbes** (⊠*Le Carré d'Or, Gustavia* ☎*0590/52–00–94*).

Hip Up (⊠*Rue Général-de-Gaulle, Gustavia* ☎*0590/27–69–33*) stocks a wonderful line of swimwear for all ages; tops and bottoms are sold separately for a practically custom fit, with cute matching accessories like sandals, cargo skirts, and T-shirt tops to complete the look.

Laurent Effel (⊠*Rue Général-de-Gaulle, Gustavia*) now has four shops in Gustavia for beautiful leather belts, colorful

linen shirts, bags, and shoes. One shop is devoted entirely
to exotic leather accessories.

Check out **Lili Belle** (⊠*Pelican Plage, St-Jean* ☎*0590/87–
46–14*), for hippie-chic drapey tops, drop-dead bikinis by
D nu D, and Stella Forest T-shirts and blouses.

Don't miss **Lolita Jaca** (⊠*Le Carré d'Or, Gustavia* ☎*0590/27–
59–98*) for trendy, tailored sportswear.

Mia Zia (⊠*Rue du Roi Oscar II, Gustavia* ☎*0590/27–55–
48*), which has relocated to big, new, purple quarters in
Gustavia, imports wonderful accessories from Morocco,
including multicolored, tassled silk and cotton shawls, caf-
tans, and colorful 6-foot-long silk cords to wrap around
your wrists, waist, or neck.

Morgan's (⊠*La Villa Créole, St-Jean* ☎*0590/27–57–22*)
has a line of popular and wearable casual wear in the
trendy vein.

Pati de Saint Barth (⊠*Passage de la Crémaillière, Gustavia*
☎*0590/29–78–04*) is the largest of the three shops that
stock the chic, locally made T-shirts that have practically
become the logo of St. Barths. The newest styles have hand-
done graffiti-style lettering.

At **Poupette** (⊠*Rue de la République, Gustavia* ☎*0590/27–
94–49*), all the brilliant color-silk and chiffon batik and
embroidered peasant skirts and tops are designed by the
owner. There also are great belts and beaded bracelets.

Stéphane & Bernard (⊠*Rue de la République, Gustavia* ☎*0590/
27–69–13*) stocks a well-edited, large selection of superstar
French fashion designers, including Rykiel, Tarlazzi, Kenzo,
Feraud, and Mugler.

Look to **St. Tropez KIWI** (⊠*St-Jean* ☎*0590/27–57–08* ⊠*Gustavia* ☎*0590/27–68–97*) for resort wear.

SUD SUD.ETC.Plage (⊠*Galerie du Commerce, St-Jean*
☎*0590/27–98–75*) stocks everything for the beach: inflat-
ables, mats, bags, and beachy shell jewelry.

Saint-Barth Stock Exchange (⊠*La Pointe-Gustavia* ☎*0590/27–
68–12*), on the far side of Gustavia's harbor, is the island's
consignment and discount shop.

COSMETICS

Don't miss the superb skin-care products made on-site from local tropical plants by **Ligne de St. Barths** (⊠*Rte. de Saline, Lorient* ☎*0590/27–82–63*).

FOODSTUFFS

A.M.C (⊠*Quai de la République, Gustavia*) is a bit older than Match but able to supply anything you might need for housekeeping in a villa, or for a picnic.

JoJo Supermarché (⊠*Lorient*) is the well-stocked counterpart to Gustavia's large supermarket and gets daily deliveries of bread and fresh produce. Prices are lower here than at the larger markets.

Match (⊠*St-Jean*), a fully stocked supermarket across from the airport, has a wide selection of French cheeses, pâtés, cured meats, produce, fresh bread, wine, and liquor.

Maya's to Go (⊠*Galleries du Commerce, St-Jean* ☎*0590/29–83–70*) is the place to go for prepared picnics, meals, salads, rotisserie chickens, and more from the kitchens of the popular restaurant.

For exotic groceries or picnic fixings, stop by St. Barths' gourmet *traiteur* (takeout) **La Rotisserie** (⊠*Rue du Roi Oscar II, Gustavia* ☎*0590/27–63–13* ⊠*Centre Vaval, St-Jean* ☎*0590/29–75–69*) for salads, prepared meats, groceries from Fauchon, and Iranian caviar.

HANDICRAFTS

The ladies of Corossol produce intricate straw work, wide-brim beach hats, and decorative ornaments by hand. Call the tourist office, which can provide information about the studios of other island artists: Christian Bretoneiche, Robert Danet, Nathalie Daniel, Patricia Guyot, Rose Lemen, Aline de Lurin, and Marion Vinot.

Look for Fabienne Miot's unusual gold jewelry at **L'Atelier de Fabienne** (⊠*Rue de la République, Gustavia* ☎*0590/27–63–31*).

Chez Pompi (⊠*On the road to Toiny* ☎*0590/27–75–67*) is a cottage whose first room is a gallery for the naive paintings of Pompi (also known as Louis Ledée).

Couleurs Provence (⊠*St-Jean* ☎*0590/52–48–51*) stocks beautiful, handcrafted French-made items like jacquard table linens in brilliant colors; decorative tableware, including trays in which dried flowers and herbs are suspended; and the home fragrance line by L'Occitane.

Kayali (⊠*Rue de la République, Gustavia* ☎*0590/27–64–48*) shows varied works by local artists.

Local works of art, including paintings, are sold in the bright **Made in St-Barth La Boutique** (⊠*La Villa Créole, St-Jean* ☎*0590/27–56–57*).

Find local stoneware, raku pottery, and other crafts at **St. Barth Pottery** (⊠*Gustavia* ☎*0590/27–69–81*), next to the post office on the harbor.

JEWELRY

Carat (⊠*Quai de la République, Gustavia*) has Chaumet and a large selection of Breitling watches.

A good selection of watches, including Patek Phillippe and Chanel, can be found at **Diamond Genesis** (⊠*Rue Général-de-Gaulle, Gustavia*).

Next door to Cartier, **Oro del Sol** (⊠*Quai de la République, Gustavia*) carries beautiful fine accessories by Bulgari, Ebel, and others.

Sindbad (⊠*Carré d'Or, Gustavia* ☎*0590/27–52–29*) is a tiny shop with funky, unique couture fashion jewelry by Gaz Bijou of St. Tropez, crystal collars for your pampered pooch, chunky ebony pendants on silk cord, and other reasonably priced, up-to-the-minute styles.

LIQUOR & TOBACCO

La Cave du Port Franc (⊠*Rue de la République, Gustavia* ☎*0590/27–65–27*) has a good selection of wine, especially from France.

La Cave de Saint-Barths (⊠*Marigot* ☎*0590/27–63–21*) has an excellent collection of French vintages stored in temperature-controlled cellars.

Le Comptoir du Cigare (⊠*Rue Général-de-Gaulle, Gustavia* ☎*0590/27–50–62*), run by Jannick and Patrick Gerthofer, is a top purveyor of cigars. The walk-in humidor has an extraordinary selection. Try the Cubans while you are on the island, and take home the Davidoffs. Refills can be shipped stateside. Be sure to try on the genuine Panama hats.

Couleur des Isles Cuban Cigar (⊠*Rue Général-de-Gaulle, Gustavia* ☎*0590/27–79–60*) has many rare varieties of smokeables and good souvenir T-shirts, too.

At **M'Bolo** (⊠*Rue Général-de-Gaulle, Gustavia* ☎*0590/27–90–54*), be sure to sample the various varieties of infused rums, including lemongrass, ginger, and, of course, the island favorite, vanilla. Bring home some in the beautiful hand-blown bottles.

Anguilla

WORD OF MOUTH

"Anguilla's water looks like you are in a swimming pool, and the sand is so white it hurts your eyes!"

—mustang8

"All [the] beaches are beautiful—long with white sand and crystal clear water—although Shoal Bay East is busier and has day trippers from St. Martin ('busy' in Anguilla is a relative term—the beaches are never really crowded)."

—MaryD

www.fodors.com/forums

By Elise
Meyer

1:00 PM: "What do you mean, you changed the menu? But my snapper," moaned the glamorous mother of three impeccably dressed children, her diamond earrings glittering in the midday sun. The maître d' listened attentively and nodded. "Don't worry, madam, I'm sure the chef will be happy to make it the way you like." "That's all right, Pierre. We'll do that tomorrow. What else would I like?" They consulted the menu together. When lunch materialized, lovely mom took one bite and realized that although she had insisted on eating the same lunch for a dozen years, she might actually like the new dish a teensy bit more.

1:00 AM: Under the full moon's glow, the beat of the rollicking calypso-tinged reggae had the whole room dancing. First-time visitors mingled with the regulars and the locals, brought together by the magic of the music, the sea air, the rum punch. At last call, they were all the best of friends and agreed to meet again the next night on the other side of the island, where a steel band might or might not appear.

Which is the "real" Anguilla? They both are. And if you want to have an incredibly special Caribbean holiday, make sure that you experience them both.

Peace, pampering, great food, and a wonderful local music scene are among the star attractions on Anguilla (pronounced ang-*gwill*-a). If you're a beach lover, you may become giddy when you first spot the island from the air; its blindingly white sand and lustrous blue-and-aquamarine waters are intoxicating. And, if you like sophisticated cuisine served in casually elegant open-air settings, this may be your culinary Shangri-La. Despite its small size, Anguilla has nearly 70 restaurants ranging from stylish temples of haute cuisine to classic, barefoot beachfront grills.

This dry limestone isle is the most northerly of the Leeward Islands, lying between the Caribbean Sea and the Atlantic Ocean. It stretches, from northeast to southwest, about 16 mi (26 km) and is 3 mi (5 km) across at its widest point. The highest spot is 213 feet above sea level, and there are neither streams nor rivers—only saline ponds once used for salt production. The island's name, a reflection of its shape, is most likely a derivative of *anguille,* which is French for "eel." (French explorer Pierre Laudonnaire is credited with having given the island this name when he sailed past it in 1556.)

In 1631 the Dutch built a fort here, but so far no one has been able to locate its site. English settlers from St. Kitts colonized the island in 1650, with plans to cultivate tobacco and, later, cotton and then sugar. But the thin soil and scarce water doomed these enterprises to fail. Except for a brief period of independence, when it broke from its association with St. Kitts and Nevis in the 1960s, Anguilla has remained a British colony ever since.

From the early 1800s various island federations were formed and disbanded, with Anguilla all the while simmering over its subordinate status and enforced union with St. Kitts. Anguillians twice petitioned for direct rule from Britain and twice were ignored. In 1967, when St. Kitts, Nevis, and Anguilla became an associated state, the mouse roared; citizens kicked out St. Kitts's policemen, held a self-rule referendum, and for two years conducted their own affairs. To what *Time* magazine called "a cascade of laughter around the world," a British "peacekeeping force" of 100 paratroopers from the Elite Red Devil unit parachuted onto the island, squelching Anguilla's designs for autonomy but helping a team of royal engineers stationed there to improve the port and build roads and schools. Today Anguilla elects a House of Assembly and its own leader to handle internal affairs, while a British governor is responsible for public service, the police, the judiciary, and external affairs.

The territory of Anguilla includes a few islets (or cays, pronounced "keys"), such as Scrub Island, Dog Island, Prickly Pear Cay, Sandy Island, and Sombrero Island. The 10,000 or so residents are predominantly of African descent, but there are also many of Irish background, whose ancestors came over from St. Kitts in the 1600s. Historically, because the limestone land was unfit for agriculture, attempts at enslavement never lasted long; consequently, Anguilla doesn't bear the scars of slavery found on so many other Caribbean islands. Instead, Anguillians became experts at making a living from the sea and are known for their boat-building and fishing skills. Tourism is the stable economy's growth industry, but the government carefully regulates expansion to protect the island's natural resources and beauty. New hotels are small, select, and definitely casino-free; Anguilla emphasizes its high-quality service, serene surroundings, and friendly people.

EXPLORING ANGUILLA

Exploring on Anguilla is mostly about checking out the spectacular beaches and resorts. The island has only a few roads; some are in bad condition, but the lack of adequate signage is being addressed. Locals are happy to provide directions, but having a good map—and using it—is the best strategy. Get one at the airport, the ferry dock, your hotel, or the tourist office in the Valley.

WHAT TO SEE

Heritage Museum Collection. Don't miss this remarkable opportunity to learn about Anguilla. Old photographs and local records and artifacts trace the island's history over 4 millennia, from the days of the Arawaks. The museum is painstakingly curated by Colville Petty. High points include the historical documents of the Anguilla Revolution and the albums of photographs chronicling island life, from devastating hurricanes to a visit from Queen Elizabeth in 1964. You can see examples of ancient pottery shards and stone tools along with fascinating photographs of the island in the early 20th century—many depicting the heaping and exporting of salt and the christening of schooners—and a complete set of beautiful postage stamps issued by Anguilla since 1967. ⊠*East End at Pond Ground* ☎*264/497–4092* 💰*$5* ⏰*Mon.–Sat. 10–5.*

★ **Island Harbour.** Anguillians have been fishing for centuries in the brightly painted, simple handcrafted fishing boats that line the shore of the harbor. It's hard to believe, but skillful pilots take these little boats out to sea as far as 50 mi or 60 mi (80 km or 100 km). Late afternoon is the best time to see the day's catch. Hail the boat to Gorgeous Scilly Cay, a classic little restaurant offering sublime lobster and Eudoxie Wallace's knockout rum punches on Wednesday, Friday, and Sunday.

Sandy Ground. Almost everyone who comes to Anguilla stops by its most developed beach. Little open-air bars and restaurants line the shore, and there are several boutiques, a dive shop, the Pyrat Rum factory, and a small commercial pier. This is where you catch the ferry for tiny Sandy Island, just 2 mi (3 km) offshore.

Wallblake House. The only surviving plantation house in Anguilla, Wallblake House was built in 1787 by Will Blake (Wallblake is probably a corruption of his name) and has recently been thoroughly and thoughtfully restored. The

Ram's Head

Masara

Flat Cap Point

Little Bay

ATLANTIC OCEAN

Sandy Island

North Hill

Road Bay

Sandy Ground

Wallblake Airport

South Hill

1 **2**

3 **4**

Long Bay

21 **16**

11

19 **20**
14 **15**

Meads Bay

Wallblake House

Barnes Bay

12 **13**

12

6 **5**

Rendezvous Bay

Blowing Point Harbour

Little Harbour

West End

17 **18**

7

Cove Bay

16 **11**

15

Maundays Bay

Anguillita Island

Shoal Bay West

10

13 **14**

8 **9**

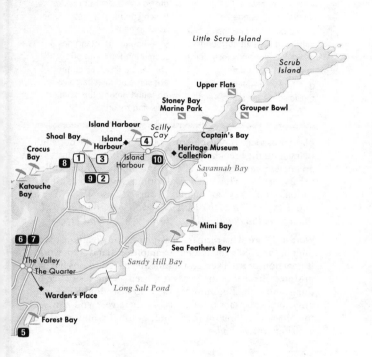

Anguilla

Little Scrub Island

Scrub Island

Upper Flats

**Stoney Bay
Marine Park**

Grouper Bowl

Island Harbour

Captain's Bay

Shoal Bay

**Island
Harbour**

*Scilly
Cay*

4

**Crocus
Bay**

8 **1** **3**

**Island
Harbour**

9 **2**

10

**Heritage Museum
Collection**

Savannah Bay

**Katouche
Bay**

Mimi Bay

Sea Feathers Bay

6 **7**

The Valley

The Quarter

Sandy Hill Bay

Long Salt Pond

Warden's Place

Forest Bay

5

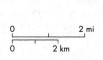

0 — 2 mi

0 — 2 km

KEY

⌐ *Beaches*

◺ *Dive Sites*

1 *Restaurants*

1 *Hotels*

Anguilla Best Bets

Anguilla is a little island with a lot to offer.

■ Miles of brilliant beaches ensure you have a quality spot on which to lounge.

■ The dining scene offers fine cuisine in elegant surroundings as well as delicious local food in casual restaurants.

■ A funky late-night local music scene for reggae and string band fans means you don't have to go to bed early.

■ Excellent luxury resorts coddle you in a level of comfort to which you may or may not be accustomed.

■ Although the island has a reputation for being pricey, if you look a little closer, there are some relative bargains to be found among the smaller inns and resorts.

place is associated with many a tale involving murder, high living, and the French invasion in 1796. On the grounds are an ancient vaulted stone cistern and an outbuilding called the Bakery (which wasn't used for making bread at all but for baking turkeys and hams). Tours are usually at 10 AM and 2 PM. ⊠ *Wallblake Rd., The Valley* ☎ *264/497–6613* ⊕ *www.wallblake.ai* ☞ *Free* ☉ *Mon., Wed., and Fri.*

Warden's Place. This former sugar-plantation greathouse was built in the 1790s and is a fine example of island stonework. It now houses KoalKeel restaurant and a sumptuous bakery upstairs. But for many years it served as the residence of the island's chief administrator, who also doubled as the only medical practitioner. Across the street you can see the oldest dwelling on the island, originally built as slave housing. ⊠ *The Valley.*

WHERE TO EAT

Anguilla has an extraordinary number of excellent restaurants, ranging from elegant establishments to down-home seaside shacks. Many have breeze-swept terraces, where you can dine under the stars. Anguillian restaurant meals are leisurely events, and service is often at a relaxed pace, so settle in and enjoy. Most restaurant owners are actively and conspicuously present, especially at dinner. It's a special treat to take the time to get to know them a bit when they stop by your table to make sure that you are enjoying your meal.

ABOUT THE RESTAURANTS

Call ahead—especially in winter—to make a reservation; in late summer and fall (especially between August and December) to confirm if the place you've chosen is open since many restaurants close for the off-season, when several of the island's larger resorts are also closed.

WHAT IT COSTS IN U.S. DOLLARS				
$$$$	$$$	$$	$	¢
RESTAURANTS				
over $30	$20–$30	$12–$20	$8–$12	under $8

Restaurant prices are for a main course and do not include taxes or service charges.

WHAT TO WEAR

During the day, casual clothes are widely accepted: shorts will be fine, but don't wear bathing suits and cover-ups unless you're at a beach bar. Note that the topless bathing common on some of the French islands is strictly forbidden here. In the evening, shorts are okay at the extremely casual eateries. Elsewhere, women should wear sundresses or nice casual slacks; men will be fine in short-sleeved shirts and casual pants. Some hotel restaurants are more formal and may have a jacket requirement in high season; ask when you make your reservation.

AMERICAN

$$$$ Fodor'sChoice **Blanchard's.** This absolutely delightful restaurant, a mecca for foodies, is considered one of the best in the Caribbean. Proprietors Bob and Melinda Blanchard moved to Anguilla from Vermont in 1994 to fulfill their culinary dreams. A festive atmosphere pervades the handsome, airy white room, which is accented with floor-to-ceiling teal-blue shutters to let in the breezes, and colorful artworks by the Blanchards' son Jesse on the walls. A masterful combination of creative cuisine, an upscale atmosphere, attentive service, and an excellent wine cellar (including a selection of aged spirits) pleases the star-studded crowd. The nuanced contemporary menu is ever-changing but always delightful; house classics like corn chowder, lobster cakes, and a Caribbean sampler are crowd pleasers. For dessert, you'll remember concoctions like the key lime "pie-in-a-

glass" or the justly famous "cracked coconut" long after your suntan has faded. ✉ *Meads Bay* ☎*264/497–6100* ⚖*Reservations essential* ☲*AE, MC, V* ⊘*No lunch. Closed Sun., Aug., and Sept.*

$$$–$$$$ ✕ **Zurra.** The Blanchard's heavenly outpost at the St. Regis Temenos Clubhouse is named for a white, Spanish, tropical-fruit sangria, and the restaurant is as fresh and lovely as its namesake. Sitting on the broad patio, gazing at the glittering sea is a treat for lunch or dinner. Prime aged steaks and chops are char-grilled to perfection, salads sparkle, and the desserts are simply delectable. The afternoon bar menu adds snacks and grilled skewers—it's popular with golfers and their friends. Don't miss a peek at the glass wine cellar, and a tour of Jesse Blanchard's large-scale paintings. ✉ *Temenos Golf Club* ☎*264/222–8300* ⊕*www. zurrarestaurant.com* ⚖*Reservations essential* ☲*AE, MC, V* ⊘*Closed Aug. and Sept.*

ASIAN-FUSION

★ FodorsChoice ✕ **Hibernia.** Some of the island's most creative
$$$–$$$$ dishes are served in this wood-beam cottage restaurant–art gallery overlooking the water at the far eastern end of Anguilla. Unorthodox yet delectable culinary pairings—inspired by chef–owners Raoul Rodriguez and Mary Pat's annual travels to the Far East—include Asian mushroom soup topped with cream of cauliflower, duck breast with Chinese plum and five-spice sauce with black-sesame-crusted gnocchi; a crayfish casserole with steamed rice noodles in basil and coconut milk; and roasted lobster, served with Lao purple rice and artichoke hearts filled with spinach and pine nuts in a vanilla-bean sauce. Every visit here is an opportunity to share in Mary Pat and Raoul's passion for life, expressed through the vibrant combination of setting, art, food, unique tableware, beautiful gardens, and thoughtful hospitality. ✉ *Island Harbour* ☎*264/497–4290* ☲*MC, V* ⊘*Closed mid-Aug.–mid-Oct. Call for seasonal hrs.*

BARBECUE

$–$$$ ✕ **Smokey's.** There's no sign, so you'll have to ask the way
★ to Cove Bay to find this quintessential Anguillian beach barbecue, part of the Gumbs family mini-empire of authentic and delicious eateries. African-style hot wings, honey-coated ribs, salt-fish cakes, curried chicken roti, and grilled lobsters are paired with local staple side dishes such as

spiced-mayonnaise coleslaw, hand-cut sweet-potato strings, and crunchy onion rings. If your idea of the perfect summer lunch is a roadside lobster roll, be sure to try the version here, served on a home-baked roll with a hearty kick of hot sauce. The dinner menu includes crayfish tails and chicken in orange sauce. On Saturday afternoon a popular local band, the Musical Brothers, enlivens the casual, laid-back atmosphere. ⊠*Cove Rd., Cove Bay* ☎*264/497–6582* ▭*AE, MC, V* ☉*May–Nov., closed Mon.*

3

CARIBBEAN

$–$$ ✕**English Rose.** Lunch finds this neighborhood hangout packed with locals: cops flirting with sassy waitresses, entrepreneurs brokering deals with politicos, schoolgirls in lime-green outfits doing their homework. The decor is not much to speak of, but this is a great place to eavesdrop or people-watch while enjoying island-tinged specialties like beer-battered shrimp, jerk chicken Caesar salad, snapper creole, and baked chicken. ⊠*Main St., The Valley* ☎*264/497–5353* ▭*MC, V* ☉*Closed Sun.*

$$$–$$$$ ✕**Overlook.** Perched on a cliff high above the bustling harbor of Sandy Ground, chef Deon Thomas's popular and friendly eatery showcases flavorful dishes that combine local and Continental cuisine with a sure hand and a distinct flair. The verandah is pretty, and the orange-and-blue dining room is decorated in island art. The soups stand out: try the carrot-and-apple or pumpkin to start, or perhaps a refreshingly brash gazpacho topped with a basil-Worcestershire granité. At dinner, main courses like roasted grouper curry with coconut-mango chutney as well as braised goat with fragrant rice and peas reflect local flavors, while international touches yield such dishes as oven-crisp duck with Chambord sauce or roasted rack of lamb with rosemary and eggplant tomato ragout. It's closed in summer, when Thomas cooks for lucky fans on Martha's Vineyard. Reservations are recommended. ⊠*Back St., South Hill* ☎*264/497–4488* ▭*AE, MC, V* ☉*Closed May–Oct.*

$$–$$$$ ✕**Tasty's.**
★ Once your eyes adjust to the quirky kiwi, lilac, and coral color scheme, you'll find that breakfast, lunch, or dinner at Tasty's is, well, very tasty. It's open all day long, so if you come off a mid-afternoon plane starving, head right here—it's right near the airport. Chef–owner Dale Carty trained at Malliouhana, and his careful, confident preparation bears the mark of French culinary training, but the menu is classic Caribbean. It's worth leaving the beach

at lunch for the lobster salad here. A velvety pumpkin soup garnished with roasted coconut shards is superb, as are the seared jerk tuna and the garlic-infused marinated conch salad. Yummy desserts end meals on a high note. This is one of the few restaurants that do not allow smoking, so take your Cubans elsewhere for an after-dinner puff. Dale also cooks lunch at Bankie Banx's Dune Preserve on the white sands of Rendevous Bay. ⊠*On main road in South Hill* ☎*264/497–2737* ⚇*Reservations essential* ⊟*AE, MC, V* ⊙*Closed Thurs.*

ECLECTIC

$$ ✗**Kemia.** Cap Juluca's seaside "hors d'oeuverie" looks like
★   a posh pasha's oasis transported to the Caribbean. Arches, tables, and lamps are embedded with jewel-like mosaic and colored glass; cushy throw pillows and billowing tent ceilings complete the fantasy. Chef Vernon Hughes prepares a truly global selection of small tapaslike plates that are perfect for sharing in this romantic retreat at the edge of the cerulean waves. Spanish-style shrimp in garlic butter, tiny pots of curries, rare Thai beef salad—it's all delicious. ⊠*Cap Juluca, Maundays Bay* ☎*888/858–5822 in U.S., 264/497–6666* ⚇*Reservations essential* ⊟*AE, MC, V* ⊙*Closed Sun., Mon., Sept., and Oct. No lunch May–Nov.*

$$$–$$$$ ✗**Pimms.** The most coveted tables in this enchanted venue at
★   Cap Juluca are so close to the water that you can actually see fish darting about as you dine. Innovative fare utilizes ultraluxe ingredients from around the world, and the menu includes such creations as organic heirloom tomato sampler with 28-year-old balsamic vinegar, duck confit Greek salad, house-cured duck prosciutto with foie gras, and for a major splurge, Kobe beef rib eye. There are excellent choices for vegetarians, too. A sterling wine list complements the menu (look for regular winemaker dinners). Your perfect meal could end with chocolate mousse, an aged rum, and a pre-Castro *Cubano.* ⊠*Cap Juluca, Maundays Bay* ☎*264/497–6666* ⚇*Reservations essential* ⊟*AE, MC, V* ⊙*Closed Sept. and Oct. No lunch.*

$$$–$$$$ ✗**Straw Hat.** Seven picture windows frame seascapes, from
★   floodlighted coral reefs to fishing flotillas, from this covered dock built on pilings directly over the water. By night, the lights of St. Martin and St. Barths twinkle in the distance. But charming owners Peter and Ann Parles, and the sophisticated and original food is the real reason that the

restaurant recently celebrated its 10th anniversary. The curried goat here sets the bar for the island. And "fish of the day" here means the fish that was truly caught that day. ✉*Forest Bay* ☎264/497–8300 ▤AE, D, MC, V ⊘*Closed Sun. No lunch.*

★ **Fodor'sChoice** ✕**Veya.** The stylishly appointed tables glow with

$$$–$$$$ flickering candlelight (white-matte sea-urchin votive holders made of porcelain) lining the suavely minimalist, draped, four-sided verandah. A lively lounge where chic patrons mingle and sip mojitos to the purr of soft jazz anchors the room. Inventive, sophisticated, and downright delicious, Carrie Bogar's "Cuisine of the Sun" features thoughtful but ingenious preparations of first-rate provisions. Ample portions are sharable works of art—sample Moroccan-spiced shrimp "cigars" with roast tomato–apricot chutney or Vietnamese-spiced calamari. Jerk-spiced tuna is served with a rum coffee glaze on a juicy slab of grilled pineapple with curls of plantain crisps. Dessert is a must. Sublime warm chocolate cake with chili-roasted banana ice cream and carmelized bananas steals the show. ✉*Sandy Ground* ☎264/498–8392 ⌂*Reservations essential* ▤AE, MC, V ⊘*Closed Sun. No lunch.*

$$–$$$$ ✕**Zara's.** Chef Shamash Brooks presides at this cozy restaurant with beamed ceilings, terra-cotta floors, colorful artwork, and poolside seating. His kitchen turns out tasty fare that combines Caribbean and Italian flavors with panache. Standouts include a velvety pumpkin soup with coconut milk, crunchy calamari, lemon pasta scented with garlic, herbed rack of lamb served with a roasted apple sauce, and spicy fish fillet steamed in banana leaf. ✉*Allamanda Beach Club, Upper Shoal Bay* ☎264/497–3229 ▤AE, D, MC, V ⊘*No lunch.*

FRENCH

$$$$ ✕**Covecastles.** Elegant, intimate, and—above all—healthy dinners are served here in a garden overlooking beautiful Shoal Bay West. Each season, Dominique Thevenet devises a new menu, innovatively mating French culinary traditions with Caribbean ingredients. The current menu features grilled organic beef tenderloin with lavender oil, spinach and crayfish ravioli in a tomato-garlic sauce, and grilled tuna steak with a juniper berry and port wine cream sauce. Villa guests receive priority for the seven tables, so call ahead for reservations. ✉*Shoal Bay West* ☎264/497–6801

⚴*Reservations essential* ☰*AE, D* ☉*Closed Sept.–Nov. No lunch.*

¢–$$ ✕**Geraud's Patisserie.** A stunning array of absolutely deli-
★ cious French pastries and breads—and universal favorites
like cookies, brownies, and muffins—are produced in this
tiny shop by Cordon Bleu dynamo Geraud Lavest. Come
early morning for cappuccino and croissants, and pick up
fixings for a wonderful lunch later (or choose from among
the list of tempting daily lunch specials). ☒*South Hill Plaza*
☏*264/497–5559* ☰*AE, MC, V* ☉*No dinner.*

★ Fodor'sChoice ✕**KoalKeel.** Originally part of a sugar and cot-
$$$–$$$$ ton plantation, KoalKeel is owned by descendants of the
slaves once housed on this very site. A tour is a high point
of any meal here, as the buildings are rich in history. A 200-
year-old rock oven is used by the on-site bakery upstairs.
With a day's notice, you can enjoy a whole chicken that
has been slow-roasted from the inside. The menu features a
combination of classic French and West Indian specialties.
Start with goat cheese baked in puff pastry in a pool of
honey vinaigrette; then continue with rack of lamb served
with pumpkin gratin or veal chop in a rosemary sauce
with caramelized shallots and truffled mashed potato. Be
sure to save room for the incredible desserts. Wine lovers
take note of the exceptional 15,000-bottle wine cellar,
in an underground cistern. Anguilla's savvy early risers
show up here for the fresh French bread, croissants, and
pain au chocolat that are sold out by 9 AM. ☒*Coronation
Ave., The Valley* ☏*264/497–2930* ⚴*Reservations essential*
☰*AE, MC, V.*

$–$$ ✕**Madeariman Reef Bar & Restaurant.** This casual, feet-in-the-
sand bistro right on busy, beautiful Shoal Bay is open for
breakfast, lunch, and dinner; the soups, salads, and simple
grills here are served with a bit of French flair. Come for
lunch and stay to lounge on the beach chaises, or bar-hop
between here and Uncle Ernie's barbecue next door. ☒*Shoal
Bay East* ☏*264/497–5750* ☰*AE, MC, V.*

$$$–$$$$ ✕**Michael Rostang at Malliouhana.** Sparkling crystal and fine
★ china, attentive service, a wonderful 25,000-bottle wine
cellar, and a spectacularly romantic, open-air room comple-
ment exceptional haute cuisine rivaling any in the French
West Indies. Consulting chef Michael Rostang, renowned
for his exceptional Paris bistros, and chef Alain Laurent
revamp the menu seasonally, incorporating local ingredi-
ents in both classic and contemporary preparations. The
ultimate in hedonism is sipping champagne as the setting
sun triggers a laser show over the bay, before repairing to

your table. ⊠*Meads Bay* ☎*264/497–6111* ⚑*Reservations essential* ▤*AE, D, MC, V* ☉*Closed Sept. and Oct.*

ITALIAN

$$–$$$$ ✕**Luna Rosa.** Classic upscale Italian favorites, light and tasty
★ pastas, and luscious vegetables prepared with sensitivity to the importance of authentic ingredients is a winning formula for this 2007 newcomer. The eggplant Parmesan is crisp and light with an intense tomato ragout, and the wild-mushroom risotto is so delicious you may be tempted to lick your plate. The thrilling sea view and charming management are icing on the cake. ⊠*Lower South Hill* ☎*264/497–6810* ⚑*Reservations essential* ▤*AE, MC, V* ☉*Closed Sun.*

$$$–$$$$ ✕**Trattoria Tramonto & Oasis Beach Bar.** The island's only Italian restaurant features a dual (or dueling) serenade of Andrea Bocelli on the sound system and gently lapping waves a few feet away. Chef Valter Belli artfully adapts recipes from his home in Emilia-Romagna. Try the delicate lobster ravioli in truffle-cream sauce, or go for a less Italian option: kangaroo steak. For dessert, don't miss the authentic tiramisu. Though you might wander in here for lunch after a swim, when casual dress is accepted, you'll still be treated to the same impressive menu. You can also choose from a luscious selection of champagne fruit drinks, a small but fairly priced Italian wine list, and homemade grappas. Denzel Washington celebrated his 50th birthday here with such close friends as Robert De Niro and Sean "P. Diddy" Combs. ⊠*Shoal Bay West* ☎*264/497–8819* ⚑*Reservations essential* ▤*MC, V* ☉*Closed Mon., Sept., and Oct.*

SEAFOOD

★ **Fodor'sChoice** ✕**Mango's.** One meal at Mango's and you'll
$$$–$$$$ understand why it's a perennial favorite of repeat visitors to Anguilla. Sparkling-fresh fish specialties have starring roles on the menu here. Light and healthy choices like a spicy grilled whole snapper are deliciously perfect. Save room for dessert—the warm apple tart and the coconut cheesecake are worth the splurge. There's an extensive wine list, and the Cuban cigar humidor is a luxurious touch. The proprietor, a former New Jerseyan known islandside as Mango Dave, keeps a watchful eye over his chic domain and over his stylish clientele, a veritable *People* magazine spread in high season. Excellent local live music several nights a week adds to the cheerful party atmosphere. ⊠*Barnes Bay*

☎264/497–6479 ⚘*Reservations essential* ▭*AE, MC, V* ☺*Closed Tues. No lunch.*

SOUTHWESTERN

$-$$$ ✕ **Picante.** This casual, bright-red roadside Caribbean
⚙ *taqueria*, opened by a young California couple, serves
★ huge, tasty burritos with a choice of fillings, fresh warm
tortilla chips with first-rate guacamole, and tequila-lime
chicken grilled under a brick. Mexican chocolate pud-
ding makes a great choice for dessert. Seating is at picnic
tables; the friendly proprietors cheerfully supply pillows
on request. Reservations are recommended. ✉ *West End
Rd., West End* ☎*264/498–1616* ▭*AE, MC, V* ☺*Closed
Tues. No lunch.*

WHERE TO STAY

Tourism on Anguilla is a fairly recent phenomenon—most
development didn't begin until the early 1980s, so most
hotels and resorts are of relatively recent vintage. The
lack of native topography and, indeed, vegetation, and the
blindingly white expanses of beach have inspired building
designs of some interest; architecture buffs might have fun
trying to name some of the most surprising examples. Inspi-
ration largely comes from the Mediterranean: the Greek
Islands, Morocco, and Spain, with some Miami-style art
deco thrown into the mixture.

Anguilla accommodations basically fall into two categories:
grand, sumptuous resorts and luxury resort-villas, or low-
key, simple, locally owned inns and small beachfront com-
plexes. The former can be surprisingly expensive, the latter
surprisingly reasonable. In the middle are some condo-type
options, with full kitchen facilities and multiple bedrooms,
which are great for families or for longer stays. At this
writing, many properties are in the building, expanding,
or planning stages, and by 2009 there may be upward of
1,000 new guest rooms on the island, many in super-deluxe
projects. Private villa rentals are becoming more common
and are increasing in number and quality every season as
development on the island accelerates.

ABOUT THE HOTELS

A good phone chat or e-mail exchange with the manage-
ment of any property is a good idea, as some lodgings
don't have in-room TVs, a few have no air-condition-

ing, and units within the same complex can vary greatly in layout, accessibility, distance to the beach, and view. When calling to reserve a room, ask about special discount packages, especially in spring and summer. Most hotels include continental breakfast in the price, and many have meal-plan options. But keep in mind that Anguilla is home to dozens of excellent restaurants before you lock yourself into an expensive meal plan that you may not be able to change; consider the more flexible voucher offerings. All hotels charge a 10% tax, a $1 per room/per day tourism marketing levy, and—in most cases—an additional 10% service charge.

Assume that hotels operate on the European Plan (EP—with no meals) unless we specify that they use either the Continental Plan (CP—with a continental breakfast), Breakfast Plan (BP—with full breakfast), or the Modified American Plan (MAP—with breakfast and dinner). Other hotels may offer the Full American Plan (FAP—including all meals but no drinks) or may be All-Inclusive (AI—with all meals, drinks, and most activities).

WHAT IT COSTS IN U.S. DOLLARS				
$$$$	$$$	$$	$	¢
HOTELS*				
over $350	$250–$350	$150–$250	$80–$150	under $80
HOTELS**				
over $450	$350–$450	$250–$350	$125–$250	under $125

*EP, BP, CP **AI, FAP, MAP; Hotel prices are for two people in a double room in high season and do not include 8% tax, 10%–15% service charge, or meal plans.

HOTELS

$$$ ☒ **Anguilla Great House Beach Resort.** These traditional West Indian–style bungalows strung along one of Anguilla's longest beaches evoke an old-time Caribbean feel with their cotton-candy colors, and the gentle prices and interconnected rooms appeal to families and groups of friends traveling together. Gingerbread trim frames views of the ocean from charming verandahs. Rather basic rooms are decked

with local artwork, mahogany and wicker furnishings, tropical-print fabrics, and ceiling fans; some have hand-painted floral borders. Those numbered 111 to 127 offer beach proximity and the best views; newer units aren't as well situated and lack views but have television and Internet access. The restaurant serves a mix of West Indian, Italian, and Continental cuisines; the bartenders proudly ask you to sample their special concoctions, exemplifying the friendly service. The hotel can arrange in-room massage and other spa treats. **Pros:** Real, old-school Caribbean, young crowd, gentle prices. **Cons:** Rooms are very simple, and bathrooms are the bare basics. ⊠*Rendezvous Bay* ⌂*Box 157, The Valley* ☎*264/497–6061 or 800/583–9247* ☎*264/497–6019* ⊕*www.anguillagreathouse.com* ⬐*35 rooms* ♿*In-room: refrigerator, dial-up (some). In-hotel: restaurant, pool, gym, beachfront, water sports* ☐*AE, MC, V* ⑩*EP.*

$$–$$$ ▥**Arawak Beach Inn.** These breezy, hexagonal two-story villas are a good choice for a funky, low-key island respite. The pricier units on the top floors are more spacious and a bit quieter and enjoy spectacular views of the rocky shores of boat-dotted Island Harbor and beyond to Scilly Key. Some rooms have large four-poster rattan beds, and some have kitchenettes. Most aren't air-conditioned, and those that are cost more, but the harbor breezes are usually sufficient. The inn's manager, Maria Hawkins, will make you feel like one of the family by the time you leave. Mix your own drinks at the bar—or, if co-owner Maurice Bonham-Carter is around, have him mix you the island's best Bloody Mary. The Arawak Cafe, splashed in psychedelic colors, serves special pizzas and lip-smacking Caribbean comfort food. A small private cove with a sandy beach is a five-minute walk. The common areas have Wi-Fi. **Pros:** Funky, casual crowd, friendly owners, gentle rates. **Cons:** Not on the beach, location makes a car a must, plumbing problems. ⌂*Box 1403, Island Harbour* ☎*264/497–4888, 877/427–2925 reservations only* ☎*264/497–4889* ⊕*www.arawakbeach. com* ⬐*13 rooms, 4 suites* ♿*In-room: no a/c (some), safe, kitchen (some), no TV (some). In-hotel: restaurant, bar, pool, beachfront, water sports, no elevator, public Wi-Fi* ☐*AE, D, MC, V* ⑩*EP.*

$$$$ ▥**Cap Juluca.** Sybaritic and serene, this 179-acre resort
☾   wraps around breathtaking Maundays Bay, the glittering
★   sand rivaled only by the dramatic domed, white, Moorish-style villas, caring staff, and first-rate sports facilities. Enormous and private, guest rooms are furnished with Moroccan textiles and Brazilian hardwood furniture and

3

have huge marble bathrooms, a few with tubs big enough for two. But the property could stand some maintenance and refurbishing. Private patios, balconies, or sunroofs render sea, sky, and sand part of the decor. The romantic atmosphere makes this resort popular for honeymoons and destination weddings. Ask about special golf packages if you're interested in playing nearby Temenos course. Facilities include a fitness center, an aqua-golf driving range, and an extensive water-sports pavilion. There are three room categories, but even the standard ("luxury") accommodations are well laid out, spacious, and comfortable. Flexible multibedroom private villas are beautifully furnished and include a 24-hour-a-day butler. A high point: each morning at the exact moment you specify, continental breakfast appears on your private verandah—the meal includes a basket of fresh-baked pastries, a platter of delicious fresh fruit, and piping-hot coffee. Room TVs are available by request only. At this writing, there was a possibility of the resort changing hands and possibly expanding. **Pros:** Lots of space to stretch out on miles of talcum-soft sand, warm service; romantic atmosphere (no kids). **Cons:** It's sometimes hard to find your room, as the units have strange names or numbers, bathrooms are dated, room TVs only by request. ✎ *Box 240, Maundays Bay* ☎ *888/858–5822 in U.S., 264/497–6779* 🖷 *264/497–6617* ⊕ *www.capjuluca. com* 🛏 *72 rooms, 7 patio suites, 6 pool villas* 🚼 *In-room: refrigerator, no TV, Ethernet. In-hotel: 3 restaurants, room service, bar, tennis courts, pool, gym, spa, beachfront, water sports, no elevator, children's programs (ages 3–14), laundry service* 🝙 *AE, D, MC, V* ☻ *Closed Sept. and Oct.* 🝙 *CP.*

★ **Fodor's**Choice ☂**CuisinArt Resort & Spa.** This family-friendly
$$$$ beachfront resort's design—gleaming white-stucco build-
☉ ings, blue domes and trim, glass-block walls—blends art deco with a Greek Isle feel. Huge rooms were refurnished and redecorated in 2008, painted in a calming sky-blue and fitted with flat-screen TVs. Guests return in droves to enjoy the casual atmosphere, full-service spa, extensive sports facilities, and the fulfill-every-wish concierge crew, who provide everything from vacation-long nannies to local cell phones to dinner reservations. Continuing facility upgrades include a spacious health club and spa with thalassotherapy tubs. High-season children's programs give parents a chance to enjoy the holiday, too. A hydroponic farm provides ultrafresh organic produce for the two restaurants; tours of the greenhouse, lush tropical gardens,

and orchards are fun and engaging. Cooking classes and demonstrations are conducted in the teaching kitchen, and enjoyed at a Chef's Table twice a week. Six private villas are planned for 2009. **Pros:** Family-friendly, great spa and sports, gorgeous beach and gardens. **Cons:** Food service can be slow, pool area is noisy, public areas not inviting. ⌂*Box 2000, Rendezvous Bay* ☎264/498–2000 or 800/943–3210 📠264/498–2010 ⊕*www.cuisinartresort.com* ⤙*93 rooms, 2 penthouses* &*In-room: safe, refrigerator, Ethernet. In-hotel: 3 restaurants, bars, tennis courts, pool, gym, spa, beachfront, water sports, bicycles, laundry service* ⊟*AE, D, MC, V* ⊗*Closed Sept. and Oct.* ⍟*EP.*

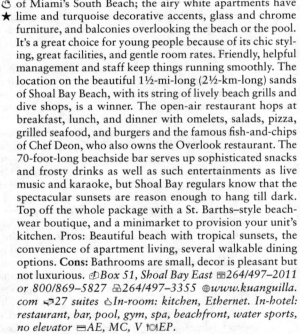

$$$–$$$$ ⌑ **Kú.** This all-suites hotel is modeled on the barefoot chic
☾ of Miami's South Beach; the airy white apartments have
★ lime and turquoise decorative accents, glass and chrome furniture, and balconies overlooking the beach or the pool. It's a great choice for young people because of its chic styling, great facilities, and gentle room rates. Friendly, helpful management and staff keep things running smoothly. The location on the beautiful 1½-mi-long (2½-km-long) sands of Shoal Bay Beach, with its string of lively beach grills and dive shops, is a winner. The open-air restaurant hops at breakfast, lunch, and dinner with omelets, salads, pizza, grilled seafood, and burgers and the famous fish-and-chips of Chef Deon, who also owns the Overlook restaurant. The 70-foot-long beachside bar serves up sophisticated snacks and frosty drinks as well as such entertainments as live music and karaoke, but Shoal Bay regulars know that the spectacular sunsets are reason enough to hang till dark. Top off the whole package with a St. Barths–style beachwear boutique, and a minimarket to provision your unit's kitchen. **Pros:** Beautiful beach with tropical sunsets, the convenience of apartment living, several walkable dining options. **Cons:** Bathrooms are small, decor is pleasant but not luxurious. ⌂*Box 51, Shoal Bay East* ☎264/497–2011 or 800/869–5827 📠264/497–3355 ⊕*www.kuanguilla. com* ⤙*27 suites* &*In-room: kitchen, Ethernet. In-hotel: restaurant, bar, pool, gym, spa, beachfront, water sports, no elevator* ⊟*AE, MC, V* ⍟*EP.*

$$$$ ⌑ **Malliouhana Hotel and Spa.** European refinement in a tran-
☾ quil beach setting, attentive service, stellar dining, and
★ a plethora of activities keep the mostly mogul clientele returning year after year, despite nearly universal agreement that a general refurbishment is overdue. An elegant air surrounds the resort's white arches and soaring columns, accented by tile stairways that wrap dramatically around

a rocky bluff. With high ceilings, large balconies, marble baths, and sumptuous—if somewhat dated—decor, rooms are so comfortable you might never want to leave. Some suites even have private hot tubs; one has a private swimming pool. Extensive facilities allow you to be as active—or sedentary—as you wish: spend your days snorkeling, water-skiing, or fishing, or just relax at the spa or take a leisurely stroll along mile-long Meads Bay. Those with young ones need not be deterred by the opulence here—Malliouhana is family-friendly. Kids enjoy a beachside pirate-ship playground, playroom, and separate dining facilities. Summertime packages offer two rooms for the price of one. Note the 10% service charge and an additional $20/day electricity surcharge. **Pros:** Huge rooms, elite international clientele, stellar dining on a beautiful terrace over the sea. **Cons:** The beach drops off at the edge, and the water can be rough, guests need to bring lots of cash, shabby outdoor furniture. ✉*Box 173, Meads Bay* ☎*264/497–6111 or 800/835–0796* 🖷*264/497–6011* ⊕*www.malliouhana.com* ⇌*34 double rooms, 6 junior suites, 7 1-bedroom suites, 2 2-bedroom suites, 2 Jacuzzi suites, 1 honeymoon suite, 1 pool suite* ♿*In-room: safe, refrigerator, no TV, Ethernet. In-hotel: 2 restaurants, room service, bar, tennis courts, 3 pools, gym, spa, beachfront, water sports, no elevator, laundry service, public Internet* ⊟*AE, MC, V* ⊘*Closed Sept. and Oct.* ⋈*EP.*

$$$$ 🖼**Sheriva.** This intimate, luxury-villa hotel, opened in 2006,
☯ offers a glimpse into the future of Anguilla's high-end lodg-
★ ings. Three cavernous private villas containing a total of 20 guest rooms and 7 private swimming pools overlook a broad swath of turquoise sea. The villas can be divided into one- to seven-bedroom residences, completely outfitted with all kinds of amenities: fully equipped offices, exercise rooms, multiple plasma TVs, video libraries, and poker tables. Besides these perks you have a concierge, a private chef to prepare your meals (meals cost extra), and an attentive housekeeping staff that even does your laundry. Private golf carts shuttle Sheriva guests to nearby Cap Juluca for beach, tennis, spa, and restaurants, with signing privileges. Pros: Incredible staff to fulfill every wish, all the comforts of home and more, good value for large family groups. **Cons:** Not on the beach, you risk being spoiled for life by the staff's attentions. ✉*Maundays Bay Rd., West End* ☎*264/498–9898* ⊕*www.sheriva.com* ⇌*20 rooms* ♿*In-room: kitchen, DVD, Wi-Fi. In-hotel: pools, laundry service* ⊟*AE, MC, V* ⋈*EP.*

$$$ ⊞ **Sirena.** Young management and a hip, modern look please
★ new and repeat visitors to this low-key resort overlook-
ing Meads Bay. Although small, the attractively redone
standard rooms have fresh white paint, flat-screen TVs,
comfy beds, and touches of Asian decor. Budget-conscious
travelers appreciate the garden suites and larger villas,
which have full kitchens. Junior suites have kitchenettes,
big granite bathrooms, and whirlpool baths. The restau-
rant is a gathering spot for guests, many of whom choose
a meal plan that includes breakfast and dinner or, for more
flexibility, purchase meal vouchers for a part of their stay.
Though the five-minute walk to the beach is not the pret-
tiest, you'll find thatched umbrellas and chaises when you
get there. **Pros:** Modern, clean, and well-equipped, good
value, nice tech amenities. **Cons:** Long walk to the beach
with many stairs, ongoing construction next door. ⌂Box
200, Meads Bay ☎264/497–6827 ⌂264/497–6829 ⊕www.
sirenaresort.com ⇨20 rooms, 4 suites, 6 villas ♿In-room:
safe, kitchen (some), no TV. In-hotel: restaurant, bar, pools,
diving, bicycles, no elevator, public Internet ▤AE, D, MC,
V ⦿CP.

VILLAS & CONDOMINIUMS

The tourist office publishes an annual **Anguilla Travel Plan-
ner** with informative listings of available vacation apart-
ment rentals.

You can contact the **Anguilla Connection** (⌂Box 1369, Island
Harbour ☎264/497–9852 or 800/916–3336 ⌂264/497–
9853 ⊕www.luxuryvillas.com) for condo and villa listings.
myCaribbean (☎877/471–2733 ⊕www.mycaribbean.com) is
the largest local private villa rental company. Gayle Gurvey
and her staff manage and rent more than 100 local villas,
and have been in business for almost 10 years.
Ricketts Luxury (☎264/497–6049 ⊕www.anguillaluxury
collection.com) is operated by Sue and Robin Ricketts,
longtime Anguilla real estate experts who manage a col-
lection of first-rate villas.

$$ ⊞ **Allamanda Beach Club.** Youthful, active couples from
☾ around the globe happily fill this casual, three-story, white-
stucco building hidden in a palm grove just off the beach.
Units are neat and simply furnished, with tile floors and
pastel matelassé bedspreads; ocean views are best from
the top floor. On the ground floor are four large deluxe

apartment suites that are great for families. People return year after year, thanks to the management's dedicated hospitality. The creative restaurant, Zara's, is a popular draw, as is the less expensive Gwen's Reggae Grill, a boisterous and colorful beachside joint with an upscale, frat-party atmosphere. Look into special summer packages. **Pros:** Right on Shoal Bay's action, young crowd, good restaurant. **Cons:** Location requires a car; rooms are clean, but not at all fancy, beach and pool lounges are aging poorly. ⌂*Box 662, Upper Shoal Bay Beach* ☎*264/497–5217* ☏*264/497–5216* ⊕*www.allamanda.ai* ⌿*20 units* ♿*In-room: kitchen. In-hotel: 2 restaurants, pool, gym, water sports, public Internet* ☐*AE, D, MC, V* ⑩*EP.*

$$$$ ▦**Altamer.** Architect Myron Goldfinger's geometric symphony of floor-to-ceiling windows, cantilevered walls, and curvaceous floating staircases is fit for any king (or CEO)—as is the price tag that goes along with it. Each of the three villas here has a distinct decorative theme and must be rented in its entirety; choose from Russian Amethyst, Brazilian Emerald, or African Sapphire. Striking interiors are filled with custom-made and antique pieces—Murano fixtures, Florentine linens, Turkish kilims, Fabergé ornaments, Tsarist silver candelabras—but still manage to feel airy rather than cluttered. They're also outfitted with the latest gadgetry, from touch-pad stereo systems to wireless Internet. A private butler and eight staff, including a chef, anticipate your every whim. Full conference facilities make this an ideal location for corporate or family retreats of up to 40 people. Planned renovations, slated to begin around 2010, include a luxury yacht marina and additional villas. **Pros:** The last word in luxury and electronic diversions. **Cons:** Construction of proposed marina might be bothersome. ✉*Shoal Bay West* ⌂*Box 3001, The Valley* ☎*264/498–4000* ☏*264/498–4010* ⊕*www.altamer.com* ⌿*3 5-bedroom villas* ♿*In-room: kitchen, VCR (some), Wi-Fi (some). In-hotel: tennis courts, pool, gym, beachfront, water sports, laundry service, public Internet* ☐*AE, D, DC, MC, V* ⌕*1-week minimum* ⑩*AI.*

$$$$ ▦**Baccarat Hotel and Residences at Temenos.** "Temenos" is
★ Greek for "sanctuary," and the name is certainly justified. These incomparably glamorous villas were inspired by the pure, spare architecture of Mykonos and Santorini: sparkling white buildings contrast with the serene blues and greens of the ocean. At this writing, building continues on the 116 new one-, two-, and three-bedroom villas, modeled on the original three super-luxe villas favored by celebrity

visitors to Anguilla. The first wave of these is expected to open around 2010. All will have cathedral ceilings, louvered French doors, infinity pools, and enormous marble bathrooms with indoor-outdoor showers. Textural elements are mixed beautifully; marble, granite, wrought iron, mosaic tiles, and woven rugs offset state-of-the-art kitchen and entertainment equipment. The private staff is friendly yet unobtrusive. Of course, sanctuary comes with a high price, but celebrities like Janet Jackson know that you get what you pay for. The beautiful Greg Norman–designed golf course is up and running; as are a state-of-the-art fitness center, three restaurants, four tennis courts, and a 60,000-square-foot clubhouse. **Pros:** Luxurious perfection, amazing bathrooms, super service. **Cons:** You'll spend your whole vacation trying to come up with a "con." ⑀*Box 1656, Long Bay* ☎*264/498–9000* 🖷*264/498–9050* ⊕*www. temenosanguilla.com* ⌦*1 5-bedroom villa, 2 4-bedroom villas* ⌂*In-room: kitchen, DVD, Ethernet. In-hotel: tennis courts, pools, gym, beachfront, water sports, laundry service, public Internet* ▭*AE, D, MC, V* ⌦*1-week minimum* ⦿*CP.*

$$$$ 🏨**Caribella.** These spacious Mediterranean-style villas on the broad sands of Barnes Bay are a terrific bargain, especially at the discounted weekly rate. The two-bedroom, two-bathroom villas have full kitchens and daily maid service. The decor is not much to speak of, but the beach is beautiful. **Pros:** Huge amount of space for the cost, beautiful views from huge balconies. **Cons:** Somewhat noisy due to location next to restaurant and construction, very basic décor. ⑀*Box 780, Barnes Bay, West End* ☎*264/497–6045* 🖷*264/497–8929* ⊕*www.lambertventures.com* ⌦*6 villas* ⌂*In-room: kitchen. In-hotel: no elevator* ▭*MC, V* ⦿*EP.*

$$$$ 🏨**Carimar Beach Club.** This horseshoe of bougainvillea-draped Mediterranean-style buildings on beautiful Meads Bay has the look of an upscale Sun Belt condo. Although only two units—No. 1 and No. 6—stand at the water's edge, all have balconies or patios with ocean views. Bright, white, one- and two-bedroom apartments are individually owned and thus reflect their owners' tastes, but most are well-appointed, fully equipped, and carefully maintained. The cordial staff, supreme beachfront location, and several fine restaurants within walking distance make this a popular spot. Portable air-conditioners can be rented for a fee. **Pros:** Tennis courts, easy walk to restaurants and spa, right next door to Malliouhana. **Cons:** No pool or restaurant, no TV,

not great a/c. *Box 327, The Valley* ☎*264/497–6881 or 800/235–8667* ☖*264/497–6071* ⊕*www.carimar.com* ⌨*24 apartments* ⌂*In-room: kitchen, no TV. In-hotel: tennis courts, beachfront, water sports, no elevator, public Internet* ⊟*AE, D, MC, V* ⊘*Closed Sept. and Oct.* ⌂*EP.*

$$$$ 　🏨**Covecastles Villa Resort.** Though this secluded Myron Gold-finger–designed enclave resembles a series of giant concrete baby carriages from the outside, the sensuous curves and angles of the skylighted interiors bespeak elegance and comfort. Decor in the soaring one- to six-bedroom villas is luxurious but unstuffy: custom-made wicker furniture, raw-silk cushions, and hand-embroidered linens in muted, soothing colors. Louvered Brazilian walnut doors and windows perfectly frame tranquil views of St. Martin, creating living canvases. Units are filled with such high-tech amenities as DVD and CD players. The Point, a super-luxe five-bedroom villa right on the beach, is one of the island's, if perhaps the world's, premier accommodations. The restaurant melds organic to French-Caribbean, the beach beckons, and an unobtrusive staff allows tranquillity to reign. **Pros:** Private beach with reef for snorkeling, great service, classy modern decor. **Cons:** Beach is small and rocky, located at the far end of the island. *Box 248, Shoal Bay West* ☎*264/497–6801 or 800/223–1108* ☖*264/497–6051* ⊕*www.covecastles.com* ⌨*15 apartments* ⌂*In-room: DVD (some), Ethernet. In-hotel: restaurant, room service, tennis courts, beachfront, water sports, bicycles, laundry service, no elevator* ⊟*AE, MC, V* ⌂*EP.*

$$–$$$$ 　🏨**Paradise Cove.** This pretty complex of reasonably priced
⌂ one- and two-bedroom apartments compensates for its
★ location away from the beach with two whirlpools, a large pool, and tranquil tropical gardens where you can pluck fresh guavas for breakfast. The beautiful Cove and Rendezvous bays are just a few minutes' stroll away. Spotless units are attractively appointed with white rattan and natural wicker furniture, gleaming white-tile floors, large kitchens, and soft floral or pastel fabrics from mint to mango. Second-floor units have high beamed ceilings. Maid service and private cooks are available. Families will appreciate such thoughtful touches as cookies-and-cream pool parties and weekend pizza-making lessons. Very reasonable seven-night packages include a car. **Pros:** Reasonable rates, great pool, lovely gardens. **Cons:** It's a bit far to the beach, decor is bland. *Box 135, The Cove* ☎*264/497–6959 or 264/497–6603* ☖*264/497–6927* ⊕*www.paradise.ai* ⌨*12 studio suites, 17 1- and 2-bedroom apartments* ⌂*In-room:*

kitchen (some), dial-up. In-hotel: restaurant, bar, pools, gym, laundry facilities, laundry service, public Internet ☰*AE, D, MC, V* ⊚*EP.*

$$–$$$ ☒ **Serenity Cottages.** Despite the name of this property, it ☾ comprises not cottages but rather large, fully equipped, and relatively affordable studios and one- and two-bedroom apartments in a small complex at the farthest end of glorious Shoal Bay Beach. The restaurant is located on a breezy verandah near the beach. Guests gather on mismatched Adirondack-type chairs for sundowner cocktails. But there isn't much attention from staff. **Pros:** Big apartments, quiet end of beach, snorkeling right outside the door. **Cons:** Generic decor, more condo than hotel in terms of staff, location at the end of Shoal Bay pretty much requires a car, and some extra time to drive to the West End. ⊠*Shoal Bay East, Upper Bay* ☎*264/497–3328* ⊕*www.serenity. ai* ⊅*8 2-bedroom apartments, 2 1-bedroom suites* ⚷*In-room: kitchen. In-hotel: restaurant, bar, beachfront, public Internet* ☰*AE, MC, V* ⊙*Closed Sept.* ⊚*EP.*

NIGHTLIFE & THE ARTS

In late February or early March, reggae star and impresario Bankie Banx stages Moonsplash, a three-day music festival that showcases local and imported talent around the nights of the full moon. At the end of July is the International Arts Festival, which hosts artists from around the world. BET (Black Entertainment Television) sponsors Tranquility Jazz Festival in November, attracting major musicians such as Hilton Ruiz, James Moody, Bobby Watson, and Vanessa Rubin.

NIGHTLIFE

Most hotels and many restaurants offer live entertainment in high season and on weekends, ranging from pianists and jazz combos to traditional steel and calypso bands. Check the local tourist magazines and newspaper for listings. Friday and Saturday, Sandy Ground is the hot spot; Wednesday and Sunday the action shifts to Shoal Bay East.

The nightlife scene here runs late into the night—the action doesn't really start until after 11 PM. If you do not rent a car, be aware that taxis are not readily available at night. If you plan to take a taxi back to your hotel or villa at the end of the night, be sure to make arrangements in advance with the driver who brings you or with your hotel concierge.

★ ~~Fodor's~~Choice The funky **Dune Preserve** (⊠*Rendezvous Bay* ☎*264/497–6219*) is the driftwood-fabricated home of Bankie Banx, Anguilla's famous reggae star. He performs here weekends and during the full moon. Kevin Bacon also plays here when he's on the island. There's a dance floor and a beach bar, and sometimes you can find a sunset beach barbecue in progress. In high season there's a $15 cover charge.

★ **Elvis' Beach Bar** (⊠*Sandy Ground* ☎*264/772–0637*) is the perfect locale (it's actually a boat) to hear great music and sip the best rum punch on earth. Check to see if there's a Full-Moon Lunasea party.

★ Things are lively at **Johnno's Beach Stop** (⊠*Sandy Ground* ☎*264/497–2728*), with live music and alfresco dancing every night and on Sunday afternoon, when just about everybody drops by. This is *the* classic Caribbean beach bar, attracting a funky eclectic mix, from locals to movie stars.

★ At the **Pumphouse** (⊠*Sandy Ground* ☎*264/497–5154*), in the old rock-salt factory, you can find live music most nights—plus surprisingly good pub grub, celebrities like Bruce Willis and Charlie Sheen, and a minimuseum of artifacts and equipment from 19th-century salt factories. There's calypso-soca on Thursday; it's open from noon until 3 AM daily, except Sunday.

BEACHES

Renowned for their beauty, Anguilla's 30-plus dazzling white-sand beaches are the best reason to visit. You can find long, deserted stretches ideal for walking and beaches lined with bars and restaurants—all accompanied by surf that ranges from wild to glassy-smooth. As anywhere, exercise caution in remote locations, and never swim alone. ⚠**Do not leave personal property in cars.** Swimming is not recommended at Captain's Bay and Katouche Bay, due to strong westerly currents and potentially dangerous undertows. Do not leave personal items in cars parked at beaches—this can be a problem especially at Little Bay.

NORTHEAST COAST

Captain's Bay. On the north coast just before the eastern tip of the island, this quarter-mile stretch of perfect white sand is bounded on the left by a rocky shoreline where Atlantic waves crash. If you make the grueling four-wheel-drive-only trip along the inhospitable dirt road that leads to the northeastern end of the island toward Junk's Hole, you'll be rewarded with peaceful isolation. The surf here slaps the sands with a vengeance, and the undertow is strong—so wading is the safest water sport.

Island Harbour. These mostly calm waters are surrounded by a slender beach. For centuries Anguillians have ventured from these sands in colorful handmade fishing boats. There are several bars and restaurants (Arawak Cafe, Cote Mer, and Smitty's are best for casual lunches), and this is the departure point for the three-minute boat ride to Scilly Cay, where a thatched beach bar serves seafood. Just hail the restaurant's free boat and plan to spend most of the day (the all-inclusive lunch starts at $40 and is worth the price), Wednesday, Friday, and Sunday only.

Barnes Bay. Between Meads Bay and West End Bay, this beach is a superb spot for windsurfing and snorkeling, though in high season it can get a bit crowded with day-trippers from St. Martin. The only public access is on the road to Mango's restaurant and Caribella resort.

Little Bay. Little Bay is on the north coast between Crocus Bay and Shoal Bay, not far from the Valley. Sheer cliffs embroidered with agave and creeping vines rise behind a small gray-sand beach, usually accessible only by water (it's a favored spot for snorkeling and night dives). The easiest way to get here is a five-minute boat ride from Crocus Bay (about $10 round-trip). The hale and hearty can also clamber down the cliffs by rope to explore the caves and surrounding reef; this is the only way to access the beach from the road and is not recommended to the inexperienced climber. Do not leave personal items in cars parked here.

Road Bay. The clear blue waters here are usually dotted with yachts and cargo boats. Several restaurants, including evergreen classic Johnno's, a water-sports center, and lots of windsurfing and waterskiing activity make this area—often called Sandy Ground—a commercial one. The snorkeling isn't very good here, but the sunset vistas are glorious.

Sandy Island. A popular side excursion for Anguilla visitors, Sandy Island is a tiny islet with a lagoon, nestled in coral reefs about 2 mi (3 km) from Road Bay.

SOUTHEAST COAST

Sandy Hill. Not far from Sea Feathers Bay, this base for anglers sits between the Valley and Junks Hole at East End. Here you can buy fish and lobster right off the boats and snorkel in the warm waters. Don't plan to sunbathe—the beach is too narrow. But there's very good snorkeling here, and you'll also find great views of St. Martin and St. Barths.

★ Fodor'sChoice **Shoal Bay.** Anchored by sea grape and coconut trees and covered in the most exquisite powdery-white coral sand, Shoal Bay—not to be confused with Shoal Bay West at the other end of the island—is one of the Caribbean's prettiest beaches. Restaurants like Gwen's Reggae Grill, Kú, and Madeariman Beach Club offer seafood and tropical drinks; shops sell T-shirts and sunscreen; and the water-sports center arranges diving, sailing, and fishing trips. You can even enjoy a beachside massage.

SOUTHWEST COAST

Cove Bay. Lined with coconut palms, this is a quiet spot between Rendezvous Bay and Maundays Bay. You can walk here from Cap Juluca for a change of pace or a beach lunch at Smokey's. There's a fishing boat pier, a dive shop, and a place where you can rent floats, umbrellas, and mats.

Maundays Bay. The dazzling, 1-mi-long (1½-km-long) beach is known for good swimming and snorkeling. You can also rent water-sports gear.

Rendezvous Bay. Here you'll find 1½ mi (2½ km) of pearl-white sand lapped by calm water and with a view of St. Martin. The rockier stretch provides marvelous snorkeling. The expansive crescent houses three resorts, with plenty of open space to go around; stop in for a drink or a meal at one of the hotels. For public access to Rendezous Bay Beach, take the turn off from the main road for Anguilla Great House (between South Hill Plaza and CuisinArt) and follow this road straight to the water.

Shoal Bay West. This glittering bay is a lovely place to spend the day. This mile-long sweep of sand, home to some major restaurants and resorts, is rimmed with mangroves, and there are coral reefs not too far from shore. Punctuate your day with a meal at beachside Trattoria Tramonto. You can reach Shoal Bay West by taking the main road to the West End and turning left at the end of the pavement on a gravel

CLOSE UP

A Day at the Boat Races

If you want a different kind of trip to Anguilla, try for a visit during Carnival, which starts on the first Monday in August and continues for about 10 days. Colorful parades, beauty pageants, music, delicious food, arts-and-crafts shows, fireworks, and nonstop party-ing are just the beginning. The music starts at sunrise jam sessions—as early as 4 AM—and continues well into the night. The high point? The boat races. They are the national passion and the official national sport of Anguilla.

Anguillians from around the world return home to race old-fashioned, made-on-the-island wooden boats that have been in use on the island since the early 1800s. Similar to some of today's fastest sailboats, these are 15 to 28 feet in length and sport only a mainsail and jib on a single 25-foot mast. The sailboats have no deck, so heavy bags of sand, boulders, and sometimes even people are used as ballast. As the boats reach the finish line, the ballast—including some of the sailors—gets thrown into the water in a furious effort to win the race. Spectators line the beaches and follow the boats on foot, by car, and by even more boats. You'll have almost as much fun watching the fans as the races.

road around the pond. Note that similarly named Shoal Bay is a separate beach on a different part of the island.

SPORTS & THE OUTDOORS

Anguilla's expanding sports options are enhanced by its beautiful first golf course, designed by Greg Norman to accentuate the natural terrain and maximize the stunning ocean views over Rendezvous Bay. Players say the par-72, Troon-managed course is reminiscent of Pebble Beach. Personal experience says: bring a lot of golf balls! The Anguilla Tennis Academy, designed by noted architect Myron Goldfinger, operates in the Blowing Point area. The 1,000-seat stadium, equipped with pro shop and seven lighted courts, was created to attract major international matches and to provide a first-class playing option to tour-ists and locals.

BOATING & SAILING

Anguilla is the perfect place to try all kinds of water sports. The major resorts offer complimentary Windsurfers, paddleboats, and water skis to their guests.

If your hotel lacks facilities, you can get in gear at **Sandy Island Enterprises** (⊠*Sandy Ground* ☎264/476–6534), which rents Sunfish and Windsurfers and arranges fishing charters. **Island Yacht Charters** (⊠*Sandy Ground* ☎264/497–3743 or 264/235–6555) rents the 35-foot, teak *Pirate* powerboat and the 30-foot Beneteau *Eros* sailboat and organizes snorkeling, sightseeing, and fishing expeditions.

DIVING

Sunken wrecks; a long barrier reef; terrain encompassing walls, canyons, and hulking boulders; varied marine life, including greenback turtles and nurse sharks; and exceptionally clear water—all of these make for excellent diving. Prickly Pear Cay is a favorite spot. **Stoney Bay Marine Park,** off the northeast end of Anguilla, showcases the late-18th-century *El Buen Consejo,* a 960-ton Spanish galleon that sank here in 1772. Other good dive sites include **Grouper Bowl,** with exceptional hard-coral formations; **Ram's Head,** with caves, chutes, and tunnels; and **Upper Flats,** where you are sure to see stingrays.

Anguillian Divers (⊠*Meads Bay* ☎264/497–4750 ⊕*anguil liandivers.com*) is a full-service dive operator with a PADI five-star training center. At Shoal Bay, contact **Shoal Bay Scuba & Watersports** (☎264/497–4371 ⊕*www.shoalbay scuba.ai*). Single-tank dives start at $50, two-tank dives, $80. Daily snorkel trips at 1 PM are $25 per person.

FISHING

Albacore, wahoo, marlin, barracuda, and kingfish are among the fish angled after off Anguilla's shores. You can strike up a conversation with almost any fisherman you see on the beach, and chances are, you'll be a welcome addition on his next excursion. If you'd rather make more formal arrangements, **Johnno's Beach Stop** (☎264/497–2728) in Sandy Ground has a boat and can help you plan a trip.

GOLF

Temenos Golf Club (☎264/498–7000), designed by super-star Greg Norman, is an 18-hole, 7,200-yard champion-ship course, managed by Troon Golf. The course features sweeping sea vistas and an ecologically responsible water-ing system of ponds and lagoons that snake through the grounds. Greens fees top $400 per person, but include cart, caddie, driving range, and water, but not the service charge of $15.

HORSEBACK RIDING

The scenic Gibbons nature trails, along with any of the island's miles of beaches, are perfect places to ride, even for the novice. Ride English- or western-style or take lessons at **El Rancho Del Blues** (☎264/497–6334). Prices start at $25 to $35 per hour ($50 for two-hour rides).

SEA EXCURSIONS

A number of boating options are available for airport trans-fers, day trips to offshore cays or neighboring islands, night trips to St. Martin, or just whipping through the waves en route to a picnic spot.

Chocolat (⊠*Sandy Ground* ☎264/497–3394) is a 35-foot catamaran available for private charter or scheduled excursions to nearby cays. Captain Rollins is a knowl-edgeable, affable guide. Rates for day sails with lunch are about $80 per person. For an underwater peek without getting wet, catch a ride ($20 per person) on **Junior's Glass Bottom Boat** (⊠*Sandy Ground* ☎264/235–1008 ⊕*www.junior.ai*). Snorkel trips and instruction are available, too. Picnic, swimming, and diving excursions to Prickly Pear Cay, Sandy Island, and Scilly Cay are available through **Sandy Island Enterprises** (☎264/476–6534). **No Fear Sea Tours** (⊠*The Cove* ☎264/235–6354) has three 32-foot speed-boats and a 19-foot ski boat. **Funtime Charters** (⊠*The Cove* ☎264/497–6511) operates five powerboats ranging in size from 32 to 38 feet.

SHOPPING

Anguilla is by no means a shopping destination. In fact, if your suitcase is lost, you will be hard-pressed to secure even the basics on-island. If you're a hard-core shopping enthusi-ast, a day trip to nearby St. Martin will satisfy. Well-heeled visitors sometimes organize boat or plane charters through their hotel concierge for daylong shopping excursions to St. Barths. The island's tourist publication, *What We Do in Anguilla,* has shopping tips and is available free at the airport and in shops. Pyrat rums—golden elixirs blending up to nine aged and flavored spirits—are a local specialty available at the Anguilla Rums distillery and several local shops. For upscale designer sportswear, check out the small boutiques in hotels (some are branches of larger stores in Marigot on St. Martin). Outstanding local artists sell their work in galleries, which often arrange studio tours (you can also check with the Antigua Tourist Office).

SPECIALTY STORES

CLOTHING

Boutique at Malliouhana (⊠*Malliouhana, Meads Bay* ☎*264/497–6111*) specializes in such upscale designer specialties as jewelry by Oro De Sol, luxurious swim fashion by Manuel Canovas and LaPerla, and Robert LaRoche
★ sunglasses. **Capri Boutique** (⊠*CuisinArt Resort & Spa, Rendezvous Bay* ☎*264/498–2000*) carries custom designs by the renowned jewelers Alberto & Lina, as well as Helen Kaminski accessories and more brand-name merchandise. **Caribbean Fancy** (⊠*George Hill* ☎*264/497–3133*) sells Ta-Tee's line of crinkle-cotton resort wear, plus books, spices, perfumes, wines, and gift items. **Caribbean Silkscreen** (⊠*South Hill* ☎*264/497–2272*) creates designs and prints them on golf shirts, hats, sweatshirts, and jackets. **Irie Lite** (⊠*South Hill* ☎*264/497–6526*) sells vividly hued beach and resort wear, Reef flip-flops, and French bikinis that appeal to the younger set who also jive to the java and the wireless Internet connection. **Sunshine Shop** (⊠*South Hill* ☎*264/497–6964*) stocks cotton pareus (saronglike beach cover-ups), silkscreen items, cotton resort wear, and hand-painted Haitian wood items. **Why Knot.** ⊠ *West End Rd., right past golf course* ☎*264/772–7685.* for Fabiana's jewel-color cotton tie-able garments, and the beads and sandals that perfectly accessorize them. If the road sign says "Knot Today" come back later. **Whispers** (⊠*Cap Juluca, Maundays Bay* ☎*264/497–6666*) sells Asian handicrafts and designer resort wear for men and women.

HANDICRAFTS

★ **Anguilla Arts & Crafts Center** (✉ *The Valley* ☎264/497–2200) carries island crafts, including textiles and ceramics. Of particular interest are unique ceramics by Otavia Fleming, lovely spotted glaze items with adorable lizards climbing on them. Look for special exhibits and performances—ranging from puppetry to folk dance—sponsored by the Anguilla

★ National Creative Arts Alliance. **Cheddie's Carving Studios** (✉ *West End Rd., The Cove* ☎264/497–6027) showcases Cheddie Richardson's fanciful wood carvings and coral

★ and stone sculptures. **Devonish Art Gallery** (✉ *West End Rd., George Hill* ☎264/497–2949) purveys the wood, stone, and clay creations of Courtney Devonish, an internationally known potter and sculptor, plus creations by his wife, Carolle, a bead artist. Also available are works by other Caribbean artists and regional antique maps. **Hibernia Restaurant & Gallery** (✉ *Island Harbour* ☎264/497–4290) has striking pieces culled from the owners' travels, from contemporary Eastern European artworks to traditional Indo-Chinese crafts. In the historic Rose Cottage, **Loblolly Gallery** (✉ *Coronation St., Lower Valley* ☎264/497–6006) showcases the work of three expats (Marge Morani, Paula Warden, Georgia Young) working in various media and also mounts exhibits from Anguilla's artistic grande dame, Iris Lewis. **Savannah Gallery** (✉ *Coronation St., Lower Valley* ☎264/497–2263) specializes in works by local Anguillian artists as well as other Caribbean and Central American art, including watercolors, oil paintings from the renowned Haitian St. Soleil group, Guatemalan textiles, Mexican pottery, and brightly painted metal work. The peripatetic proprietors of **World Arts Gallery** (✉ *Cove Rd., West End* ☎264/497–5950 or 264/497–2767), Nik and Christy Douglas, display a veritable United Nations of antiquities: exquisite Indonesian ikat hangings to Thai teak furnishings, Aboriginal didgeridoos to Dogon tribal masks, Yuan Dynasty jade pottery to Uzbeki rugs. There is also handcrafted jewelry and handbags.

St. Maarten, St. Barths & Anguilla Essentials

PLANNING TOOLS, EXPERT INSIGHT, GREAT CONTACTS

There are planners and there are those who, excuse the pun, fly by the seat of their pants. We happily place ourselves among the planners. Our writers and editors try to anticipate all the issues you may face before and during any journey, and then they do their research. This section is the product of their efforts. Use it to get excited about your trip to St. Maarten, St. Barths & Anguilla, to inform your travel planning, or to guide you on the road should the seat of your pants start to feel threadbare.

GETTING STARTED

We're proud of our Web site: Fodors.com is a great place to begin any journey. Scan Travel Wire for suggested itineraries, travel deals, restaurant and hotel openings, and other up-to-the-minute info. Check out Booking to research prices and book plane tickets, hotel rooms, rental cars, and vacation packages. Head to Talk for on-the-ground pointers from travelers who frequent our message boards. You can also link to loads of other travel-related resources.

▌ RESOURCES

ONLINE TRAVEL TOOLS

All About St. Maarten, Anguilla & St. Barths The Web site of the **Anguilla Hotel & Tourism Association** (⊕www.ahta.ai) focuses mainly on lodging choices on the island. In addition to advertising, there are useful links to the Web sites of most of the island's hotels and resorts. The **Anguilla Guide** (⊕http://net.ai) is a useful and comprehensive Web site with information on the island.

St. Barths Online (⊕www.st-barths. com) has information on the island, links to island establishment Web sites, and some pretty good maps, including maps that show where the island's grocery stores and beaches are located.

The web site **SXM-Info** (⊕www. sxm-info.com) has a lot of information, as well as a lot of advertising, for both St. Maarten and St. Martin.

Currency Conversion Google (⊕www.google.com) does currency conversion. Just type in the amount you want to convert and an explanation of how you want it converted (e.g., "14 Swiss francs in dollars"), and then voilà. **Oanda.com** (⊕www.oanda.com) also allows you to print out a handy table with the current day's conversion rates. **XE.com** (⊕www.xe.com) is a good currency conversion Web site.

Weather Accuweather.com (⊕www.accuweather.com) is an independent weather-forecasting service with good coverage of hurricanes. **Weather.com** (⊕www. weather.com) is the Web site for the Weather Channel.

VISITOR INFORMATION

In St. Barths, a daily news sheet called *News* lists local happenings like special dinners or music and is available at markets and newsstands. Also, the free weekly *Journal de Saint-Barth*—mostly in French—is useful for current events. The small *Ti Gourmet Saint-Barth* is a free pocket-size guidebook that's invaluable for addresses and telephone numbers of restaurants and services.

Look for the annual *Saint-Barth Tables* for full restaurant menus. Its counterpart, *Saint-Barth Leisures* contains current information about sports, spas, nightlife, and the arts.

Anguilla Anguilla Tourist Office (✉Coronation Ave., The Valley ⊕www.anguilla-vacation.com ☎264/497–2759, 800/553–4939 from U.S.).

St. Barths French Government Tourist Office (☎900/990–0040 charges a fee ⊕www.franceguide. com ☎213/272–2661 in Beverly Hills, CA ☎312/337–6301 in Chicago, IL). **St-Barths Office du Tourisme** (✉Quai Général-de-Gaulle ☎0590/27–87–27 ✑odtsb@ wanadoo.fr).

St. Maarten/St. Martin St. Maarten Tourist Information Bureau (✉Cyrus Wathey Sq., Philipsburg ☎599/542-2337). **St. Maarten Tourist Office** (☎800/786–2278, 212/953–2084 in New York ⊕www.st-maarten. com). **St. Martin Office of Tourism** (☎877/956–1234, 212/475–8970 in New York 🖷212/260-8481 ✉Rte. de Sandy Ground, near Marina Port-Royale, Marigot ☎590/87–57–21 or 590/87–57–21 ⊕www.st-martin.org).

▌ THINGS TO CONSIDER

PASSPORTS & VISAS

A passport and a returning or continuing ticket is required for entry to Anguilla, St. Barths, and St. Maarten.

U.S. Passport Information U.S. Department of State (☎877/487–2778 ⊕http://travel.state.gov/passport).

TRIP INSURANCE

Comprehensive travel policies typically cover trip-cancellation and interruption, letting you cancel or cut your trip short because of a personal emergency, illness, or, in some cases, acts of terrorism in your destination. Such policies also cover evacuation and medical care. Some also cover you for trip delays because of bad weather or mechanical problems as well as for lost or delayed baggage. Another type of coverage to look for is financial default—that is, when your trip is disrupted because a tour operator, airline, or cruise line goes out of business. Generally you must buy this when you book your trip or shortly thereafter, and it's only available to you if your operator isn't on a list of excluded companies.

At the very least, consider buying medical-only coverage. Neither Medicare nor some private insurers cover medical expenses anywhere outside of the United States (including time aboard a cruise ship, even if it leaves from a U.S. port). Medical-only policies typically reimburse you for medical care (excluding that related to pre-existing conditions) and hospitalization abroad, and provide for evacuation. You still have to pay the bills and await reimbursement from the insurer, though.

Expect comprehensive travel insurance policies to cost about 4% to 7% or 8% of the total price of your trip (it's more like 8%–12% if you're over age 70). A medical-only policy may or may not be cheaper than a comprehensive policy. Always read the fine print of your policy to make sure that you are covered for the risks that are of most concern to you. Compare several policies to make sure you're getting the best price and range of coverage available.

■TIP➔ OK. You know you can save a bundle on trips to warm-weather destinations by traveling in rainy season. But there's also a chance that a severe storm will disrupt your plans. The solution? Look for hotels and resorts that offer storm/hurricane guarantees. Although they rarely allow refunds, most guarantees do let you rebook later if a storm strikes.

Insurance Comparison Sites Insure My Trip.com (☎800/487-4722 ⊕www.insuremytrip.com). **Square Mouth.com** (☎800/240-0369 or 727/490-5803 ⊕www.squaremouth.com).

Medical Assistance Companies AirMed International Medical Group (⊕www.airmed.com). **International SOS** (⊕www.internationalsos.com). **MedjetAssist** (⊕www.medjetassist.com).

Medical-Only Insurers International Medical Group (☎800/628-4664 ⊕www.imglobal.com).. **Wallach & Company** (☎800/237-6615 or 540/687-3166 ⊕www.wallach.com).

Comprehensive Travel Insurers Access America (☎866/729-6021 ⊕www.accessamerica.com). **AIG Travel Guard** (☎800/826-4919 ⊕www.travelguard.com). **CSA Travel Protection** (☎800/873-9855 ⊕www.csatravelprotection.com). **HTH Worldwide** (☎610/254-8700 ⊕www.hthworldwide.com). **Travelex Insurance** (☎888/228-9792 ⊕www.travelex-insurance.com). **Travel Insured International** (☎800/243-3174 ⊕www.travelinsured.com).

BOOKING YOUR TRIP

Unless your cousin is a travel agent, you're probably among the millions of people who make most of their travel arrangements online.

▍ONLINE

You really have to shop around. A travel wholesaler such as Hotels. com or HotelClub.net can be a source of good rates, as can discounters such as Hotwire or Priceline, particularly if you can bid for your hotel room or airfare. Indeed, such sites sometimes have deals that are unavailable elsewhere. They do, however, tend to work only with hotel chains (which makes them just plain useless for getting hotel reservations outside of major cities) or big airlines (so that often leaves out upstarts like jetBlue and some foreign carriers like Air India).

Also, with discounters and wholesalers you must generally prepay, and everything is nonrefundable. And before you fork over the dough, be sure to check the terms and conditions, so you know what a given company will do for you if there's a problem and what you'll have to deal with on your own.

▍TIP→ **To be absolutely sure everything was processed correctly, confirm reservations made through online travel agents, discounters, and wholesalers directly with your hotel before leaving home.**

Booking engines like Expedia, Travelocity, and Orbitz are actually travel agents, albeit high-volume, online ones. And airline travel packagers like American Airlines Vacations and Virgin Vacations—well, they're travel agents, too. But they may still not work with all the world's hotels.

An aggregator site will search many sites and pull the best prices for airfares, hotels, and rental cars from them. Most aggregators compare the major travel-booking sites such as Expedia, Travelocity, and Orbitz; some also look at airline Web sites, though rarely the sites of smaller budget airlines. Some aggregators also compare other travel products, including complex packages—a good thing, as you can sometimes get the best overall deal by booking an air-and-hotel package.

▍WITH A TRAVEL AGENT

If you use an agent—brick-and-mortar or virtual—you'll probably pay a fee for the service. And know that the service you get from some online agents isn't comprehensive. For example Expedia and Travelocity don't search for prices on all budget airlines or small foreign carriers. That said, some agents (online or not) *do* have access to fares that are difficult to find otherwise, and the savings can more than make up for any surcharge.

■TIP→Remember that Expedia, Travelocity, and Orbitz are travel agents, not just booking engines. To resolve any problems with a reservation made through these companies, contact them first.

Agent Resources American Society of Travel Agents (☎703/739–2782 ⊕www.travelsense.org).

■ ACCOMMODATIONS

St. Maarten/St. Martin has the widest array of accommodations of any of the three islands, with a range of large resort hotels, small resorts, time-shares, condos, private villas, and small B&Bs scattered across the island. Most of the larger resorts are concentrated in Dutch St. Maarten. Visitors find a wide range of choices in many different price ranges.

Anguilla has several large luxury resorts, a few smaller resorts and guesthouses, and a rather large mix of private condos and villas. Lodging on Anguilla is generally fairly expensive, but there are a few more modestly priced choices.

The vast majority of accommodations on St. Barths are in private villas in a wide variety of levels of luxury and price; villas are often priced in U.S. dollars. The island's small luxury hotels are exceedingly expensive, made more so for Americans because prices are in euros. A few modest and moderately priced hotels do exist on the island, but there's nothing on St. Barths that could be described as cheap.

Most hotels and other lodgings require you to give your credit-card details before they will confirm your reservation. If you don't feel comfortable e-mailing this information, ask if you can fax it (some places even prefer faxes). However you book, get confirmation in writing and have a copy of it handy when you check in.

Be sure you understand the hotel's cancellation policy. Some places allow you to cancel without any kind of penalty—even if you prepaid to secure a discounted rate—if you cancel at least 24 hours in advance. Others require you to cancel a week in advance or penalize you the cost of one night. Small inns and B&Bs are most likely to require you to cancel far in advance. Most hotels allow children under a certain age to stay in their parents' room at no extra charge, but others charge for them as extra adults; find out the cutoff age for discounts.

■TIP→Assume that hotels operate on the European Plan (EP, no meals) unless we specify that they use the Breakfast Plan (BP, with full breakfast), Continental Plan (CP, continental breakfast), Full American Plan (FAP, all meals), Modified American Plan (MAP, breakfast and dinner) or are all-inclusive (AI, all meals and most activities).

APARTMENT & HOUSE RENTALS

Private villas are common in all three islands, but condos (particularly time-shares) are common only on St. Maarten. Wimco is the primary villa broker on St. Barths and represents private villas on both Anguilla and St. Maarten/St.

Martin. St. Barth Properties, Incl. also represents many villas on St. Barths.

🏠 At Home Abroad (☎212/421–9165 ⊕www.athomeabroadinc.com). **Barclay International Group** (☎516/364–0064 or 800/845–6636 ⊕www.barclayweb.com). **Forgetaway** (⊕www.forgetaway.weather.com). **Home Away** (☎512/493–0382 ⊕www.homeaway.com). **St. Barth Properties, Inc.** (☎508/528–7727 or 800/421–3396 🖷508/528–7789 ⊕www.stbarth.com). **Villanet** (☎206/417–3444 or 800/964–1891 ⊕www.rentavilla.com). **Villas & Apartments Abroad** (☎212/213–6435 or 800/433–3020 ⊕www.vaanyc.com). **Villas International** (☎415/499–9490 or 800/221–2260 ⊕www.villasintl.com). **Villas of Distinction** (☎707/778–1800 or 800/289–0900 ⊕www.villasofdistinction.com). **Wimco** (☎800/449–1553 ⊕www.wimco.com).

AIRLINE TICKETS

All U.S. domestic airline tickets are now electronic; most international airline tickets are also electronic, though some smaller Caribbean airlines still use paper tickets. With an e-ticket the only thing you receive is an e-mailed receipt citing your itinerary and reservation and ticket numbers. The greatest advantage of an e-ticket is that if you lose your receipt, you can simply print out another copy or ask the airline to do it for you at check-in.

RENTAL CARS

When you reserve a car, ask about cancellation penalties, taxes, drop-off charges (if you're planning to pick up the car in one city and leave it in another), and surcharges (for being under or over a certain age, for additional drivers, or for driving across state or country borders or beyond a specific distance from your point of rental). All these things can add substantially to your costs. Request car seats and extras such as GPS when you book.

Rates are sometimes—but not always—better if you book in advance or reserve through a rental agency's Web site. There are other reasons to book ahead, though: for popular destinations, during busy times of the year, or to ensure that you get certain types of cars (vans, SUVs, exotic sports cars).

■TIP→ **Make sure that a confirmed reservation guarantees you a car. Agencies sometimes overbook, particularly for busy weekends and holiday periods.**

Major Agencies Alamo (☎800/522–9696 ⊕www.alamo.com). **Avis** (☎800/331–1084 ⊕www.avis.com).**Budget** (☎800/472–3325 ⊕www.budget.com). **Hertz** (☎800/654–3001 ⊕www.hertz.com). **National Car Rental** (☎800/227–7368 ⊕www.nationalcar.com).

CAR-RENTAL INSURANCE

Everyone who rents a car wonders whether the insurance that the rental companies offer is worth the expense. No one—including us—has a simple answer. It all depends on how much regular insurance you have, how comfortable you are with risk, and whether or not money is an issue.

If you own a car, your personal auto insurance may cover a rental to some degree, though not all policies protect you abroad; always read your policy's fine print. If you don't have auto insurance, then seriously consider buying the collision- or loss-damage waiver (CDW or LDW) from the car-rental company, which eliminates your liability for damage to the car.

Some credit cards offer CDW coverage, but it's usually supplemental to your own insurance and rarely covers SUVs, minivans, luxury models, and the like. If your coverage is secondary, you may still be liable for loss-of-use costs from the car-rental company. But no credit-card insurance is valid unless you use that card for *all* transactions, from reserving to paying the final bill. All companies exclude car rental in some countries, so be sure to find out about the destination to which you are traveling.

■TIP➔ Diners Club offers primary CDW coverage on all rentals reserved and paid for with the card. This means that Diners Club's company—not your own car insurance—pays in case of an accident. It *doesn't* mean your car-insurance company won't raise your rates once it discovers you had an accident.

Some rental agencies require you to purchase CDW coverage; many will even include it in quoted rates. All will strongly encourage you to buy CDW—possibly implying that it's

required—so be sure to ask about such things before renting. In most cases it's cheaper to add a supplemental CDW plan to your comprehensive travel-insurance policy (➔ *Trip Insurance under Things to Consider in Getting Started, above*) than to purchase it from a rental company. That said, you don't want to pay for a supplement if you're required to buy insurance from the rental company.

■TIP➔ You can decline the insurance from the rental company and purchase it through a third-party provider such as Travel Guard (www.travelguard.com)—$9 per day for $35,000 of coverage. That's sometimes just under half the price of the CDW offered by some car-rental companies.

CAR RENTALS IN ANGUILLA

You may or may not want to rent a car in Anguilla depending on where you're staying. It's possible to base yourself in Sandy Grand, Rendezvous Bay, Meads Bay, or Upper Shoal Bay and do without a car, but restaurants and resorts are quite spread out, so for the sake of convenience, you may wish to rent a car for a few days or for your entire stay. Taxis are fairly expensive on Anguilla, another reason to rent a car. You must purchase a temporary Anguilla driver's license ($20, good for three months) if you rent a car on the island; you will purchase it at the car-rental agency at the time you pick up your car. Rental rates are about $45 to $55 per day, plus insurance.

🚗 **Apex/Avis** (✉Airport Rd. ☎264/497–2642). **Triple K Car**

Rental/Hertz (✉Airport Rd. ☎264/497–5934).

CAR RENTALS IN ST. BARTHS

Most travelers to St. Barths rent a car. The new St. Barth Shuttle service can be convenient and much less expensive than a taxi if you're just one or two people, but it still doesn't completely negate the need for a car. You'll find major rental agencies at the airport. You must have a valid driver's license and be 25 or older to rent, and in high season there may be a three-day minimum. During peak periods, such as Christmas week and February, be sure to arrange for your car rental ahead of time. When you make your hotel reservations, ask if the hotel has its own cars available to rent; some hotels provide 24-hour emergency road service—something most rental companies don't offer. If there are only two of you, think about renting a Smart car. Tiny but powerful on the hills, it's a blast to buzz around in, and also a lot easier to park than larger cars.

🚗 Avis (☎0590/27–71–43). Budget (☎0590/27–66–30). Europcar (☎0590/27–74–34 ⊕www.st-barths.com/europcar/index.html). Gumbs (☎0590/27–75–32). Hertz (☎0590/27–71–14). Gust: Smart of St-Barth (☎0690/41–66–72). St. Barth Shuttle (✉At the Mangliers, St. Jean ☎0590/29–44–19). Turbe (☎0590/27–71–42 ⊕www.saint-barths.com/turbecarrental).

CAR RENTALS IN ST. MAARTEN/ST. MARTIN

Most people rent a car so they can more easily reach both sides of the island and interesting beaches. Depending on the time of year, a subcompact car will cost between $25 and $50 a day with unlimited mileage. You can rent a car on the French side, but this rarely makes sense for Americans because of the unfavorable exchange rates.

🚗 Avis (☎599/545–2847 or 590/87–50–60). Budget (☎599/545–4030 or 866/978–4447). Dollar (☎599/545–3281). Empress Car Rental (☎866/978–0849). Golfe Car Rental (☎599/545–4541 or 590/51–94–81). Hertz (☎599/545–4541 or 590/87–83–71). Sunshine Car Rental (☎599/545–2685). Thrifty (☎599/545–2393). Unity Car Rental (☎599/557–6760).

▌ VACATION PACKAGES

Packages *are not* guided excursions. Packages combine airfare, accommodations, and perhaps a rental car or other extras (theater tickets, guided excursions, boat trips, reserved entry to popular museums, transit passes), but they let you do your own thing. During busy periods packages may be your only option, as flights and rooms may be sold out otherwise.

Packages will definitely save you time. They can also save you money, particularly in peak seasons, but—and this is a really big "but"—you should price each part of the package separately to be sure. And be aware that prices advertised on Web sites and in newspapers rarely include service charges or taxes, which can up your costs by hundreds of dollars.

■TIP➔ **Some packages and cruises are sold only through travel agents. Don't always assume that you can get the best deal by booking everything yourself.**

Each year consumers are stranded or lose their money when packagers—even large ones with excellent reputations—go out of business. How can you protect yourself?

First, always pay with a credit card; if you have a problem, your credit-card company may help you resolve it. Second, buy trip insurance that covers default. Third, choose a company that belongs to the United States Tour Operators Association, whose members must set aside funds to cover defaults. Finally, choose a company that also participates in the Tour Operator Program of the American Society of Travel Agents (ASTA), which will act as mediator in any disputes.

Packages for travel to St. Maarten/St. Martin are very common, for Anguilla less so though still available. You're unlikely to find a package for travel to St. Barths.

Organizations American Society of Travel Agents (ASTA ☎703/739–2782 or 800/965–2782 ⊕www.astanet.com). **United States Tour Operators Association** (USTOA ☎212/599–6599 ⊕www.ustoa.com). ■TIP➔**Local tourism boards can provide information about lesser-known and small-niche operators that sell packages to only a few destinations.**

TRANSPORTATION

St. Maarten/St. Martin, Anguilla, and St. Barths are all in relatively close proximity to each other and are connected by either ferries or short airplane rides. St. Maarten is the immediate region's major air hub.

▌ BY AIR

TO ANGUILLA

There are no nonstop flights to Anguilla. American Eagle flies several times a day from San Juan, with connecting flights from other destinations through Continental and Delta. Caribbean Star/TransAnguilla offers daily flights from Antigua, St. Thomas, and St. Kitts and provides air-taxi service on request from neighboring islands. Windward Islands Airways (Winair) wings in daily from St. Thomas and several times a day from St. Maarten. Anguilla Air Services is a reliable charter operation that flies to any Caribbean destination and runs day trips between Anguilla and St. Barths at the very reasonable round-trip rate of $175 per person (4-person minimum). LIAT comes in from Antigua, Nevis, St. Kitts, St. Maarten, St. Thomas, and Tortola. Note that LIAT requires all passengers to reconfirm 72 hours in advance, to avoid cancellation of their reservations.

🛪 **American Eagle** (☎264/497–3500). **Anguilla Air Services** (☎264/498–5922). **Caribbean Star/TransAnguilla** (☎264/497–8690). **LIAT** (☎264/497–5002). **Windward Islands Airways** (☎264/497–2748).

AIRPORTS

Wallblake Airport is the hub on Anguilla; it receives only smaller propeller-drive planes.

🛪 **Wallblake Airport** (✉Anguilla ☎264/497–2719).

TO ST. BARTHS

There are no direct flights to St. Barths. Most North Americans fly first into St. Maarten's Queen Juliana International Airport, from which the island is only 10 minutes by air. Flights leave at least once an hour between 7:30 AM and 5:30 PM on Winair. Air Caraïbes, based in Guadeloupe, flies among the French West Indies and to the Dominican Republic. Anguilla Air Services is an excellent charter company that flies to any Caribbean destination and runs day trips between Anguilla and St. Barths, at the very reasonable rate of $175 per person (4-person mininum). St. Barth Commuter is a small, private charter company that can also arrange service. Tradewind Aviation offers charters and regularly scheduled daily nonstop Premium service from San Juan, Puerto Rico. Flights are timed conveniently to meet early flights from the United States.

You must confirm your return interisland flight, even during off-peak seasons, or you may very well lose your reservation. Do not be upset if your luggage has not made the trip with you. It frequently will arrive on a later flight, and your hotel will send a porter to receive it; villa-rental companies may also help you retrieve luggage from the airport, but you may have to beg. It's a good idea to pack a change of clothes, required medicines, and a bathing suit in your carry-on.

🛪 **Air Caraïbes** (☎0590/27-71-90, 877/772-1005 in U.S. ⊕www. aircaraibes.com). **Anguilla Air Services** (☎264/498-5922 ⊕www. anguillaairservices.com). **St. Barth Commuter** (☎0590/27-54-54 ⊕www.stbarthcommuter.com). **Tradewind Aviation** (☎800/376-7922 ⊕www.tradewindaviation. com). **Winair** (☎0590/27-61-01 or 800/634-4907 ⊕www.fly-winair. com).

AIRPORTS
St. Barths has only a small airstrip and receives regular service by three small regional carriers. Pilots must be specially trained to land here, but the descent to the airstrip is thrilling.

🛪 **Aéroport de St-Jean** (✉St-Jean, St. Barthélemy ☎0590/27-75-81).

TO ST. MAARTEN/ST. MARTIN
St. Maarten is the immediate region's major airline hub. You'll find good and frequent service to the island from the U.S. American, Delta, Continental, JetBlue, United, and US Airways offer daily nonstop and connecting service; most of these flights are nonstops from the U.S. mainland. Air Canada flies from Toronto, and Air Transat flies from Toronto and Montreal. Air Caraïbes, BWIA, DAE, LIAT, and Winair (Windward Islands Airways) offer service from other islands in the Caribbean. Be aware that LIAT has a reputation for being unreliable.

🛪 **Air Caraïbes** (☎590/52-05-10 ⊕www.aircaraibes.com). **Air France** (☎590/51-02-02 or 599/546 7602 ⊕www.airfrance.com). **Air Transat** (☎877/872-6728 in U.S. ⊕www. airtransit.com). **American Airlines** (☎599/546-2050, 800/433-7300 in U.S. ⊕www.aa.com). **Caribbean Airlines** (☎599/546-7610 ⊕www. caribbean-airlines.com). **Continental Airlines** (☎599/546-7671, 800/231-0856 in U.S. ⊕www. continental.com). **Delta Airlines** (☎599/599/546-7615, 800/241-4141 in U.S. ⊕www.delta. com). **Dutch Antilles Express** (☎599/546-7842 ⊕www.flydae. com). **Insel Air** (☎599/546-7690 ⊕www.fly-inselair.com). **jetBlue** (☎599/545-5757, 800/538-2583 in U.S. ⊕www.jetblue.com). **KLM** (☎599/546-7695 ⊕www.klm.com). **LIAT** (☎599/546-7677 ⊕www. liatairline.com). **Spirit Airlines** (☎599/546-7621, 800/772-7117 in U.S. ⊕www.spirit.com). **United** (☎599/546-7681, 800/538-2929 in U.S. ⊕www.united.com). **US Airways** (☎599/546-7683, 800/622-1015 in U.S. ⊕www.usairways.com). **Winair** (☎599/546-7690 ⊕www.fly-winair. com).

AIRPORTS
In St. Maarten/St. Martin, Aéroport de L'Espérance, on the French side, is small and handles only island-hoppers. Jumbo jets fly into Princess Juliana International Airport,

on the Dutch side, and this airport is reasonably modern and efficient with a brand-new terminal.

⚑ Aéroport de L'Espérance (✉Grand Case, St. Martin ☎590/87–53–03). **Princess Juliana International Airport** (✉Simpson Bay, St. Maarten ☎599/546–7542 ⊕www.pjiae.com).

▌ BY BIKE & MOPED

ST. BARTHS

Several companies rent motorbikes, scooters, mopeds, and mountain bikes. Motorbikes go for about $30 per day and require a $100 deposit. Helmets are required. Scooter and motorbike rental places are mostly along rue de France in Gustavia and around the airport in St-Jean. They tend to shift locations slightly.

⚑ Barthloc Rental (✉Rue de France, Gustavia ☎0590/27–52–81). **Chez Béranger** (✉Rue de France, Gustavia ☎0590/27–89–00). **Ets Denis Dufau** (✉St-Jean ☎0590/27–70–59).

ST. MAARTEN/ST. MARTIN

Though traffic can be heavy, speeds are generally slow, so a moped can be a good way to get around. Parking is easy, filling the tank is affordable, and you've got that sea breeze to keep you cool. Scooters rent for as low as €25 per day and motorbikes for €37 a day at Eugene Moto, on the French side. At Go Scoot the bikes are in good repair and the counter clerks are helpful. If you're in the mood for a more substantial bike, contact the Harley-Davidson dealer, on the Dutch side, where you can rent a big hog for $150 a day or $900 per week.

⚑ Eugene Moto (✉Sandy Ground Rd., Sandy Ground ☎590/87–13–97). **Go Scoot** (✉20 Airport Rd., Simpson Bay ☎599/545–4553 ⊕www.aquaworld-goscoot.com). **Harley-Davidson** (✉71 Union Rd., Cole Bay ☎599/544–2704 ⊕www.h-dstmartin.com).

▌ BY BOAT & FERRY

Ferries link St. Barths and St. Maarten/St. Martin as well as Anguilla and St. Maarten/St-Martin, but not Anguilla and St. Barths.

ANGUILLA

Ferries run frequently between Anguilla and St-Martin. Boats leave from Blowing Point on Anguilla approximately every half hour from 7:30 AM to 6:15 PM and from Marigot on St-Martin every half hour from 8 AM to 7 PM. Check for evening ferries, whose schedules are more erratic. You pay a $3 departure tax before boarding, in addition to the $12 one-way fare ($15 in the evening). Don't buy a round-trip ticket, as it restricts you to the boat for which it is purchased. On very windy days the 20-minute trip can be bouncy, so bring medication if you suffer from motion sickness. An information booth outside the customs shed in Blowing Point is usually open daily from 8:30 AM to 5 PM, but sometimes the attendant wanders off. For schedule information, and info on special boat charters, contact Link Ferries. The larger resort hotels usually offer private transfers by speedboat, which meets arrivals at the local boat dock at a cost of about $65 per person. If you desire this service, mention it to your reservations representative who will make the arrangements.

🚢 **Link Ferries** (☎264/497–2231 ⊕www.link.ai).

ST. BARTHS

Voyager offers ferry service for day trips between St. Barths, St-Martin (Marigot), and Saba. Round-trips are offered for about $60 per person. There's an additional €12 surcharge for fuel and port fees. All service is from Quai de la République. Private boat charters are also available.

🚢 **Voyager** (☎0590/87–10–68 ⊕www.voyager-st-barths.com).

ST. MAARTEN/ST. MARTIN

The *Voyager II* offers daily service from Marigot to St. Barths Tuesday through Saturday. The cost for the 75-minute ride is €88 round-trip. The price includes an open bar, tasty snacks, and port fees; children under 12 travel for about half price. It takes about 30 to 40 minutes to get to St. Barths on the new *Rapid Explorer*, a high-speed catamaran, which departs from the Chesterfield Marina. It's €89 round-trip. Link Ferries make the 20-minute trip between the Marigot waterfront and Blowing Point, on Anguilla, every half hour from 8 AM until 7 PM daily. The fare is $26 round-trip.

The *Dawn II* sails Tuesday, Thursday and Saturday to Saba. The fare is $80 round-trip. High-speed passenger ferries *Edge I* and *Edge II* motor from Simpson Bay's Pelican Marina to Saba on Wednesday, Friday, and Sunday in just an hour ($100 round-trip) and to St. Barths on Wednesday, Thursday, and Saturday in 45 minutes ($90 round-trip).

🚢 **Dawn II** (☎599/416–3671 ⊕www.sabactransport.com). Edge I and Edge II (☎599/544–2640 ⊕www.stmaarten-activities.com). **Link Ferries** (☎264/497–2231 or 264/497–3290 ⊕www.link.ai). Rapid Explorer (☎590/27–60–33 ⊕www.sbhonline.com). Voyager II (☎590/87–10–68 ⊕www.voyager-st-barths.com).

▌ BY CAR

ANGUILLA

Although most of the rental cars on-island have the driver's side on the left as in North America, Anguillian roads are like those in the United Kingdom—driving is on the left side of the road. It's easy to get the hang of, but the roads can be rough, so be cautious, and observe the 30 mph (48 kph) speed limit. Roundabouts are probably the biggest driving obstacle for most. As you approach, give way to the vehicle on your right; once you're in the rotary you have the right of way.

A temporary Anguilla driver's license is required—you can get into real trouble if you're caught driving without one. You get it for $20 (good for three months) at any of the car-rental agencies at the time you pick up your car; you'll also need your valid driver's license from home.

ST. BARTHS

Roads are sometimes unmarked, so be sure to get a map. Instead of road signs, look for signs pointing to a destination. These will be nailed to posts at all crossroads. Roads are narrow and sometimes very steep, so check the brakes and gears of your rental car before you drive away, and make a careful inventory of the existing dents and scrapes on the vehicle. Maximum speed on the island is 30 mph (50 kph). Driving is on the right, as in the United States and Europe. St. Barths drivers often seem to be in an unending grand prix and thus tend to keep their cars maxed out, especially and inexplicably when in reverse. Parking is an additional challenge.

There are two gas stations on the island, one near the airport and one in Lorient. They aren't open after 5 PM or on Sunday, but you can use the one near the airport at any time with some credit cards, including Visa, JCB, or Carte Blanche. Considering the short distances, a full tank of gas should last you most of a week.

ST. MAARTEN/ST. MARTIN

Most roads are paved and in generally good condition. However, they can be crowded, especially when the cruise ships are in port. Be alert for potholes and speed bumps, as well as the island tradition of stopping in the middle of the road to chat with a friend or yield to someone entering traffic. Few roads are identified by name or number, but most have signs indicating the destination. International symbols are used.

BY TAXI

ANGUILLA

Taxis are fairly expensive, so if you plan to explore the island's many beaches and restaurants, it may be more cost-effective to rent a car. Taxi rates are regulated by the government, and there are fixed fares from point to point, which are listed in brochures the drivers should have handy and are also published in the local guide, *What We Do in Anguilla*. It's $24 from the airport or $22 from Blowing Point Ferry to West End hotels. Posted rates are for one or two people; each additional passenger adds $4 to the total and there is sometimes a charge for luggage. You can also hire a taxi by the hourly rate of $25. Surcharges of $2–$5 apply to trips after 6 PM. You'll always find taxis at the Blowing Point Ferry landing and at the airport. You will need to call them to pick you up from hotels and restaurants, and arrange ahead with the driver who took you if you will require a taxi late at night from one of the nightclubs or bars.

📋 **Airport Taxi Stand** (☎264/235–3828). **Blowing Point Ferry Taxi Stand** (☎264/497–6089).

ST. BARTHS

Taxis are expensive and not particularly easy to arrange, especially in the evening. There's a taxi station at the airport and another in Gustavia; from elsewhere you must contact a dispatcher in Gustavia or St-Jean. Technically, there's a flat rate for rides up to five minutes long. Each additional three minutes is an additional amount. In reality, however, cabbies usually name a fixed rate—and will not budge. Fares are 50% higher from 8 PM to 6 AM and on Sunday and holidays.

🚖 **Gustavia taxi dispatcher** (☎0590/27-66-31). **St-Jean taxi dispatcher** (☎0590/27-75-81).

ST. MAARTEN/ST. MARTIN
The government regulates taxi rates. You can hail cabs on the street or call the taxi dispatch to have one sent for you. On the French side of the island, the minimum rate for a taxi is $4, $2 for each additional passenger. There's a taxi service at the Marigot port near the tourist information bureau. Fixed fares apply from Juliana International Airport and the Marigot ferry to the various hotels around the island. Fares are 25% higher between 10 PM and midnight, 50% higher between midnight and 6 AM.

🚖 **Dutch taxi dispatch** (☎147). **French taxi dispatch** (☎590/87-56-54).

ON THE GROUND

▌COMMUNICATIONS

INTERNET

In Anguilla, Internet access is common at hotels, but independent Internet cafés are not. In many hotels, however, only Wi-Fi is offered, so you must bring your own laptop if you want to go online.

In St. Barths, most hotels provide Internet and e-mail access for guests at the front desk, if not right in the room, but if yours does not, make a visit to the Internet Service at Centre Alizes, which has fax service and 10 computers online. It's open weekdays from 8:30 to 12:30 and 2:30 to 7, as well as on Saturday morning. France Télécom can provide you with temporary Internet access that may let you connect your laptop. If you have a Wi-Fi-equipped laptop, there are hot spots at the port area, the Guanahani, and in the parking lot of the Oasis Shopping Center in Lorient; service is provided by Antilles Référencement, an excellent computer shop that can set you up with a temporary Internet account or provide other computer support.

In St. Maarten/St. Martin, any hotels offer Internet service—some complimentary and some for a fee. There are cybercafés scattered throughout the island and Wi-Fi hot spots on the boardwalk behind Front Street in Philipsburg.

Internet Cafés in St. Barths

Antilles Référencement (✉Oasis Shopping Centre, Lorient ☎0590/58–97–97). **Centre Alizes** (✉Rue de la République, Gustavia ☎0590/29–89–89). **France Télécom** (✉Espace Neptune, St-Jean ☎0590/27–67–00).

Internet Cafés in St. Maarten

Coconets (✉29 Hope Estate, Grand Case). **Cyber Link** (✉53 Front St., Philipsburg). **Internet Corner** (✉105 rue de Hollande, Marigot).

PHONES

The good news is that you can now make a direct-dial telephone call from virtually any point on earth. The bad news? You can't always do so cheaply. Calling from a hotel is almost always the most expensive option; hotels usually add huge surcharges to all calls, particularly international ones. In some countries you can phone from call centers or even the post office. Calling cards usually keep costs to a minimum, but only if you purchase them locally. And then there are mobile phones (⇨below), which are sometimes more prevalent—particularly in the developing world—than land lines; as expensive as mobile phone calls can be, they are still usually a much cheaper option than calling from your hotel.

If you have a multiband phone (some countries use different frequencies than what's used in the United States) and your service provider uses the world-standard GSM network (as do T-Mobile, Cingular, and Verizon), you can probably use your phone abroad. Roaming fees can be steep, however: 99¢ a minute is considered reasonable. And overseas you normally pay the toll charges for incoming calls. It's almost always cheaper to send a text message than to make a call, since text messages have a very low set fee (often less than 5¢).

If you just want to make local calls, consider buying a new SIM card (note that your provider may have to unlock your phone for you to use a different SIM card) and a prepaid service plan in the destination. You'll then have a local number and can make local calls at local rates. If your trip is extensive, you could also simply buy a new cell phone in your destination, as the initial cost will be offset over time.

■TIP→ **If you travel internationally frequently, save one of your old mobile phones or buy a cheap one on the Internet; ask your cell phone company to unlock it for you, and take it with you as a travel phone, buying a new SIM card with pay-as-you-go service in each destination.**

◪ **Cellular Abroad** (☎800/287-5072 ⊕www.cellularabroad.com) rents and sells GMS phones and sells SIM cards that work in many countries. **Mobal** (☎888/888-9162 ⊕www.mobalrental.com) rents mobiles and sells GSM phones (starting at $49) that will operate in 140 countries. Per-call rates vary throughout the world. **Planet Fone** (☎888/988-4777 ⊕www.planet fone.com) rents cell phones, but the per-minute rates are expensive.

ANGUILLA

To make a local call, dial the seven-digit number. Most hotels will arrange with a local provider for a cell phone to use during your stay. Try to get a prepaid, local one for the best rates. Some GSM international cell phones will work, some not; check with your service before you leave. Hotels usually add a hefty surcharge to all calls.

Cable & Wireless is open weekdays 8–6, Saturday 9–1, and Sunday 10–2. Here, you can rent a cell phone for use during your stay, or purchase Caribbean phone cards for use in specially marked phone booths. Inside the departure lounge at the Blowing Point Ferry dock and at the airport there's an AT&T USADirect access phone for collect or credit-card calls to the United States.

To call Anguilla from the United States, dial 1 plus the area code 264, then the local seven-digit number. From the United Kingdom dial 001 and then the area code and the number. From Australia and New Zealand dial 0011, then 1, then the area code and the number.

To call internationally, dial 1, the area code, and the seven-digit number to reach the United States and Canada; dial 011, 44, and the local number for the United Kingdom; dial 011, 61, and the local number for Australia; and dial 011, 64, and the local number for New Zealand.

◪ **Cable & Wireless** (✉Wallblake Rd., Anguilla ☎264/497-3100).

ST. BARTHS

MCI and AT&T services are available. Public telephones do not accept coins; they accept *télécartes,* prepaid calling cards that you can buy at the gas station next to the airport and at post offices in Lorient, St-Jean, and Gustavia. Making an international call using a télécarte is much less expensive than making it through your hotel.

If you bring a cell phone to the island and wish to activate it for local use, visit St. Barth Eléctronique across from the airport. You can also buy an inexpensive cell phone with prepaid minutes for as little as €20, including some initial air time. Many hotels will rent you a local-service cell phone; ask the manager or concierge.

The country code for St. Barths is 590. Thus, to call St. Barths from the U.S., dial 011 + 590 + 590 and the local six-digit number. Some cell phones use the prefix 690, in which case you would dial 590 + 690. For calls on St. Barths, you must dial 0590 plus the six-digit local number; for St. Martin dial just the six-digit number for the French side, for the Dutch side (Sint Maarten) dial 00–599–54 plus the five-digit number, but remember that this is an international call and will be billed accordingly. To call the United States from St. Barths, dial 001 plus the area code plus the local seven-digit number.

▣ **France Télécom** (⊠Espace Neptune, St-Jean ☎0590/27-67-00).
St. Barth Eléctronique (⊠St-Jean ☎0590/27-50-50).

ST. MAARTEN/ST. MARTIN

Calling from one side of the island to another is an international call. To phone from the Dutch side to the French, you first must dial 00–590–590 for local numbers, or 00–590–690 for cell phones, then the six-digit local number. To call from the French side to the Dutch, dial 00–599, then the seven-digit local number. Because of this, many businesses will have numbers on each side for their customers.

To call a local number on the French side, dial 0590 plus the six-digit number. On the Dutch side, just dial the seven-digit number with no prefix.

For calls to the Dutch side from the United States, dial 011–599/54 plus the local number; for the French side, 011–590–590 plus the six-digit local number. At the Landsradio in Philipsburg, there are facilities for overseas calls and a USADirect phone, where you're directly in touch with an operator who will accept collect or credit-card calls. To call direct with an AT&T credit card or operator, dial 001–800/872–2881. On the French side, AT&T can be accessed by calling 080–099–00–11. If you need to use public phones, go to the special desk at Marigot's post office and buy a *télécarte.* There's a public phone at the tourist office in Marigot where you can make credit-card calls: the operator takes your card number (any major card) and assigns you a PIN (Personal Identification Number), which you then use to charge calls to your card.

▌CUSTOMS & DUTIES

You're always allowed to bring goods of a certain value back home without having to pay any duty or import tax. But there's a limit on the amount of tobacco and liquor you can bring back duty-free, and some countries have separate limits for perfumes; for exact figures, check with your customs department. The values of so-called "duty-free" goods are included in these amounts. When you shop abroad, save all your receipts, as customs inspectors may ask to see them as well as the items you purchased. If the total value of your goods is more than the duty-free limit, you'll have to pay a tax (most often a flat percentage) on the value of everything beyond that limit.

U.S. Information U.S. Customs and Border Protection (⊕www.cbp.gov).

▌DAY TOURS & GUIDES

ANGUILLA

A round-the-island tour by taxi takes about 2½ hours and costs $40 for one or two people, $5 for each additional passenger. Bennie's Tours is one of the island's more reliable tour operators. Malliouhana Travel & Tours will create personalized package tours of the island. The Old Valley Tour, created by longtime resident Frank Costin, ambles the road up Crocus Hill, a treasure trove of Anguilla's best-preserved historic edifices, including Ebenezer's Methodist Church (the island's oldest), the Warden's Place, and typical turn-of-the-20th-century cottages (most housing galleries). The tour is by appointment only and offers a fascinating insight into Anguillian architecture, past and present.

Contact the Anguilla Tourist Board or call 264/497–2711 to arrange the tour by Sir Emile Gumbs, the island's former chief minister, of the Sandy Ground area. This tour, which highlights historic and ecological sites, is on Tuesday at 10 AM. The $10 fee benefits the Anguilla Archaeological Historical Society. Gumbs also organizes bird-watching expeditions that show you everything from frigate birds to turtle doves.

▐ Anguilla Tourist Office (⊠Coronation Ave., The Valley ☎264/497–2759 or 800/553–4939 ⊕www.anguilla-vacation.com). **Bennie's Tours** (⊠Blowing Point ☎264/497–2788). **Malliouhana Travel & Tours** (⊠The Quarter ☎264/497–2431). **Old Valley Tour** (☎264/497–2263).

ST. BARTHS

You can arrange island tours by minibus or car at hotel desks or through any of the island's taxi operators in Gustavia or at the airport. The tourist office runs a variety of tours with varying itineraries that run about €46 for a half day for up to eight people. Mat Nautic can help you arrange to tour the island by water on a Jet Ski or Waverunner. St-Barth Tours and Travel will customize a tour of the island. Wish Agency can arrange customized tours as well as take care of airline ticketing, event planning, maid service, and private party arrangements.

🚢 **Mat Nautic** (✉Quai du Yacht Club, Gustavia ☎0690/49–54–72). **St-Barth Tours & Travel** (✉Rue Jeanne d'Arc, Gustavia ☎0590/27–52–14). **Wish Agency** (☎0590/29–83–74 ✉wish.agency@wanadoo.fr).

ST. MAARTEN/ST. MARTIN
A 2½-hour taxi tour of the island costs $50 for one or two people, $18 for each additional person. Your hotel or the tourist office can arrange it for you. Elle Si Belle offers island tours by van or bus for $15.

🚢 **Elle Si Belle** (✉Airport Blvd., Simpson Bay ☎599/545–4954).

▌ EATING OUT

St. Maarten/St. Martin, Anguilla, and St. Barths are known for their fine restaurants. For more information on local cuisine and dining possibilities, see the individual island chapters. *For information on food-related health issues, see Health below.*

PAYING
Credit cards are widely accepted on all three islands. For more information, see the individual island chapters.

For guidelines on tipping see Tipping below.

▌ ELECTRICITY

Generally, the Dutch St. Maarten and Anguilla operate on 110 volts AC (60-cycle) and have outlets that accept flat-prong plugs—the same as in North America.

The French St. Martin and St. Barths operate on 220 volts AC (60-cycle), with round-prong

plugs, as in Europe; you need an adapter and sometimes a converter for North American appliances. The French outlets have a safety mechanism—equal pressure must be applied to both prongs of the plug to connect to the socket.

Consider making a small investment in a universal adapter, which has several types of plugs in one lightweight, compact unit. Most laptops and mobile phone chargers are dual voltage (i.e., they operate equally well on 110 and 220 volts), so require only an adapter. These days the same is true of small appliances such as hair dryers. Always check labels and manufacturer instructions to be sure. Don't use 110-volt outlets marked FOR SHAVERS ONLY for high-wattage appliances such as hair-dryers.

🚢 **Steve Kropla's Help for World Traveler's** (⊕www.kropla.com) has information on electrical and telephone plugs around the world. **Walkabout Travel Gear** (⊕www.walkabouttravelgear.com) has a good coverage of electricity under "adapters."

▌EMERGENCIES

ANGUILLA
As in the United States, dial 911 in any emergency.

Ambulance & Fire Ambulance (☎264/497–2551). **Fire** (☎911).

Hospitals Hotel de Health (✉Palm Court at Sea Feathers Bay ☎264/497–4166) is a well-regarded private medical facility. **Princess Alexandra Hospital** (✉Sandy Ground ☎264/497–2551). Emergency room and ambulance operate 24 hours a day.

Police Police emergencies (☎911). **Police nonemergencies** (☎264/497–2333).

ST. BARTHS
Emergency Services Ambulance & Fire (☎0590/27–62–31). **Police** (☎17 or 0590/27–66–66).

Hospitals Hospital De Bruyn (✉Gustavia ☎0590/27–60–35).

ST. MAARTEN/ST. MARTIN
Emergency Services Dutch-side emergencies (☎911 or 599/542–2222). **French-side emergencies** (☎17 or 590/52–25–52). **Ambulance or fire emergencies Dutch side** (☎120, 130 for ambulances, 599/542–6001). **Ambulance or fire emergencies French side** (☎18, 590/87–95–01 in Grand Case, 590/87–50–08 in La Savanne). **Police emergencies Dutch side** (☎111 or 599/542–2222). **Police emergencies French side** (☎17 or 590/87–88–35 in Marigot, 590/87–19–76).

Hospitals Hôpital de Marigot (✉Rue de l'Hôpital, Concordia ☎590/52–25–25). **St. Maarten** Medical Center (✉Cay Hill ☎599/543–1111).

▌ETIQUETTE & BEHAVIOR

In general, people in the Caribbean are polite and very sociable. They will always greet you with warmth and will expect to exchange polite comments about the day or the weather before getting down to business. It's considered quite rude not to do so—so smile and join in the pleasantries; you might even make a friend. Swimming attire is suitable only for the beach or at beachside restaurants (and then only at lunch); for dinner, on all three islands dress is generally casual, though you'll see more dressing up in St. Barths and Anguilla than in St. Maarten.

Topless bathing is permitted on several beaches in St. Barths even though it is technically illegal. The south end of Baie Orientale is nude; you'll notice the difference as you travel south from the more family-oriented north end, and it's not unusual to see nude sunbathers at Cupecoy Beach, particularly on the rocks. Topless bathing is never permitted on Anguilla.

▌HEALTH

An increase in dengue fever has been reported across the Caribbean since early 2007. While Puerto Rico, Martinique, and Guadeloupe have been the islands most heavily affected, instances have been reported in other parts of the Caribbean as well, including St. Barths. Since there are no effective vaccines to prevent dengue fever, visitors to the region should protect themselves with mosquito repellent (particularly repellant containing DEET, which has been deemed the most effective) and keep arms and legs covered at sunset, when mosquitoes are particularly active.

There are no particular problems regarding food and water safety in St. Maarten/St. Martin, Anguilla, or St. Barths. If you have an especially sensitive stomach, you may wish to drink only bottled water; also be sure that food has been thoroughly cooked and is served to you fresh and hot. Peel fruit. If you have problems, mild cases of traveler's diarrhea may respond to Pepto-Bismol. Generally, Imodium (known generically as loperamide) just makes things worse, but it may be necessary if you have persistent problems. Be sure to drink plenty of fluids; if you can't keep fluids down, seek medical help immediately.

If you travel a lot internationally—particularly to developing nations—refer to the CDC's *Health Information for International Travel* (aka Traveler's Health Yellow Book). Info from it is posted on the CDC Web site (www.cdc.gov/travel/yb), or you can buy a copy from your local bookstore for $24.95.

Health Warnings **National Centers for Disease Control & Prevention** (CDC ☎877/394–8747 international travelers' health line ⊕www.cdc.gov/travel). **World Health Organization** (WHO ⊕www.who.int).

LANGUAGE

English is the official language in Anguilla.

French is the official language in St. Barths, so it can't hurt to pack a phrase book and/or French dictionary. If you speak any French at all, don't be shy. You may also hear Creole, the regional French dialect called patois, and even the Creole of Guadeloupe. Most hotel and restaurant employees speak some English—at least enough to help you find what you need.

Dutch is the official language of St. Maarten, and French is the official language of St. Martin, but almost everyone speaks English. If you hear a language you can't quite place, it may be Papiamento—a mix of Spanish, Portuguese, Dutch, French, and English—spoken throughout the Netherlands Antilles.

MAIL

ANGUILLA

Airmail postcards and letters cost EC$1.50 (for the first ½ ounce) to the United States, Canada, and the United Kingdom and EC$2.50 to Australia and New Zealand. The only post office is in the Valley; it's open weekdays 8 to 4:45. When writing to the island, you don't need a postal code; just include the name of the establishment, address (location or post-office box), and "Anguilla, British West Indies."

The post office, located in the Valley, is open weekdays 8 to 3:30. There's a FedEx office near the airport. It's open weekdays 8 to 5 and Saturday 9 to 1.

🏠 **Anguilla Post Office** (✉Wallblake Rd., The Valley ☎264/497–2528). **FedEx** (✉Hallmark Bldg., 227 Old Airport Rd., The Valley ☎264/497–3575).

ST. BARTHS

Mail is slow. Correspondence between the United States and the island can take up to three weeks to arrive. The main post office is in Gustavia, in season it's open daily 7:30–3, (except for Wed. and Sat., when it closes at noon), but smaller post offices are in St-Jean and Lorient. These are open a few hours each morning. When writing to an establishment on St. Barths, be sure to include "French West Indies" at the end of the address. Because of the slow mail service, faxes are widely used.

🏠 **Main post office** (✉Rue Jeanne d'Arc, Gustavia ☎0590/27–62–00). **Lorient post office** (✉Lorient ☎0590/27–61–35). **Saint-Jean post office** (✉Saint-Jean ☎0590/27–64–02).

ST. MAARTEN/ST. MARTIN

The main Dutch-side post office is on Walter Nisbeth Road in Philipsburg. There's a branch at Simpson Bay on Airport Road. The main post office on the French side is in Marigot, on rue de la Liberté. Letters from the Dutch side to North America and Europe cost ANG2.85; postcards to all destinations are ANG1.45. From the French side, letters up to 20 grams and postcards are €1 to North America. When writing to Dutch St. Maarten, call it "Sint Maarten"

and make sure to add "Netherlands Antilles" to the address. When writing to the French side, the proper spelling is "St. Martin," and you add "French West Indies" to the address. Postal codes are used only on the French side.

▮ MONEY

Though the legal tender in Anguilla is the Eastern Caribbean (EC) dollar, U.S. dollars are widely accepted. (You'll often get change in EC dollars, though.) The exchange rate between U.S. and EC dollars is set at EC$2.68 to the U.S. dollar. Be sure to carry lots of small bills; change for a $20 bill is often difficult to obtain.

Legal tender in Dutch St. Maarten is the Netherlands Antilles florin (guilder), written NAf or ANG. At this writing, ANG1 equals 56 cents.

In French St. Martin and in St. Barths, the currency is the euro. The exchange rate at this writing was €1 equals US$1.60.

Prices quoted in this chapter are in U.S. dollars unless otherwise noted.

Prices throughout this guide are given for adults. Substantially reduced fees are almost always available for children, students, and senior citizens.

ATMS & BANKS

Your own bank will probably charge a fee for using ATMs abroad; the foreign bank you use may also charge a fee. Nevertheless, you'll usually get a better rate of exchange at an ATM than you will at a currency-exchange office or even when changing money in a bank. And extracting funds as you need them is a safer option than carrying around a large amount of cash.

■ TIP→ **PIN numbers with more than four digits are not recognized at ATMs in many countries. If yours has five or more, remember to change it before you leave.**

ANGUILLA
Most ATMs dispense both American and Eastern Caribbean dollars.

🏧 **Scotiabank** (☎264/497-3333 ⊕www.scotiabank.com).

ST. BARTHS
Banks and ATMs are well located throughout the island, so getting money is rarely a problem. The official currency in St. Barths is the euro; however, dollars are accepted in almost all shops and in many restaurants, though you will probably receive euros in change.

ST. MAARTEN/ST. MARTIN
It's generally not necessary to change your money in St. Maarten/St. Martin. All banks now have ATMs that accept international cards. Remember, though, that they may issue just dollars or just euros. On the Dutch side, try RBTT or Windward Islands Bank, both of which have several branches on the island. On the French side, try Banque des Antilles Françaises or Banque Française Commerciale.

🏧 **Banque des Antilles Françaises** (⊠Rue de la République, Marigot ☎590/29-13-30). **Banque Française Commerciale** (⊠Rue de Hollande, Marigot ☎590/87-53-80).

Credit Mutuel (⊠Rue de la République, Marigot ☎590/29-54-90). **RBTT** (⊠Emnaplein, Philipsburg ☎599/542-5908 ⊠Union Rd., Cole Bay ☎599/544-3078). **Windward Islands Bank** (⊠Cannegieter St., Philipsburg ☎599/542-2313).

CREDIT CARDS
Throughout this guide, the following abbreviations are used: **AE,** American Express; **D,** Discover; **DC,** Diners Club; **MC,** MasterCard; and **V,** Visa.

It's a good idea to inform your credit-card company before you travel, especially if you're going abroad and don't travel internationally very often. Otherwise, the credit-card company might put a hold on your card owing to unusual activity—not a good thing halfway through your trip. Record all your credit-card numbers—as well as the phone numbers to call if your cards are lost or stolen—in a safe place, so you're prepared should something go wrong. Both MasterCard and Visa have general numbers you can call (collect if you're abroad) if your card is lost, but you're better off calling the number of your issuing bank, since MasterCard and Visa usually just transfer you to your bank; your bank's number is usually printed on your card.

If you plan to use your credit card for cash advances, you'll need to apply for a PIN at least two weeks before your trip. Although it's usually cheaper (and safer) to use a credit card abroad for large purchases (so you can cancel payments or be reimbursed if there's a problem), note that some credit-card companies *and* the banks that issue them add substantial percentages to all foreign transactions, whether they're in a foreign currency or not. Check on these fees before leaving home, so there won't be any surprises when you get the bill.

Major credit cards are widely accepted on St. Maarten, Anguilla, and St. Barths. A few restaurants may have a surcharge if you pay by credit card. A few places also take only cash.

Reporting Lost Cards **American Express** (☎800/528–4800 in the U.S. or 336/393–1111 collect from abroad ⊕www.americanexpress. com). **Diners Club** (☎800/234–6377 in the U.S. or 303/799–1504 collect from abroad ⊕www.diners club.com). **Discover** (☎800/347–2683 in the U.S. or 801/902–3100 collect from abroad ⊕www.discover card.com). **MasterCard** (☎800/627–8372 in the U.S. or 636/722–7111 collect from abroad ⊕www.master card.com). **Visa** (☎800/847–2911 in the U.S. or 410/581–9994 collect from abroad ⊕www.visa.com).

▌SAFETY

Anguilla is a quiet, relatively safe island, but crime reports have increased since 2007, including a few burglaries of private villas; however, crime is far from a major problem for visitors.

There's relatively little crime on St. Barths. Visitors can travel any-where on the island with confidence, though petty crime has been reported since 2007. Don't walk

barefoot outside at night. There are venomous centipedes that can inflict a remarkably painful sting.

Petty crime can be a problem on both sides of St. Maarten/St. Martin. Robberies—and on occasion armed robberies—and purse snatchings have been on the upswing. While the level of crime does not rise to the same level as in a large U.S. city, many travelers to the island have been reporting more problems than usual since 2007.

There are several general safety rules that it's prudent to follow on all three islands. Always lock your valuables and travel documents in your room safe or your hotel's front-desk safe. When sightseeing in a rental car, keep valuables locked in the trunk or car, or better yet, don't leave anything in the car. Never leave your things unattended at the beach. Despite the romantic imagery of the Caribbean, it's not good policy to take long walks along the beach at night.

■TIP→ **Distribute your cash, credit cards, IDs, and other valuables between a deep front pocket, an inside jacket or vest pocket, and a hidden money pouch. Don't reach for the money pouch once you're in public.**

▌TAXES

ANGUILLA
The departure tax is $20 for adults and $10 for children, payable in cash at the airport, $3 payable in cash at Blowing Point Ferry Terminal. A 10% accommodations tax

is added to hotel bills along with a $1 per night marketing tax.

ST. BARTHS

The island charges a $5 departure tax when your next stop is another French island, $10 if you're off to anywhere else. This is payable in cash only, dollars or euros, at the airport. At this writing, some hotels added an additional 10% to 15% service charge to bills, though most include it in their tariffs. There are no other additional taxes on either hotels or villa rentals.

ST. MAARTEN/ST. MARTIN

Departure tax from Juliana Airport is $10 to destinations within the Netherlands Antilles and $30 to all other destinations. This tax is included in the cost of many airline tickets, so it's best to check with your airline. If it's not included, the tariff must be paid in cash (dollars, euros, or local currency) at a booth before you get on your plane. If you arrive on the island by plane and depart within 24 hours, you'll be considered "in transit" and will not be required to pay the departure tax. It will cost you €3 (usually included in the ticket price) to depart by plane from L'Espérance Airport and $4 by ferry to Anguilla from Marigot's pier.

Hotels on the Dutch side add a 15% service charge to the bill as well as a 5% government tax, for a total of 20%. Hotels on the French side add 10% to 15% for service and a *taxe de séjour*; the amount of this visitor tax differs from hotel to hotel and can be as high as 5%.

▌ TIME

St. Maarten, Anguilla, and St. Barths are in the Atlantic Standard Time zone, which is one hour later than Eastern Standard and four hours earlier than GMT. Caribbean islands don't observe daylight saving time, so during the period when it's in effect, Atlantic Standard and Eastern Standard are the same.

▌ TIPPING

In St. Barths and French St. Martin, a service charge is always added to restaurant bills, but it's common practice to tip a bit more (perhaps 5% to 10%) in cash (even if you have paid by credit card). In Anguilla and Dutch St. Maarten, you may see a service charge added to your bill, but if not, tip about 15%.

Almost all Caribbean hotels add a service charge, but this doesn't always go directly to the staff. It's generally expected that you will tip more. Leave something for the maid in your hotel or resort (best left at the beginning of each day since the cleaning staff can change); $1 to $5 is appropriate depending on the resort and level of service. Tip the concierge at your resort if you receive helpful service; tip beach attendants and waiters when they provide service to you; tip porters when at least $1 per bag when they carry your bags.

Tip taxi drivers on Anguilla and St. Maarten/St. Martin; taxi drivers on St. Barths do not expect to be tipped.

▌WEDDINGS

ANGUILLA

Anguilla's beaches and sybaritic resorts, such as Cap Juluca and Malliouhana, provide ideal settings for destination weddings and honeymoons. Several resorts will help plan everything in advance. Some people are discouraged by a fairly lengthy residency period to get an inexpensive marriage license: if one partner lives on Anguilla at least 15 days before the wedding date, the license costs $40; otherwise, you must pay a fee of $284. Allow two working days to process applications, which can be obtained weekdays from 8:30 to 4 at the Judicial Department. Both parties must present proof of identity (valid passport, birth certificate, or driver's license with photo), as well as an original decree of divorce where applicable and death certificate if widowed. Blood tests are not required. There are additional requirements if you wish to marry in the Catholic Church.

ST. BARTHS

Because of the long legal residency requirement, it's not really feasible to get married on St. Barths unless you are a French citizen, though unofficial wedding celebration are not uncommon on the island.

ST. MAARTEN/ST. MARTIN

Marriages on St. Maarten follow the same rules as on the other Netherlands Antilles islands; getting married on the French side really isn't feasible because of stringent residency requirements, identical to those in France. Couples must be at least 18 years old and submit their documents at least 14 days prior to the wedding date. The application requires notarized original documents to be submitted to the registrar, including birth certificates, passports (for non-Dutch persons), divorce decrees from previous marriages, death certificates of deceased spouses, and passports for six witnesses if the ceremony is to take place outside of the Marriage Hall. The documents must be submitted in Dutch or English—or else they must be translated into Dutch. The cost for this process is $285.90. Any questions should be directed to the chief registrar.

🛈 **Chief Registrar** (✉Census Office, Soualiga Rd., Philipsburg ☎599/542–5647 📠599/542–4267).

INDEX

NOTES

NOTES

NOTES

ABOUT OUR WRITERS

Puja Chugani, who has contributed to *Fodor's London*, among other guides, is a freelance travel writer who is willing to search high and low for the world's best restaurants. A part-time resident of St. Maarten, she covered the island's dining scene for this book.

Elise Meyer's friends insist that her middle name is "Let's Go." With an academic background in art history, she opened a gallery in SoHo in the 1970s, which was a great excuse to travel frequently to Europe. A life-long resident of New England, she believes that her regular trips to the Caribbean have always been a wintertime necessity despite a passion for skiing. For 20 years, St. Barths and Anguilla have been frequent destinations, when she is not pursuing (and chronicling) interests in gardening, food, golf, the arts, and things that are funny. Now that the two kids are off on their own adventures, she's been enjoying longer and more exotic trips with a husband who shares her wanderlust, as well as a firm resolve never to check in luggage. A long-time contributor to *Fodor's Caribbean*, she has covered Anguilla and St. Barths for this guide.

An award-winning travel junkie, Roberta Sotonoff writes to support her habit. She can be found anywhere—in a plane feasting on pretzels, in the water exploring the deep, destroying her body while swinging from jungle canopies, or stumbling up and down mountains. Her family often complains that she spends more time with gate agents than with them. Her work has been published in dozens of domestic and international newspapers, magazines, Web sites, and guidebooks including several Fodor's publications. Though she loves exploring her hometown, Chicago, most of her time at home is spent chained to her computer. For this book, she explored St. Maarten and St. Martin, covering everything from hotels to deep-sea fishing guides to shops.